THE CHANGING

Pacific Northwest

INTERPRETING its PAST

Sherman and Mabel Smith Pettyjohn
Lectures in Pacific Northwest History

THE CHANGING

Pacific Northwest

INTERPRETING its PAST

EDITED by
DAVID H. STRATTON and GEORGE A. FRYKMAN

Washington State University Press
Pullman, Washington
1988

Washington State University Press, Pullman, Washington 99164-5910

Library of Congress Cataloging-in-Publication Data

The Changing Pacific Northwest.

(Sherman and Mabel Smith Pettyjohn lectures in
Pacific Northwest history)
Bibliography: p.
Includes index.
1. Northwest, Pacific—History. 2. Northwest,
Pacific—Social conditions.   I. Stratton, David H.
(David Hodges), 1927-   .   II. Frykman, George A.,
1917-   .   III. Series.
F851.C53 1987   979.5   88-1146
ISBN 0-87422-023-8
ISBN 0-87422-020-3 (pbk.)

This book is printed on pH neutral, acid-free paper.

Research grants for this study were provided by
The Pettyjohn Endowment, Washington State University

Front and back cover photos: Picnic Party on the Coeur d'Alene River near
Kingston, Idaho, *from the Barnard Stockbridge Collection, University of Idaho,
Moscow, Idaho.*

Hudson's Bay Company mill, from the *Pacific Railroad Reports.*
Manuscripts, Archives, and Special Collections, Washington State University Library,
Pullman, Washington

Contents

Paloose Falls in Washington Territory, a lithograph from the Mullan Road
Survey, drawn by Gustavus Sohon.
Private Collection

Introduction

The Pacific Northwest, once regarded as an "American Siberia" of dense forests and stormy coasts, is a relatively new region in the nation's development when compared with older sections, such as New England or the South. Perhaps for that reason Northwest history has been slighted and thus offers an unusually fertile field for investigation. In addition, the broad expanse of Oregon, Washington, Idaho, western Montana, and — in the context of a "Greater Northwest" — Alaska has experienced dramatic changes in the past four decades. Spectacular economic and population growth marked the wartime years of the 1940s as the beginning of a new historical period, comparable in significance to the "New Northwest" introduced during the transitional decade of the 1880s. This pattern of change, although with less acceleration, has also characterized the years from the 1940s to the 1980s. It will probably continue, if for no other reason, as the population increases due to attractive living conditions and as industry and commerce follow in the wake of human migration. Yet even among those who already live in the Northwest, knowledge and understanding are woefully inadequate about the economic, social, and political milieu which should have a bearing on the formation of this emerging society. At this particularly opportune time scholars and the general public alike need to explore new approaches for interpretation of the region's past.

Fortunately there are many signs of increasing interest in Pacific Northwest history. One of these hopeful indications is the Pettyjohn Distinguished Lecture Series at Washington State University, Pullman. The estate of Margaret Pettyjohn, a long-time Walla Walla area resident and patron of historical organizations, provided WSU with an endowment designated for the promotion of Northwest history. The University of Washington and the University of Idaho also shared in the estate of Miss Pettyjohn, whose family farmed a large acreage near Prescott, Washington. She died in 1978. In memory of her parents, both pioneers of Walla Walla County, WSU established the Sherman and Mabel Smith Pettyjohn Distinguished Lectureship of Pacific Northwest History.

During the week of October 27-November 1, 1980, the WSU History Department started using these funds by bringing noted historian Norman A. Graebner of the University of Virginia to the Pullman campus as the first Pettyjohn Distinguished Lecturer. In conjunction with his week-long visit, the department sponsored jointly with the National Endowment for the Humanities a two-day research symposium (October 30-31) entitled "A Changing Historiography for the Pacific Northwest," in which Graebner delivered the keynote address. He was joined for the symposium by a group of regional scholars and interested individuals from the general public who assessed current historical writing in the Northwest and identified future research priorities.

Besides the Pettyjohn Lecturer, eight other persons presented major papers or addresses and a three-member panel consisting of an architect and two archaeologists conducted a discussion on the value and use of nondocumentary sources. Nine other participants served as primary discussants for the major presentations, thereby providing a "bridge" for questions and comments from the audience. Among those gathered from all six states of the "Greater Northwest" were academic scholars, professional or public historians, officials of five state historical societies (Oregon, Washington [two societies represented], Montana, and Idaho), and the editors of three regional historical journals (*Pacific Northwest Quarterly, Montana Magazine,* and *Idaho Yesterdays*). The relatively small attendance (about seventy-five) fostered informality, lengthy exchanges of information, and frank evaluations—in short, a thorough airing of the problems and advantages of regional history.

All but one of the essays in this anthology were delivered in the symposium, and all have been revised in varying degrees. The chapter by Alvin M. Josephy, Jr., originated separately as the Fall 1982 Pettyjohn Distinguished Lecture. In the symposium's keynote address Norman A. Graebner not only views the Northwest Coast as an American region but also as a coveted prize in nineteenth-century international diplomacy. The other essays fall into three broad categories, beginning with *the nature of the region.* Richard Maxwell Brown suggests a wholly new interpretation for the "nature" of the Pacific Northwest, linking its character and social development to the influence of climate. Josephy's account, which comes next, challenges scholars and other modern-day Americans to recognize Indian spiritual systems as key forces in the pervasive historical theme of Indian-white relations. In the essay on Alaska's painful experiences Claus-M. Naske points out the reasons why that far northern state must be accepted as an integral part of the region and the nation, rather than as an obscure appendage.

A second category contains essays that address some of the questions posed by the studies of *social history and political culture* that are providing new interpretations of regions as well as of ethnic and minority groups, including women. Ronald H. Limbaugh discusses the complex problem of political elites in early Idaho and, by implication, in other western territories, a matter of special importance to Washington, Montana, and Alaska as well, since they, too, endured lengthy territorial apprenticeships. In the essay by Michael P. Malone (with Dianne Dougherty) the authors contend that political elites are the natural product of a particular culture and environment, with Montana serving as a prime example. The burden of Carlos A. Schwantes's chapter is that stereotyped images of western laboring groups as merely violent men should be replaced by dispassionate investigation of their institutions, which will be more fruitful than simply concentrating on certain bizarre and murderous episodes. Susan Armitage then surveys the development of women's history as a subfield in Pacific Northwest studies and explains why historians must always ask the question: "What were women doing while men were doing the things they deemed important?" A concluding category, represented by Robert E. Burke's sage observations on editing, explores the ways to establish *standards of publication* which should be met by editors and authors who want to develop new themes of regional history.

In addition, the following symposium participants made important contributions to this project either as primary discussants or by presiding over sessions:

William L. Lang, Editor, *Montana, the Magazine of Western History;* the late Robert Hitchman, President, Washington State Historical Society; Terrence O'Donnell, Oregon Historical Society; Judith Austin, Editor, *Idaho Yesterdays;* Patricia Roppel, historical writer, Ketchikan, Alaska; Kent D. Richards, Central Washington University; Patricia Jones, Indian Education Coordinator, Pullman School District; Norman H. Clark, Everett Community College; William S. Greever, Siegfried B. Rolland, and Roderick Sprague, all of the University of Idaho; Virginia Guest Ferriday, architect and historic preservationist, Portland; and Margaret Andrews, James F. Short, Jr., Allan H. Smith, and Richard D. Daugherty, all of Washington State University. Several of our colleagues at WSU also gave us special assistance in the symposium: Glenn Terrell, WSU President; Edward M. Bennett; Clifford E. Trafzer; John Slaughter, Academic Vice President and Provost; and Andrew J. Gregg, who served as Symposium Coordinator. John Alexander Williams and Katherine Abramovitz, Division of Research Programs, National Endowment for the Humanities, provided helpful advice and evaluation for the symposium. Stuart B. Bradley of Chicago, McMurray, Black & Snyder, Attorneys at Law, gave generous support to this publication. At the WSU Press, Fred C. Bohm, Editor in Chief, J. D. Britton, Project Editor, and Sharon White, Designer, worked their special miracles with the publication process. We acknowledge the individual efforts of those named here, but hold ourselves accountable for any missteps in the overall project.

David H. Stratton
George A. Frykman

The Northwest Coast in World Diplomacy, 1790-1846

EDITORS' NOTE

Few first books have had the great scholarly impact of Norman A. Graebner's *Empire on the Pacific: A Study in American Continental Expansion* (1955). In what came to be called the "Graebner thesis," he challenged fundamental Turnerian dogmas by arguing that American objectives of expansion in the 1840s were not agrarian and territorial, as Frederick Jackson Turner had maintained, but rather maritime and commercial. More specifically, Graebner contended that neither migrating pioneers nor the spirit of Manifest Destiny determined the course of diplomacy that culminated in acquisition by the United States of both Oregon and California. Instead, he asserted that two generations of American presidents and statesmen steadfastly pursued the major goal of obtaining the harbors at San Diego, San Francisco, and Puget Sound as gateways for commerce with Asia. With this initial book Graebner not only contributed a significant reinterpretation of Manifest Destiny, but stimulated a great deal of lively discussion among his fellow historians as well.

In the essay presented here Graebner reviews the broad framework of events and diplomatic exchanges that preceded the Oregon Treaty of 1846. His emphasis, as in *Empire on the Pacific*, rests on the primacy of the sealanes and trade. Thomas Jefferson had grasped the commercial importance of the Pacific Northwest coast even before the United States became a successful competitor for the sea otter trade in the 1790s. By the 1840s Great Britain and the United States were struggling for dominance of the coast. Yet American diplomats had long since established a traditional claim at the 49th parallel, principally because Juan de Fuca Strait and Puget Sound lay south of that line. President James K. Polk, despite the cries of his party for 54-40, became convinced, as Graebner puts it, that seaports "were all that mattered." In the end the president could claim little credit for the equitable diplomatic settlement of 1846. Both Britain and the United States, nevertheless, were well served by the Oregon Treaty in the distribution of lands and harbors; and the commercial interests of both nations were pleased with the peaceful results.

Norman A. Graebner has written extensively on American diplomatic history. Besides *Empire on the Pacific*, he is the author of *The New Isolationism* (1956) and *Cold War Diplomacy* (two editions, 1962 and 1977). He has also edited several works, including *Ideas and Diplomacy* (1964), *Manifest Destiny* (1968), and *Freedom in America: A 200-Year Perspective* (1977), and has contributed numerous articles to historical journals. Graebner received a B.S. degree (1939) at the University of Wisconsin at Milwaukee, an M.A. (1940) at the University of Oklahoma, and a Ph.D. (1949) at the University of Chicago. He has taught at Iowa State University and the University of Illinois, and is now Compton Professor of History and Public Affairs at the University of Virginia. In the fall of 1980, when he presented this paper, Graebner served as the first Pettyjohn Distinguished Lecturer at Washington State University.

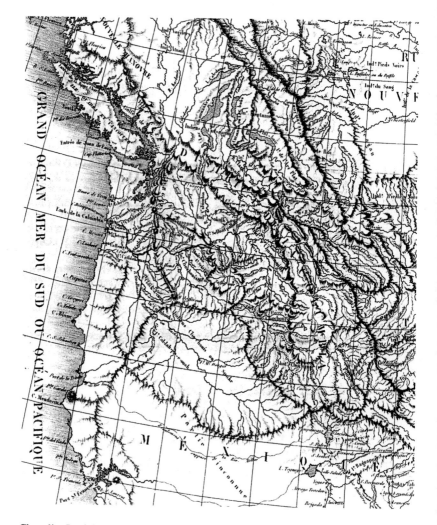

Chevalier Lapie's map of the Oregon Country in 1821.
Library of Congress, Washington, D. C.

The Northwest Coast in World Diplomacy, 1790-1846

NORMAN A. GRAEBNER

When Great Britain and Spain clashed over the possession of Nootka Sound in 1790, the Great Northwest hardly seemed worth the quarrel. For a half-century Europeans in numbers had sailed that coast in search of adventure, empire, sea otter skins, and the fabled Northwest Passage. They found adventure and fur; they discovered no passage and built no empires. For hundreds of miles to the north of San Francisco Bay they encountered a rugged coast, with rocky beaches, impermeable sand dunes, and forested headlands terminating frequently in towering cliffs that jutted precipitously from the sea. So devoid was the region of inviting coves and harbors that as late as 1790 explorers had not yet charted large portions of the shoreline between Spanish California and the Columbia River. North of the Columbia and along the shores of Juan de Fuca Strait early travelers found the coastal regions more attractive. What made these landscapes more pleasing to the eye was their gradual ascent from the generally low-lying, wooded shoreline to the crest of the coastal ranges. North of the Fraser River, wrote Captain James Cook in 1778, the coastal areas "had a very different appearance to what we had before seen." There, he noted, the mountains ran directly into the sea, creating deep inlets rather than gentle valleys along the shore. Early voyagers found the upper coasts of Vancouver Island equally forbidding.[1] Despite its grandeur, the Northwest coast in 1790 remained largely untouched. Mariners had scarcely entered, much less explored, its two most promising waterways, the Columbia River and Puget Sound. Even as an unspoiled wilderness the region seemed to belong to the past.

If eighteenth-century maritime activity in the Northwest had achieved little, it managed to give the region a momentary importance.[2] Spain claimed the Northwest under the Papal Bull of 1493 and the Spanish-Portuguese Treaty of Tordesillas of 1494; together these documents divided the New World between Spain and Portugal. Before the mid-eighteenth century Spanish explorations north of Cape Mendocino had been halting and inconclusive; they had hardly solidified, much less extended, the Spanish Empire in North America. Spanish power in the Pacific could not hold its own against the pirates and privateers that preyed on Spanish shipping. Indeed, the Spanish hegemony over the west coast of North

America was illusory and would endure only as long as that country faced no direct challenge from its European rivals. That challenge became inescapable when Vitus Bering, a Dane in the tsar's service, explored Russia's Asian coastline and, in 1728, discovered the strait that bears his name. Bering later organized an expedition which, in 1741, reached Chatham Sound south of Sitka in the vicinity of 55° north latitude. The expedition discovered portions of the Aleutian chain and took a bountiful harvest in sea otter skins. Russians now invaded the western Aleutians in search of pelts; they did not return to the coast of North America until the end of the century. Once established, the sea otter trade dominated the commerce of the North Pacific. Always, however, the Europeans relied on the natives who possessed the endurance, skill, weapons, and vessels required to pursue the prey.

Spain responded to suspected European encroachments by dispatching a series of expeditions to the northern Pacific to take formal possession of the coastal regions. On his return trip from the Queen Charlotte Islands in 1774, Juan José Pérez Hernández passed Vancouver Island and became the first European to sight Nootka Sound. When Captain James Cook, the noted English mariner, entered the Sound four years later, he purchased spoons taken from the Spaniards. Knowing that Spain claimed the Northwest coast, Cook did not take possession. After its discovery, Nootka Sound, with its large native population and its abundance of fur-bearing animals, became a center of European activity in the Northwest. Detecting the possibilities in the fur trade, British and American merchants invaded the region in large numbers. Soon such Yankees as John Kendrick and Robert Gray reached Nootka to begin their fur-trading activities. John Meares, the British sea captain, visited Nootka in 1788. To strengthen British claims, he sought and received permission from the local chief to build a house. After conducting his business, Meares dismantled the building and loaded the lumber onto one of his ships.[3] Conscious of the British and American presence at Nootka, and troubled by continuing reports of Russian movements down the coast, Spain between 1788 and 1790 dispatched further expeditions to the North Pacific to observe the Russians and take possession of additional locations along the distant shores.[4]

During 1789 the Spanish government decided to occupy Nootka and assert its special claims to the Northwest coast. To carry out this mission Spanish officials in Mexico selected Don Estéban José Martínez, an experienced mariner who had previously visited the North Pacific. Spain would now establish a permanent settlement at Nootka and remove the Russian, British, and American menaces to Spanish authority. At Nootka Martínez, finding no trace of British settlement, proclaimed the region Spanish. Kendrick and Gray had no desire to quarrel about titles; Gray believed that Spain had a better right to the coast than any other nation.[5]

Nor did British seamen aboard the *Ifigenia* at Nootka challenge Spain's claims. Nevertheless, Martínez distrusted the British. He soon discovered that the *Ifigenia*, although sailing under Portuguese registry, was actually a British vessel with instructions to resist seizure by a Russian or Spanish ship—clearly a rejection of Spanish sovereignty. Martínez seized the *Ifigenia*, held the crew on a Spanish warship, and finally sent the vessel with its officers and crew to Macao. Soon other English vessels arrived. After asserting Spanish claims to Nootka, Martínez sent them on their way. Then, in June 1789, the British seaman, Captain James Colnett, arrived at Nootka. When Martínez informed him that he commanded the garrison at Nootka in the name of the Spanish king, Colnett retorted that the Northwest coast belonged to Britain because of Captain Cook's discoveries. Suspecting a British plot to take control of Nootka, Martínez arrested Colnett, seized his ships, and sent him and his crew to San Blas.[6] Spanish officials wanted no trouble with the British; they ordered Martínez back to Mexico.

Accounts of the clash at Nootka drifted into London, embellished and distorted by the state of anti-Spanish sentiment in Britain. The Nootka controversy at last presented Britain an opportunity to demolish Spain's New World claims under the Papal Bull of 1493 by establishing the principle that Spain had no rights to territory that it did not colonize. British diplomacy, if successful, would break Madrid's economic and political monopoly in Spanish America. To coerce Spain, weak internally and isolated from its traditional ally, France, the British government charged that the Spanish seizures at Nootka in time of peace were an insult to Britain and an offense against the law of nations. Britain acknowledged no Spanish claims to sovereignty along the Pacific coast.[7]

As the crisis mounted, John Rutledge, Jr., described to Thomas Jefferson in Paris the burgeoning war spirit in the House of Commons:

> As soon as the house rose, I went amongst the members I was acquainted with, afterwards dined in company with others, and in my life I do not remember to have been amongst such insolent bullies. They were all for war, talked much of *Old England* and the *british Lion*, laughed at the Idea of drubbing the Dons', began to calculate the millions of dollars they would be obliged to pay for having insulted *the first power on Earth*, and seemed uneasy lest the Spaniards should be alarmed at the British strength, ask pardon for what they have done and come immediately to terms.[8]

Against British power and bellicosity Spanish claims based on the prior discovery and occupation of Nootka had no chance. In the Nootka negotiations British and Spanish officials found no bases of agreement in their disparate claims, but the British had the naval power to force a Spanish capitulation. In the Nootka Convention of October 28, 1790, Spain awarded the British exclusive dominion over Nootka Sound. It agreed to reparations for the seizure of the British vessels and recognized the British right to settle and conduct commerce in America wherever Spanish claims lacked the support of actual occupation.[9]

To conduct its delicate negotiations at Nootka, which were required to fulfill the terms of the Nootka Convention, Spanish officials in Mexico City chose the able Juan Francísco de la Bodéga y Quádra. By agreeing to abandon Nootka, they hoped to secure a fixed boundary between British and Spanish claims in the Northwest. They ordered Quádra to occupy a suitable harbor on Fuca Strait to protect Spanish claims to the coast between Juan de Fuca Strait and San Francisco Bay. By establishing good relations with the natives, Spanish leaders hoped to capture control of the remaining trade in sea otter skins. Quádra reached Nootka in April 1792, four months before the arrival of the British commissioner.[10]

The British admiralty commissioned George Vancouver to survey the Northwest coast north of 30° and then proceed to Nootka Sound to meet Quádra and there accept the Spanish concessions defined in the Nootka Convention. Vancouver, in command of the *Discovery* and accompanied by the tender *Chatham*, passed Cape Mendocino on the California coast on April 17, 1792, after a long voyage around the Cape of Good Hope and through the southern Pacific.[11] On April 27 Vancouver recognized Cape Disappointment, but accepted without question Meares's conclusion that no river existed in the vicinity. Soon thereafter, Vancouver approached Robert Gray's *Columbia*, sending Peter Puget and his naturalist Archibald Menzies aboard. Gray had left Nootka that spring, sailed southward almost to the northern boundary of California, then turned northward again. Vancouver assured Gray that his expedition was concerned with exploration, not furs. As Vancouver sailed northward toward Fuca Strait, Gray followed, entering the inlet since known as Grays Harbor. After trading with the Indians, Gray moved southward with the intention of entering a large river below Cape Disappointment that he had noted in April. On May 12, Gray crossed the bar and sailed into the river that he named the Columbia.[12] Meanwhile Vancouver emerged from Fuca Strait to begin his six-week task of charting the inland waters of Puget Sound. From Puget Sound Vancouver sailed through the Strait of Georgia and reentered the Pacific at Queen Charlotte Strait, demonstrating again that Vancouver was an island.[13]

When Vancouver reached Nootka, he found Quádra in an uncompromising mood, determined to contest British rights along the Northwest coast. Quádra argued that Meares had established no British claims with his small hut which did not exist when Martínez arrived in 1789. Quádra defended Martínez's behavior toward Colnett whose vessel, he said, had a Portuguese rather than an English registry. Colnett, he added, had received good treatment at San Blas, and his officers and crew, while held, received the wages of the Spanish navy. Thus Spain had nothing to deliver up, no claims to satisfy. Nevertheless, to avoid trouble the Spaniards withdrew to their new settlement at the mouth of Fuca Strait. Vancouver informed Quádra that he came to carry out the Nootka Convention, not to enter into a retrospective discussion of the relative merits of Spanish and British rights along the Northwest coast. He insisted, however, that the Nootka Convention prohibited all Spanish settlements on the coast which did not exist in April 1789. This provision eliminated all Spanish claims to the Pacific coast north of San Francisco Bay. When Quádra rejected his claims, Vancouver terminated the negotiations. Vancouver and Quádra, parting as friends, agreed to return their differences to their respective courts.[14]

At the end, both countries retreated from their claims to the Northwest coast, permitting sovereignty to return to the natives. What mattered after 1790 was due less to the claims based on discovery or elaborate acts of possession than to the decline of the sea otter trade. With the exception of the Russians at Sitka, few Europeans resided in the Great Northwest in 1800. The Aleut hunters scarcely merited the designation of settlers. Spain had relinquished Nootka as well as its tiny settlement of Fuca Strait. No British or American traders had taken up permanent residence; they had invested their earlier profits elsewhere. Despite its attractiveness the Northwest coast had convinced few that possession offered rewards commensurate with the cost of maintaining it. The Northwest trade, although linked to the Orient, offered no assurance of future profits. The Northwest coast was simply too isolated and unpromising to create a base of enterprise capable of attracting immigrants and capital.[15] Vancouver had recognized the quality of Puget Sound and its many inlets. They were, he wrote, "capable of affording great advantages to commercial pursuits, by opening communications with parts of the interior country commodiously and delightfully situated."[16] But Vancouver's writings did not visualize Puget Sound as the seat of a burgeoning Pacific commerce based on the productivity of a continent.

II

Even before Robert Gray discovered the Columbia, Thomas Jefferson had detected the true importance of the Pacific Northwest for the United States. For him, it was not a distant center of the fur trade but a gateway for American commerce in the Pacific. While still in Paris, he dispatched John Ledyard, a Connecticut adventurer, to find a continental route by entering Nootka Sound from Kamtchatka and eventually following the Missouri River to St. Louis.[17] Ledyard had reached the Yakutsk area of Siberia when Empress Catherine of Russia refused him permission to proceed further. In 1793 Jefferson, as a member of the American Philosophical Society, agreed to support the western explorations of the noted French botanist, André Michaux. He asked Michaux to "seek for and pursue that route which shall form the shortest and most convenient communication between the high parts of the Missouri and the Pacific

Ocean."[18] Jefferson's instructions to Meriwether Lewis, dated June 20, 1803, again revealed his commercial interest in the distant Northwest. "The object of your mission," the president charged the leader of the famed Lewis and Clark expedition, "is to explore the Missouri River, and such principal streams of it, as by its course and communication with the waters of the Pacific Ocean, may offer the most direct and practicable water communication across the continent, for the purposes of commerce."[19] Britain as well approached the task of empire-building in the Northwest by land rather than sea. In 1793 Alexander Mackenzie crossed the continent, reaching the Pacific on July 20 north of Vancouver Island. For Mackenzie, who published an account of his travels in 1801, Britain's future in the Northwest lay in the development of transcontinental trade.[20]

Jefferson's purchase of Louisiana bridged the gap between the Mississippi and the Pacific shores, but it left United States claims to frontage on the distant ocean uncertain and inconclusive. In the Transcontinental Treaty of 1819, which defined the southern boundary of Louisiana, Spain gave up to the United States all its claim to the territory west of the Rockies and north of the 42nd parallel. During the previous year the United States and Britain had negotiated the northern boundary of Louisiana along the 49th parallel westward from the Lake of the Woods to the Rocky Mountains. The British government had first given significance to the 49th parallel in 1719 when its representative on the Anglo-French commission, appointed to carry out the terms of the Treaty of Utrecht, suggested that line as the southern limit of the Hudson's Bay Company activity. Beyond the Rockies, however, the United States faced the expanding British Empire, reaching across Canada to the Pacific coast, with the Hudson's Bay Company in the vanguard. In the Convention of 1818 the two contestants agreed to leave the region west of the mountains equally and freely accessible for a period of ten years to the vessels and citizens of either nation without prejudice to their respective claims.[21]

What quickly brought the Northwest coast into international diplomacy again was the Russian tsar's ukase of September 1821, which demanded exclusive rights for his subjects to trade, fish, or navigate within 100 Italian miles of the Northwest coast, from Bering Strait to the 51st parallel north latitude. In June 1823 Secretary of State John Quincy Adams introduced the cabinet to the question of Russian claims. These, he argued, the United States should contest, especially since Russia had no settlements in the disputed region. On July 17 Adams informed the Russian minister in Washington that the United States would accept no Russian territorial establishment on the continent. Adams wrote several days later, "There can, perhaps, be no better time for saying, frankly and explicitly, to the Russian Government that the future peace of the world, and the interest of Russia herself, can not be promoted by Russian settlement upon any part of the American continents."[22] Adams admitted to British Minister

Stratford Canning that the United States had no territorial claims as far
north as 51°; he assumed, however, that British interests would be sufficient to counter Russian demands. Adams suggested a Russian boundary
at 55°, reserving for Britain 6° of frontage on the Pacific between the
49th and the 55th parallels. British Foreign Minister George Canning's
rejection of Adams's project for a tripartite partition of the coast did not
prevent a settlement with Russia. To keep all of Prince of Wales Island
under Russian control, the Russians proposed the boundary of 54°40′.
In the convention of April 1824 London and Washington accepted the
Russian offer; Russia, in exchange, gave up all pretensions to a *mare
clausum* in the north Pacific.[23]

The settlements of 1819 and 1824 eliminated Spanish and Russian claims
from the Northwest, leaving the long coast between 42° and 54°40′ to the
two remaining contestants, Great Britain and the United States. American
diplomats put forth claims to the 49th parallel, arguing that prior discovery
and the fur trade gave the United States rights not only to the Columbia
Valley but also to the regions extending at least to the traditional line of
49°. Even Vancouver, they noted, readily admitted that Gray had
discovered the Columbia. Its course, without question, was first explored
by Lewis and Clark. The waters of Juan de Fuca Strait and Puget Sound,
Americans conceded, had been explored over time by Spanish, British,
and American navigators, but even here American officials claimed the
Spanish rights and the prerogatives accruing from the fur trade. The Pacific
Fur Company post of Astoria at the mouth of the Columbia merely added the right of prior settlement. Lastly, American negotiators insisted that
the principle of contiguity favored the extension of the 49th parallel to
the Pacific Ocean. But what made that line the *sine qua non* of any
American settlement was more than principle; it was the knowledge that
such a settlement would serve the American interest in ocean frontage admirably; the magnificent Juan de Fuca Strait and Puget Sound were south
of that line.[24]

British diplomats were far less sanguine. They hoped that by neutraliz-
ing the American claims of prior discovery, exploration, and settlement
they could reduce the contest to a matter of actual occupation. They emphasized the early British explorations of the Columbia and the Juan de
Fuca Strait. They insisted, further, that the Spaniards had terminated their
claims to the Oregon country in the Nootka settlement of 1790; for the
United States, therefore, the Spanish rights were no rights at all. It was
the British thesis that pretensions based on discovery and exploration were
at best confused and controversial, and that Oregon should be divided
on the basis of possession.[25] This was, for Britain, a strong position
because the entire region north of the Columbia had been continuously
in the possession of the Hudson's Bay Company. Fort Vancouver, located
on the north bank of the Columbia opposite the mouth of the Willamette,

was the chief Hudson's Bay post in Oregon. For Hudson's Bay officials possession of the Columbia was essential for the maintenance of the British fur trade in Oregon; the demands of the fur trade determined the objectives of British diplomacy. While adamant on the Columbia line, the British gave up all pretensions south of the river even though the Hudson's Bay Company maintained scattered posts in that region. Thus United States claims to Oregon were unchallenged in that broad strip of land between the Columbia and the 42nd parallel. It was the struggle for frontage on the Pacific that rendered the British proposal of the Columbia unacceptable.

In the Oregon negotiations of 1826, conducted by Albert Gallatin in London, President John Quincy Adams refused to retreat from the 49th parallel despite Gallatin's willingness to concede to the British the drainage basin of Fuca Strait. British Foreign Minister George Canning admitted his own commercial motivation during the 1826 negotiations when he wrote that he would not care to have his "name affixed to an instrument by which England would have foregone the advantage of our immense direct intercourse between China and what may be, if we resolve not to yield them up, her boundless establishments on the N.W. Coast of America."[26] Keenly aware of the underlying competition for ports between the two contestants in Oregon, Canning attempted unsuccessfully to quiet the American demand for 49° by offering a frontage of isolated territory on the strait. Adams preferred to prolong the diplomatic stalemate rather than to allow Britain to endanger permanently American maritime interests in the Pacific. In his effort to contain Britain, Adams established the fundamental American diplomatic position on Oregon. In lieu of a boundary settlement, the negotiators in London extended the principle of joint occupancy indefinitely, each nation obtaining the privilege of terminating the arrangement upon a twelve-month notice of such intention.[27] As late as the 1840s Oregon was still held in this state of equilibrium by two empires struggling for mastery of the Northwest coast.

III

Oregon's still unsettled boundary troubled Daniel Webster and Lord Ashburton as they confronted the full spectrum of United States-British disputes in their Washington negotiations of 1842. London again offered a settlement at the Columbia River. When Webster predictably rejected the proposal, the two negotiators simply eliminated the Oregon question from their subsequent deliberations.[28] For American observers the Columbia had long been of questionable value as an ocean port. The writings of travelers made axiomatic the dangers of the sand bar between Cape Disappointment and Point Adams, created by the vast quantities of sand carried down the Columbia and hurled back by the surf. "Mere

description," wrote Charles Wilkes, commander of the American exploring expedition to the Pacific, "can give little idea of the terrors of the bar
of the Columbia: all who have seen it have spoken of the wildness of the
scene, and the incessant roar of the waters, representing it as one of the
most fearful sights that can possibly meet the eye of the sailor." In sharp
contrast was Wilkes's description of Fuca Strait and the sea arms to the
east of it. "Nothing," he wrote, "can exceed the beauty of these waters,
and their safety: not a shoal exists within the Straits of Juan de Fuca,
Admiralty Inlet, Puget Sound, or Hood's Canal, that can in any way in-
terrupt their navigation by a seventy-four gun ship. I venture nothing in
saying, there is no country in the world that possesses waters equal to
these."[29] Such reports—and there were others—merely reaffirmed the
American commitment to the 49th parallel.

In London, Foreign Minister Lord Aberdeen continued to insist on the
Columbia line. Troubled, however, by the failure of the negotiators in
Washington to reach a settlement, he suggested to Edward Everett, the
United States minister in London, that Britain might support Webster's
tripartite scheme whereby the United States, accepting the Columbia line,
would extend its ocean frontage southward to San Francisco Bay through
a new territorial arrangement with Mexico. Whatever the possibilities of
such a division of the coastline, Everett and Aberdeen agreed that the two
countries should seek an early settlement of the Oregon boundary.[30] In
Washington, Webster doubted that the United States could gain San Francisco through a three-nation negotiation. At the same time he discounted
the value of the Columbia as an ocean port:

> It affords [he reminded Everett privately on November 28, 1842] very small accom-
> modations to commerce, in comparison with its size, or volume of water. For nine
> months in the year the navigation of its mouth is regarded as impracticable, and for
> the rest quite uncertain and inconvenient. If we should consent to be limited by the
> river on the north, we shall not have one tolerable harbor on the whole coast. The
> straits of St. Juan de Fuca, and the inland waters with which they communicate, un-
> doubtedly contain all the good harbors between the Russian settlements and California.

What, Webster wondered, were the British interests in Oregon?

> England [he speculated] wants a good harbor in the [Puget] Sound, connected with
> the ocean through these straits; she may want also the privilege of transporting furs
> and other commodities down the [Columbia] river; and I suppose it is an object with
> her to retain the settlement at Vancouver and the other small settlements further north,
> under her jurisdiction and protection. Does she want any more? I doubt whether she
> can contemplate any considerable colonization in the regions.[31]

Webster searched for a compromise. He rejected the notion of discon-
nected territory on the Fuca Strait. As an alternative to the British proposal of 1826, Webster suggested a settlement that would begin at "the
entrance of the straits of St. Juan de Fuca, follow up these Straits, give
us a harbor at the southwest corner of these inland waters, and then continue south, striking the [Columbia] river below Vancouver, and then

following the river to its intersection with the 49th degree of latitude North." Aberdeen's response to Webster's private proposal convinced Everett that London would eventually grant the United States access to the Strait of Juan de Fuca. Everett reported as late as February 1843 that Aberdeen anticipated no difficulty in negotiating a settlement based on Webster's compromise line.[32] How the secretary intended to carry such a boundary arrangement through the Senate was not clear.

President John Tyler inadvertently aroused congressional interest in the Oregon question when, in his annual message of December 1842 he placed responsibility for his failure to achieve a satisfactory Oregon settlement that year on the British.[33] In late December Senator Lewis F. Linn of Missouri introduced a bill to encourage the American occupation of Oregon, and thereby strengthen American claims to the contested region, by establishing civil government south of the Columbia. British Minister Henry Fox immediately warned London that such action would destabilize the balance of forces in Oregon. Webster feared no less that the demands of Western politicians and editors for an immediate Oregon settlement would complicate the process of defining a boundary that would assure American access to the Strait of Juan de Fuca and Puget Sound. Webster wrote to Everett in late January 1843: "We feel the importance of settling this question if we can, but we fear embarrassments and difficulties, not, perhaps so much from the subject itself, as from the purposes of men, and of parties, connected with it."[34] The Linn Bill threatened all progress toward a diplomatic settlement. Aberdeen assured Webster that if the Linn measure, as a violation of the joint occupancy convention, passed the Congress, Britain would take whatever steps seemed essential for the maintenance of its claims. The Senate adopted the Linn Bill by a vote of 24 to 22, but the House Committee on Foreign Affairs rejected the proposal.[35]

As if to eliminate every possibility of an early Oregon settlement, a convention of delegates from six western states gathered in Cincinnati in early July 1843, and there proclaimed that the rights of the United States to all the territory between 49° and 54°40′ was clear and unquestionable.[36] The convention based its claim on the Monroe Doctrine, which declared that the American continents "were not thenceforth to be considered subjects for future colonization by any foreign power." In London this western provincialism created a mood of urgency. Aberdeen pressed Everett for a new boundary proposal, preferring to conduct the negotiations in London rather than in Washington. In August, however, Aberdeen instructed Fox to assure the Tyler administration that he was empowered to negotiate should it prefer to submit a proposition to him.[37]

Finally, in October 1843, Tyler and his new secretary of state, Abel Upshur, drafted a new Oregon boundary proposal. Tyler dropped Webster's compromise of the previous November that would have granted Britain the Columbia line except for a strip of land extending northward along the coast to the southern shore of Fuca Strait. To achieve the necessary British retreat from the Columbia, Upshur instructed Everett to assert American claims to the Russian line. "Our commerce in the Pacific Ocean," added Upshur, "is already of great extent and value, requiring the presence of armed vessels to protect it; and there is no port belonging to us to which our vessels, whether of commerce or of war, can resort, south of the Straits of Fuca." Everett, having claimed the whole of Oregon, could offer the 49th parallel as a compromise, granting the British, in exchange, the right to navigate the Columbia River. In London, Everett assured Aberdeen that the traditional American offer of 49° comprised a reasonable and equitable settlement of the Oregon dispute. Aberdeen argued that Britain, in 1824 and again in 1826, had rejected that line. "There must," he said, "be concessions on both sides." Everett responded with the proposal that Britain retain all of Vancouver Island with its frontage on Fuca Strait.[38]

Tyler, in his message of December 1843, again complicated the Oregon question by reasserting the American claim to the whole of Oregon. Without revealing what boundary he sought, the president promised the nation that he would seek a quick and satisfactory settlement of the Oregon boundary. Meanwhile, he added, Congress might protect American emigrants to the Oregon country by establishing military posts along the route and by extending American laws to assure civil order for the pioneers after their arrival.[39] The British minister in Washington detected no presidential promise in the message that would eliminate an acceptable compromise. Thus encouraged, Aberdeen now returned to the British proposal of 1826—the Columbia with an enclave of territory at the mouth of Fuca Strait and free use of all ports in British territory south of 49°, thereby, he noted, giving the United States access to good anchorages in the Pacific Northwest.[40] This British proposal would have converted Puget Sound and the coast to the Columbia into a free trade zone. Whether this arrangement would have served the American commercial interest was doubtful; the United States could never have brought its full economic power to bear on ports that lay in British territory. Richard Pakenham, the new British minister, carried Aberdeen's new proposal with him to Washington in February 1844.

Pakenham had scarcely initiated his negotiations in Washington when an explosion aboard the American war vessel *Princeton* killed Secretary of State Upshur. In March Tyler offered the position to John C. Calhoun. During the debates on the Linn Bill in January 1843, Calhoun had advised a policy of "wise and masterly inactivity" in Oregon, convinced that legislation to foster American occupation was unnecessary and unduly destructive of American relations with Britain. Calhoun argued that "time is acting for us; and if we shall have the wisdom to trust its operation, it will assert and maintain our right with resistless force, without costing a cent of money or a drop of blood."[41] Calhoun's strategy recognized the role of the pioneers in strengthening the diplomacy of the United States on the Oregon issue; it did not suggest what the ultimate settlement should be. Calhoun's policy of "masterly inactivity" seemed to be succeeding as a thousand pioneers in the spring of 1843 prepared to leave for Oregon. When in August Calhoun finally reopened the Oregon negotiations, Pakenham presented a proposal based on Aberdeen's instructions of late December 1843; Calhoun rejected the offer outright.[42] During subsequent weeks Calhoun and Pakenham set forth the traditional British and American claims to Oregon; these, Calhoun acknowledged, scarcely established any historic American rights to the 49°, much less to 54°40'. Pakenham argued that the final partition of Oregon should satisfy the interests and convenience of both countries; by giving the United States access to harbors, he wrote, the British offer had satisfied the interests of the United States.[43]

By September 1844 the two countries approached an acceptable compromise. When Calhoun again insisted on the 49th parallel, Pakenham reminded him that Britain required some concessions such as the tip of Vancouver Island and free navigations of the Columbia. In London, Aberdeen arrived at precisely the same compromise. On September 25, he revealed his private convictions in a letter to British Prime Minister Sir Robert Peel. Britain, he admitted, would not accept the traditional American proposal of the 49th parallel to the Pacific. That line would cut Britain off from the Strait of Juan de Fuca.

> But [he continued] if the line of the 49th degree were extended only to the water's edge, and should leave us in possession of all of Vancouver's Island, with the northern side of the entrance to Puget's Sound; and if all the harbors within the Sound and the Columbia, inclusive, were made free to both countries; and further, if the river Columbia from the point at which it became navigable to its mouth, were also made free to both, this would be in reality a most advantageous settlement.[44]

In Washington, Calhoun rejected what was fundamentally the Everett compromise, convinced that the Senate would not approve it. In London, Peel agreed with Aberdeen on the acceptability of the settlement, but reminded the foreign minister that the British government's opposition was not prepared to depart from the traditional British offer of the Columbia line. To avoid risk to the ministry's political future, Aberdeen recommended a settlement by arbitration. "The Oregon question," he wrote, "is principally or best suited for arbitration. Its real importance is insignificant; but the press of both countries, and public clamor, have given it a fictitious interest which renders it difficult for either government to act with moderation, or with common sense."[45] Arbitration would free responsible officials in both London and Washington from the limits imposed by their domestic detractors. For Calhoun, unlike Aberdeen, the issue was not one of minor importance; predictably, in January 1845, he rejected arbitration.[46]

IV

By 1845 British leaders had advanced the Oregon negotiations to the point of settlement. Unfortunately those Democrats campaigning for the whole of Oregon in the 1844 election seemed to eliminate the possibilities of a negotiated boundary settlement altogether. James K. Polk, the new Democratic president, had identified himself completely with his party's platform. Only by escaping his obligations to the platform and the Democrats who took the platform seriously could he accept a settlement even at 49°. In his inaugural, Polk, in declaring the American title to Oregon "clear and unquestionable," appeared concerned more with the cohesiveness of his party than with a settlement of the Oregon question.[47] Still Polk, as president, could scarcely abandon the country's diplomatic tradition that had offered Britain a boundary along the 49th parallel. What compelled his immediate return to the traditional offer was the violent reaction that his inaugural produced in both the United States and England.[48] Yet it was clear even then that politics had forever destroyed Polk's freedom to negotiate an acceptable boundary in Oregon. To insist on 54°40′, recalled Senator Thomas Hart Benton of Missouri, meant war; to recede from it was to abandon the platform. Polk met the first danger in July 1845 by offering Britain the 49th parallel to the Pacific; Pakenham rejected the proposal without referring it to London.[49]

Polk, having made a half-hearted effort at negotiation, refused thereafter to reopen the discussions. His commitment to his fellow Democrats would not permit him to abandon the platform again. When late in October T. W. Ward, the Boston agent of Baring Brothers, called on the president to seek his views, Polk noted the result in his diary: "He learned nothing, and after apologizing for making the inquiry he retired." Secretary of State James Buchanan reminded the president repeatedly that the country would not support a war for any territory north of 49°. Polk, in response, assured Buchanan that his gravest danger lay in an attack on his administration for having yielded to the position of his predecessors by offering the 49th parallel. "I told him," Polk recorded, "that if that proposition had been accepted by the British Minister my course would have met with great opposition, and in my opinion would have gone far to overthrow the administration; that, had it been accepted, as we came in on Texas the probability was we would have gone out on Oregon."[50] Polk's message to Congress in December 1845 again assured the Democratic party that he was thoroughly attuned to the declaration of the 1844 Baltimore Convention. He declared: "The extraordinary and wholly inadmissible demands of the British Government, and the rejection of the proposition made in deference alone to what had been done by my predecessors, and the implied obligation which their acts seemed to impose, afforded satisfactory evidence that no compromise which the United States ought to accept, can be effected." The American title, he repeated, was maintained "by irrefragable facts and arguments."[51] The president seemed to promise that he would not weaken again, but he carefully avoided any phraseology that would deny him the freedom to submit a compromise treaty to the Senate. He requested the necessary congressional authorization to give notice terminating joint occupancy in Oregon and he was prepared to exert pressure on Britain without assuming the diplomatic initiative.

Privately, Polk from the beginning favored a settlement at the 49th parallel. Indeed, his personal views toward Oregon differed little from those of Adams, Webster, and the commercially minded Whigs. Ports, he admitted, were all that mattered. He conceded in July 1845 that the United States could easily settle at 49° "since the entrance of the Straits of Fuca, Admiralty Inlet, and Puget's Sound, with their fine harbors and rich surrounding soil, are all south of this parallel." Polk accepted without question the verdict of travelers that the country to the north was unfit for agriculture and incapable of sustaining anything but the fur trade. With his advisors he doubted "whether the judgment of the civilized world would be in our favor in a war waged for a comparatively worthless territory north of 49°, which his predecessors had over and over again offered to surrender to Great Britain, provided she would yield her pretensions to the country south of that latitude."[52] Polk, thereafter, never lost sight of the Strait of Juan de Fuca. In his December message he declared that the United States could never accept a settlement in Oregon that "would leave on the British side two-thirds of the whole Oregon territory, including the free navigation of the Columbia and all valuable harbors on the Pacific." Later that month Polk noted in his diary that he would submit to the Senate for its previous advice any British offer that would grant to the United States the Strait of Fuca and some free ports to the north.[53]

Again Polk's interest in Pacific ports was apparent in his vigorous resistance to arbitration during the early months of 1846. He would not, he wrote, jeopardize the American acquisition of harbors on Admiralty Inlet and Puget Sound. Oregon, he asserted in his rejection, presented the avenue for commerce between Asia and the western coasts of North America. This vast region, moreover, had no safe and commodious harbors except near the 49th parallel. For commercial purposes, he informed Minister Louis McLane in London, "the United States might almost as well abandon the whole territory as consent to deprive ourselves of these harbors; because south of them, within its limits, no good harbor exists."[54]

Unable to lead the country toward the acceptance of the 49th parallel, Polk could only rely on those who favored compromise to deflate the influence of his political allies in the Democratic party. When Congress met in December 1845, there was little evidence that within six months the settlement of the disturbing Oregon question would be assured. Polk's message had followed his stated conviction that "the only way to treat John Bull is to look him straight in the eye." Enthusiasm for the whole of Oregon, enlivened by the president's message, rapidly translated United States claims in the distant Northwest into what Albert K. Weinberg once termed a "defiant anti-legalism."[55] No longer would the United States base its claims on discovery and exploration. The fact that Oregon was nearer to the United States than to Britain seemed sufficient to establish the superiority of American claims. Added to that was the assumption that an Oregon possessed by the United States would be democratic and teeming with a vigorous agricultural and commercial population, whereas a British Oregon would be monarchical and consigned to the fur trade. Edward D. Baker of Illinois informed the House of Representatives that he had little regard for "musty records and the voyages of old sea captains, or the Spanish treaties," because the United States had a better title "under the law of nature and of nations."[56] The most uncompromising Democrats in Congress were representatives from the Midwest—Ohio, Indiana, and Illinois. Senator Edward Hannegan of Indiana proposed a toast at a Philadelphia convocation: "Oregon—every foot or not an inch; 54 degrees and forty minutes or *delenda est Britannia*." It was not strange that a tenseness gripped the capital as members gathered for the opening of Congress. Few seemed willing to challenge the superior patriotism of the extremists. John C. Calhoun admitted later that when he arrived at Washington in December, it was dangerous even to whisper "forty-nine."[57]

Actually, this expanding outlook was doomed from the opening of Congress by the patent interests of American commercialism. Too many congressional eyes were narrowly trained on ports to permit the triumph of agrarian nationalism and the war that it might have produced. Samuel Gordon of New York phrased his district's cogent evaluation of Oregon in the House by stating, "It is the key to the Pacific. It will command the trade of the isles of the Pacific, of the East, and of China." Washington Hunt, also of New York, repeated this dominant theme, noting, "Its possession will ultimately secure to us an ascendancy in the trade of the Pacific, thereby making 'the uttermost parts of the earth' tributary to our enterprise, and pouring into our lap 'the wealth of Ormus and of Ind.' "[58] Salt spray had long conditioned New England's outlook. Early in January 1846, Robert Winthrop clearly defined the objectives of his constituents. "We need ports on the Pacific," he shouted. "As to land, we have millions of acres of better land still unoccupied on this side of the mountains."[59]

During the preceding year, William Sturgis, still an active member of Boston's commercial aristocracy, had popularized such particularistic notions in the Bay State. His three decades of intense maritime activity in the Pacific had channeled his attention to ports and not to land. In his famous lecture to the citizens of Boston in January 1845, Sturgis admitted that the Willamette Valley, the seat of American settlement in Oregon, was both attractive and productive, but he had never heard, he added, of any Oregon lands which were superior to millions of uncultivated acres east of the Rockies. Sturgis indicated, moreover, which ports in Oregon the United States would require to assure its future leadership in the Oriental trade. The Columbia, he warned, was always dangerous for large ships and almost inaccessible for a considerable portion of each year. Instead, this country's maritime greatness in the Pacific would derive from the possession of the Strait of Juan de Fuca and its numerous branches which were "easy of access, safe, and navigable at all seasons and in any weather."[60] This lucid analysis of American interests on the Northwest coast, complementing the writings of other travelers and merchants, determined fully the views of commercial America and its representatives in Congress toward the Oregon question.

Such assumptions, regarding Oregon and its future importance, compelled midwestern congressmen also to debate the Oregon question in commercial terms; Oregon held a special mercantile significance for their constituents as well. What disturbed these nationalists, however, was the fact that the constant reiteration of the commercial value of the Oregon coast bespoke compromise at the 49th parallel, for that boundary would give the United States access to Fuca Strait and Puget Sound.[61] Responding to the challenge, some uncompromising Democrats argued that the coastal regions north of 49° were essential for America's future in the Pacific. John McClernand of Illinois warned members of the House against the fatal error of compromise. "Commercially," he declared, "by such a concession, we voluntarily decapitate ourselves upon the Pacific seaboard; we lose that portion of Oregon which bears the same relation to the Pacific, in furnishing a commercial marine upon that ocean, which New England now bears upon the Atlantic. . . ." Furthermore, McClernand predicted, "The American or British marine, which will whiten the Pacific, . . .will be built, owned, and navigated by a similar people, who shall dwell north of the 49th parallel."[62] Similarly, Senator Hannegan warned those who favored compromise, "Let England possess Nootka Sound, the finest harbor in the world, commanding as it does the Strait of Fuca, and consequently the access to Puget's Sound, and she has all of Oregon worth possessing in a commercial and maritime point of view." He turned his abuse on men dominated by narrow commercialism. "It is the opinion of six-sevenths of the American people," he said, "that Oregon is ours — perhaps I should rather say five-sevenths, for I must leave out of the estimate the commercial and stockjobbing population of our great cities along the seaboard, a great portion of whom are English subjects, residing among us for the purpose of traffic. . . ."[63]

V

By January 1846 the movement for compromise in the United States had effectively challenged the hold of the extremists on American thought. That month the *North American Review* demanded a settlement of the Oregon question on some consideration other than that of shopworn titles that neither side intended to concede. "We have been arguing the question for thirty years," charged the writer, "and stand precisely where we did when the discussion commenced." The debate, he declared, sounded like a "solemn mummery" in which too many ambitious politicians were preventing the vast majority from regarding the issue with perfect indifference. The writer continued, "Not one in ten thousand . . . would be immediately affected by the successful assertion of our claim to the whole of Oregon."⁶⁴ Soon even the metropolitan expansionist press began to foster compromise. Throughout the commercial East, writers accused western Democrats of clinging to an unrealistic cause and employing it to play upon the nationalistic emotions of the American people, not to obtain Oregon, but to attain political power. Eastern merchants complained that threats of war were hampering United States commerce around the world, for no whaler or East India merchantman would venture freely onto the high seas with a war in the offing. "This will all do famously for the valley of the Mississippi, where they have all to gain by a war and nothing to lose," grumbled the New York merchant, Philip Hone. "But we on the seaboard must fight all, pay all, and suffer all."⁶⁵ Even from the Old Northwest, where anti-British feeling was strongest, came demands for compromise.⁶⁶

In Congress the movement for a settlement at the 49th parallel enjoyed the leadership of two powerful Democratic factions. Thomas Hart Benton and John A. Dix led the old Van Buren group in the Senate; John C. Calhoun spoke for the conservative southern bloc. Calhoun regarded himself as the Senate's chief spokesman for compromise; so the press regarded him also. The Washington correspondent of the New York *Journal of Commerce* defined his role precisely: "Mr. Calhoun, from the moment of his arrival here, had exerted himself to calm the agitated waters. He has counselled admirably, and is still engaged in promoting a good understanding between the British Minister and our Government. . . . To do this, he has used his efforts both with Whigs and Democrats, in both Houses, and has succeeded."⁶⁷ As early as February, Calhoun prepared a resolution to advise the president to reopen negotiations with England for a settlement at 49°. Whig support assured the eventual triumph of Calhoun's compromise efforts. Webster wrote in January, "Most of the Whigs in the Senate incline to remain rather quiet, and to follow the lead of Mr. Calhoun. He is at the head of a party of six or seven, and as he professes still to be an administration man, it is best to leave the work in his hands, at least for the present." The New York *Herald* described well this strange political alignment: "The chivalry of the West goes hot and strong for 54-40, while the ardent South, and the calculating East, coalesce, for once, on this point, and quietly and temperately call for 49."[68] By late February it had become obvious to the administration that a compromise at the 49th parallel would receive a two-thirds vote in the Senate.

Polk alone carried the responsibility for the nation's diplomacy. Those who favored a settlement with Britain necessarily looked to him for leadership. Politicians and the press assured the administration that the overwhelming majority of the American people would sustain its search for a compromise. "Six clear heads in Washington," argued one editor, "are much more likely to come to a correct conclusion of the Nation's welfare, than hundreds of popular meetings composed of tens of thousands of excited individuals."[69] Those who urged the president to assume the diplomatic initiative sensed correctly the peaceful intent of the administration. Yet Polk was unable to respond. The unequivocal language of his message and the pressures within his party prevented him from pursuing a settlement at the 49th parallel. Increasingly his position became untenable, for he found himself trapped between the ultimate necessity of accepting a settlement at 49° and the immediate necessity of supporting, at least publicly, the expansionists of his own party. Buchanan reminded the president that the 54-40 men were the true friends of the administration. John J. Crittenden, the Kentucky Whig, saw some discretion in Buchanan's caution. "The hardest swearers are for fifty-four forty," Crittenden wrote, "and he thinks, perhaps, by taking the same position he may escape more *curses* than in any other way." [70]

Aberdeen in the crisis assumed the leadership that politics had denied to Polk. The British foreign minister had acknowledged his retreat to 49° in September 1844. When in 1845 the Hudson's Bay Company moved its main depot from the Columbia to Vancouver Island because of the decline of the fur traffic and the growing pressure of American immigrants, it admitted that the Columbia boundary was no longer essential to its interests. The British surrender of the Columbia was the key to the Oregon settlement.[71] In April 1846 Congress passed the resolution for notice. As the administration anticipated, Britain responded with an acceptable proposal. This the president, without hesitation, forwarded to the Senate, explaining to expansionist Democrats that his own responsibilities and the state of public opinion gave him no choice.[72] When the Senate approved the British offer, Polk prepared a definitive treaty. This the Senate ratified in June.

By requesting the notice Polk undoubtedly created the occasion for the Oregon settlement. Beyond that the president assumed little responsibility for what occurred. Clinging as he did to the party platform, he denied himself the freedom to negotiate directly with the British. Webster placed credit for the treaty elsewhere: "The discussions in Congress, the discussions on the other side of the water, the general sense of the community, all protested against the iniquity of two of the greatest nations of modern times rushing into war. . . . All enforced the conviction, that it was a question to be settled by an equitable and fair consideration, and it was thus settled." Pakenham agreed. To him, Polk had remained attuned to the theme of 54-40 too long to exert any influence in bringing a final settlement. He attributed the treaty to either the "wisdom and integrity of the Senate, or the intelligence and good sense of the American people."[73] Even such Democratic leaders as Calhoun believed to the end that they had achieved the final agreement against the influence of the president.

The Oregon Treaty differed in only two respects from Polk's proposal of July 1845. The president had demanded the extension of the 49th parallel to the Pacific, with Britain ceding the southern tip of Vancouver Island. He omitted all reference to British navigation on the Columbia. Aberdeen countered with the British position: the 49th parallel to the middle of the channel between the mainland and Vancouver Island, and then a line southward through King George's Sound and westward through the Strait of Juan de Fuca to the Pacific. This boundary would convey all of Vancouver Island to Great Britain. In addition, Aberdeen demanded common use of the Columbia. McLane in London urged the acceptance of the British position, convinced that Britain would not retreat further. Polk readily conceded the loss of Vancouver Island, but he believed that concession sufficient to terminate all further negotiation over free ports to the south of Fuca Strait. He feared some future conflict along the Columbia if Britain retained navigation rights. McLane recommended that use of the Columbia be limited to the Hudson's Bay Company.[74] These modifications, agreed to in advance by both countries, comprised the only diplomatic achievement in the negotiations of 1846.

For Polk and Aberdeen, long in essential agreement over the equitable distribution of the Northwest's waterways, the Oregon Treaty was hardly a major compromise. Large portions of the British and American publics, however, viewed the final settlement as a sacrifice. The task of leadership in the crisis consisted of bringing opinion in both countries to an acceptance of the 49th parallel. Since domestic partisanship tied the president's hands, Congress and the metropolitan press led the movement for compromise in the United States. What brought easy success was the total irrelevance of the 54-40 issue to the well-defined and achievable interests of the United States. For Aberdeen the task of securing support was more difficult, because Britain, unlike the United States, retreated from a traditional offer.[75] Both nations were generally content with the distribution of land and ports. During the closing argument on the Oregon Treaty, Benton passed final judgment on the 49th parallel stating that, "With this boundary comes all that we want in that quarter, namely, all the waters of Puget's Sound, and the fertile Olympian district which borders upon them." The Oregon settlement brought to the business communities on both sides of the Atlantic relief from the evils of suspense and uncertainty. A brief poem in the New York *Herald* summed up well the attitude of the English-speaking world:

> *Old Buck and Pack*
> *Are coming back*
> *And will soon together dine.*
> *And drink a toast*
> *Upon their roast*
> *To number forty-nine.*[76]

The American Indian and Freedom of Religion: An Historic Appraisal

American historians recognized as early as 1907, when J. Franklin Jameson made it the subject of his presidential address before the American Historical Association, that religion has played an important part in the nation's social and cultural development. Jameson declared that any scholar who wanted to understand the American character, "and to that end would provide himself with data representing all classes, all periods, all regions, may find in the history of American religion the closest approach to the continuous record he desires." For the average person, religion had drawn far more universal attention than literature, philosophy, music, art, or even politics. It was true, Jameson conceded, that the main concern of the masses had always been the daily struggle to make a living, but history must be concerned "with more than mere economic matters."

Even though white Americans have long realized the importance of religion in their own culture, they have been reluctant to extend this same acknowledgement to Indian religion. Early Protestant missionaries, such as the Whitmans and Spaldings, were quickly given a place in the pantheon of Pacific Northwest history. Likewise, the diligent labors of the Catholic fathers, such as François Norbert Blanchet and Peter John DeSmet, did not go unnoticed by scholars. Yet many modern-day Americans view Indian spiritual systems as something less than valid religions and force Native Americans to continue to struggle for religious freedom.

By examining Indian-white history in the Pacific Northwest, Alvin M. Josephy, Jr., shows that Indian spiritual systems have been largely ignored as key motivating forces in Indian life and in their relations with whites. The result has been a legacy that in large measure continues to denigrate the true nature and role of Indian religions.

Josephy is one of the nation's leading authors of American Indian history. He has written several prize-winning works on Indians, including the widely read and often cited *The Nez Perce Indians and the Opening of the Northwest* (1965), as well as *The Patriot Chiefs* (1961), *The Indian Heritage of America* (1968), and *Red Power* (1971). His most recent book, *Now That the Buffalo's Gone: A Study of Today's American Indians* (1982), contains a chapter on hunting and fishing rights and includes the story of the Pacific Northwest fishing conflict. A former editor of *American Heritage Magazine*, Josephy is now senior editor of that publication. He has also been an associate editor of *Time Magazine*, a Hollywood screen writer, a World War II Marine Corps combat correspondent, a radio news director, and a reporter for the *New York Herald-Tribune*. He presently serves as president of the Institute of the American West at Sun Valley, Idaho, and as a trustee for the Museum of the American Indian in New York. His summer home is at Joseph in the Wallowa Valley of northeastern Oregon. This essay was first presented by Josephy in the Pettyjohn Distinguished Lecture Series, Washington State University, fall 1982.

A pre-1877 photograph of a group of Nez Perce who practiced the Dreamer religion.
*Manuscripts, Archives, and Special Collections Washington State University Library,
Pullman, Washington*

The American Indian and Freedom of Religion: An Historic Appraisal

ALVIN M. JOSEPHY, Jr.

On August 11, 1978, Congress passed an American Indian Religious Freedom Act. Most of the non-Indian American population was unaware of its passage. Indeed, if a large publicity splash had been made about it, many might well have wondered why such legislation had occupied the mind and time of Congress in a nation which for almost two hundred years had prided itself on the possession of a constitutional guarantee of religious freedom.

To native Americans, including those in the Northwest, and to whites who were knowledgeable about their affairs, the answer was clear. Most Americans have long recognized that—as in the case of the Mormons and those of others who from time to time have known intolerance—elements of the population have not always lived up to or enforced the constitutional guarantee. But in the case of the Indians, as late as 1978—and even continuing today—most native Americans have been unhappily aware that a majority of the rest of the population has sanctioned a widespread interference with, trampling upon, and profaning of their traditional native religions. As corroborated by current fishing and other conflicts and by accumulating court cases, it has even failed on numerous occasions to regard them as religions understood and protected by the Constitution.[1]

The testimony has been heard in the courts, in public discussions, hearings before Congress, and in the media. In Washington, Oregon, and Idaho, as well as the Great Lakes states, many whites, including state and federal officials, have readily grasped the economic competitiveness of Indian fishermen, who demand the observance of their treaty fishing rights. But whites have cynically greeted assertions that those rights also have a deep and continuing religious significance for the Indians. Somewhat begrudgingly under court decisions, they have apportioned fish to the treaty tribes for "ceremonial use"—the ceremonies, in the public mind, usually conveying the image of being a tribal civic or social event rather than a genuine and meaningful religious experience. In a similar vein, in another part of the country, the long fight of the Taos Pueblo Indians in New Mexico to regain title to their sacred Blue Lake and the forests around it, the fountainhead of their centuries-old religion, was opposed until 1970 by whites who could see no visible religious shrines in the area and charged that the Indians' religion was therefore a fraud being used to hide the tribe's economic desire to exploit the timber in the forests.[2]

A good deal of this attitude stems from history and continues as a legacy of innocence, ignorance, and stereotypic thinking, exemplified by the early Washington settler and writer George Gibbs who in 1854 informed the United States government that the Klickitat tribe "in common with the other Oregon tribes, seem to have had no distinct religious ideas previous to those introduced by the whites. . . . Their mythology consists of vague and incoherent tales. . . ."[3] Some is a holdover of cultural arrogance. Whatever may be the contemporary reasons for such thinking, the mounting litigation and persistent pressure and testimony of Indians before congressional committees in the 1970s, seeking protection for various aspects of their spiritual life, persuaded Congress that neither the government nor the general public had yet accorded traditional native religions the validity and legal rights to which they were entitled. And this was a century after the close of wars against the tribes and a half-century after Indians had been recognized, in 1924, as full citizens of the United States.

Despite its passage, the 1978 Religious Freedom Act has had, as yet, little impact on the long heritage that it was meant to overcome and reverse. Introduced by James Abourezk of South Dakota, Democratic chairman of the Senate's Select Committee on Indian Affairs, it stated, "Henceforth it shall be the policy of the United States to protect and preserve for American Indians their inherent right of freedom to believe, express, and exercise the traditional religions of the American Indian, Eskimo, Aleut, and native Hawaiians, including but not limited to access to sites, use, and possession of sacred objects and the freedom to worship through ceremonials and traditional sites."

The Act called for consultations with Indians, and government hearings were conducted around the country to "determine appropriate changes necessary to protect and preserve Native American religious cultural rights and practices." The grievances expressed by the Indians at those hearings were numerous and varied. They included resentments over the desecration of cemeteries and sacred sites, lack of access to such sites and to materials needed for holy purposes, and interference with ceremonies and rituals. One hearing was held on the Colville Reservation at Nespelem, Washington, on June 14 and 15, 1979. Tribal members from throughout the Northwest listed a host of complaints, which included the dwindling supply of salmon and other fish necessary for religious purposes; the halting of ceremonial fishing at certain sites and the lack of access to other spiritually important locations; the desecration and destruction by loggers and others of traditionally sacred areas; the disinterment of Indian remains by highway and dam builders and the failure to rebury them (holding the remains instead in boxes in museums and other public buildings); the vandalism of Indian burial sites; the inability to secure eagle feathers and animal and vegetable products needed for religious purposes; the interference by customs officials on the United States-Canadian border with the trafficking of religious objects between tribal groups in the two countries; the breaking up of religious ceremonies of Indian college students by local police; and the denial of the right of Indian prison inmates to practice their native religions and use sweat baths, Indian religious objects, and the ministrations of native religious teachers.[4]

The Act unfortunately had no teeth. Its policy — expected only to serve as an educational stimulus for the general public — was intended to be observed in principle and action by the three branches of the federal government. Some of the agencies of the executive branch, including divisions of the Departments of Justice and the Interior, have since made efforts to satisfy or ameliorate certain of the Indians' expressed grievances. These have ranged from helping to provide tribes with eagle feathers and other special products and materials required for spiritual purposes to exercising greater care than before in considering threats to Indian religious and cultural sites in government-prepared environmental impact statements. But, by and large, little else has changed. The knowledge of, and attitude toward, Indian religions by state governments and the general public have been largely unaffected, and the court cases have gone on. Even federal agencies, when it has suited their purposes, have defeated Indian attempts to make the Act effective. In Tennessee, for example, the Cherokees since 1979 were unable to prevent the TVA's Tellico Dam from flooding a host of their most sacred sites, and in Arizona a Navajo appeal for the protection of holy shrines at Rainbow Bridge was rejected by the Bureau of Reclamation and by federal courts.[5]

Today, the Indians' struggle for equality of their religious freedoms that would match that enjoyed by all other Americans has a particular relevancy for non-Indian historians. In the quest to understand the nature of present-day conflicts with Indians, we must fall back on the roots of those differences, examining how well we know what led from there to here. In doing so, it becomes clear that we have largely ignored or underemphasized a key and often decisive element in Indian-white relations: that is, the strong, pervasive force of spirituality in Indian life. Relying heavily on white witnesses and their testimony and documentation, we have focused on what have seemed to be essentially political and economic motives and clashes. Though we have also shown an appreciation for the existence of cultural differences and misunderstandings, we have only rarely given adequate attention to the role of native American spirituality as a motive for Indian actions and reactions, or compellingly seen the white impacts on the Indian's spiritual life. Even our infatuation with political and economic forces has been somewhat deficient. While we have acknowledged that among the whites religious motives were frequently intermingled with materialistic aims — as with the Puritans in New England and various missionaries in the Northwest — we have failed at the same time to recognize that among the Indians political and economic thought and actions often flowed directly and naturally from the profound religious content of their group and individual lives.

This dereliction, recognized today more by Indian scholars than by their white peers, has resulted not only in a distortion of history, but also in a heritage that continues to denigrate native Indian religions so thoroughly that most whites still know little of their actual nature or role. Being uninformed, moreover, they continue to accept the old popularized image of them — furthered by generations of cheap fiction, movies, and television — as not religions at all, but instead as backward and outmoded "medicine man" superstition or, as Gibbs wrote, something "vague and incoherent." Though most Americans are at least benign enough to feel indifferent about what spiritual beliefs and practices Indians wish to embrace for themselves, they remain skeptical about their religious validity (regarding sweat baths, for instance, as picturesque and sun dances as entertainment), and will not suffer Indian religious-based claims to interfere with the projects and wants of the dominant non-Indian society. As a result, Indian religions, when clashing with non-Indian interests over land use, the taking of fish, or other matters, are still often deemed unworthy of protection under the First Amendment.

Historically, our attitude finds roots in patterns established by the early Spanish, French, and English explorers, settlers, and entrepreneurs who came to what is now the United States. If they learned anything about Indian religious life, as some of them did, they found it strange and alien, and judged it as inferior, heathenish, malevolent, and usually unworthy of tolerance. A vast literature exists on the efforts, everywhere in this country, to convert the tribes to the religions of the whites. What is less familiar is what the tribes were being converted from.

In the Pacific Northwest, as in all parts of the Americas, there was no single Indian religion. Spiritual ideas, practices, and systems varied from one native group to another, sometimes profoundly, sometimes only in details. In view of the Euro-Americans' ideas about them, however, it was ironic that everywhere they were relentless and pervasive. The fact of the matter is that Indian religions have always been the skein that held Indian life together, from morning till night, from day to day, from year to year. All of them had evolved through the centuries to help ensure the survival, unity, and well-being of the different peoples, and, as all religions seek to do, to provide individuals and groups with answers to such fundamental questions as: "Who am I?"; "Where did I come from and where am I going?"; "What are the meaning and purpose of my existence?"; and "What is my relationship to others, to my group, to the rest of creation, and to the unseen world?"[6]

Most, if not all, of the native religions in the Northwest, as elsewhere, taught that everything in the universe — the trees, the winds, the rocks, the living creatures, and man himself — possessed a spiritual power, or life force, and that all of these spiritual forces, together with those of the unseen world, were interconnected in a delicate, harmonious balance that allowed individuals and their groups to survive and enjoy well-being. Much as we talk today of the need to maintain ecological systems, so the native religions taught that individuals, by errant thoughts or deeds, could disrupt the harmony, balance, and order of the spiritual network and imperil themselves and their communities. All behavior, all conduct, all actions, reactions, and decisions, therefore, took into account the impact they would have in either maintaining or disrupting the group's harmonious relationship with the various elements of the spiritual universe.

Some of the religions' systems appeared relatively simple in outward form, resting essentially on long-defined relationships between Indian groups or individuals and their shamans, men and women with strong spiritual powers that enabled them to communicate or intercede with the supernatural world for purposes either good or bad. Usually they assisted the people as mediums who could bring about desired aims, as foreseers of the future, or as curers. Thus, the whites termed them derogatorily "witch doctors," "wizards," or "medicine men," despite the fact that they often combined psychology and psychosomatic treatment with the use of plants and other natural products on which modern-day medicine relies. Other spiritual systems were far more complex, combining numerous intricate levels of concepts, beliefs, prayers, and rituals that, under trained leaders and teachers, united the group with its universe and oversaw the maintenance of its harmonious bond with the supernatural and with all the forces and creatures of nature.

Even the smaller and simpler societies were rich in legends, ceremonies, songs, dances, and arts, for they were integrated parts of their spiritual systems, serving to hold their societies together by instructing the people about right and wrong behavior, the position and obligations of each person within the group, and what the group expected of each of its members.

During the nineteenth century, many Indians informed whites in the Pacific Northwest that they shared the whites' belief in a single all-powerful Creator, or Creative Spirit above all other spirits. This Creator Spirit, however, was often viewed as a vague force, remote from the daily events of men's lives. More important was each individual's own guardian spirit, usually sought for and acquired in personal vision quests conducted under the supervision of a shaman or an elder while the seeker was still a youth. The guardian spirit guided, counselled, and assisted the individual throughout his or her life.

There were other important aspects of the native religions' systems that included increasing a group's collective spiritual power by adding that of allies and relying on prophecies made public by those with strong spiritual powers. From time to time—particularly in periods of anxiety or calamity—the prophecies ordained additions or changes in the religious systems such as new ceremonies, songs, special conduct, and even beliefs. Frequently after the 1780s, apprehension over the coming of white men and disastrous epidemics sometimes led to the emergence of full-blown prophetic cults. In addition, most of the religious systems, stemming basically from origin myths, united the people with great emotional and spiritual force to the land on which they lived and from which they secured their livelihood. Many of the legends among the Northwestern tribes told of a day before humans when the world was inhabited only by animals or, in some cases, by powerful cannibal monsters. At some point, a Changer or culture hero appeared—a coyote to the Nez Perces, a mink to the Quilleutes, a fox to the Puget Sound tribes. He had all the attributes, both good and bad, of humans, but he was also in many ways superhuman. It was he who finally brought forth the first humans and the different tribes and gave them the lands on which they were thereafter to live.

To the different native groups, such legends, repeated by generations of grandparents in winter stories to their grandchildren, acquired all the force that Scriptures possess for devout whites. In other parts of the country origin myths differed. They often told of a Creator or supreme spiritual power, rather than a culture hero, who gave a particular area of the earth to a tribe for its homeland. Whatever the story, the binding of the people to their homeland became sacred, and in time, landmarks and particular sites on the homeland also became sacred because they marked the boundaries of the tribe's universe, or were associated with sacred events or concepts, or with the bones of departed souls of ancestors.

In truth, this brief treatment of native American religions does little justice to them. But enough has been noted to provide the beginnings of new perspectives on Indian-white relations in which the following three points should be emphasized. First, the most important consideration of Indian groups, whether families, villages, bands, or tribes, was the survival and well-being of the people. This was achieved basically by adhering to traditional religious practices and beliefs, that is, by keeping the universe in balance through harmonious relations with the spiritual forces, and avoiding anything that might disturb them. Secondly, this adherence made religion a daily philosophy of life and conduct for the individual Indian. The worst thing that he could do was to imperil the welfare of his group. His spiritual beliefs thus became as much a part of him as his skin. The attachment of his own spirit force to the entire spiritual universe was more than an article of faith. It was his being. Thirdly, the attachment of man's spirit to the rest of creation made much of his world sacred to him. The destruction of it, or the forced separation from it, would be a soul-searing, emotional ordeal with the coloration even of death.

With all this in mind, let us examine a few episodes of Pacific Northwest history as we know it from the non-Indian point of view. The earliest whites on the coast and in the interior were essentially explorers and fur traders and trappers. Among them were the Astorians. Two anecdotes during their sojourn at the mouth of the Columbia and in the Oregon country in the period 1811-14 are instructive.

On August 26, 1813, the Astorian clerk, Alfred Seton, who had gone up the Willamette River, noted in his journal that he had met the Calapooya Indians. "They have not many articles of white men among them," he wrote, "are clothed in Dear skin robes, which, with their bows and arrows form all their riches; these are a miserable wandering set. . . ."[7] Like Lewis and Clark and others, Seton and the Astorians observed the tribes they met and judged them solely from materialistic and physical perceptions. That was the traditional way white men judged Indians, and they have, for the most part, continued to do so. The Astorians and other early whites in the Northwest compared the outward appearances of the downriver and coastal Indians with those of the plateau area or upper Columbia basin, and found the former wanting. Yet it is impossible to believe that the Calapooyas would have been regarded as inferior or judged "miserable" if Seton had been aware that they, like the upriver Indians, had other wealth—a rich and satisfying spiritual life that enabled them to live in harmony and balance with their homeland. Without concern for the religious factor, we have today a largely unflattering, stereotypic image of the Calapooyas, Chinooks, Clatsops, Cowlitz, Chehalis, and other lower Columbia peoples that does not do justice to the sophistication of their religions and the strength, dignity, and richness with which their spiritual systems endowed their societies.

Again, referring to the Astorians, we find them regularly observing but rarely understanding. On one occasion, when the Chinook chief, Comcomly, refused to let them handle the first fish caught at the commencement of a salmon run, they were amused. The whites ascribed the action to superstition or whim. But it was a Chinook article of faith, as important to them as an injunction in the Bible might be to whites. The Chinooks, like many other Pacific Northwest Indians, believed that the salmon were really humans who lived in a dwelling under the waters of the ocean, who annually assumed the guise of fish in order to provide food for the Indians. The salmon, who after being caught and ceremonially thanked, were cut and treated, then the Chinooks put their bones back in the water to return them to their homes, once again as humans, in order that they might come back again the following year as fish for the Indians. This was the Chinooks' understanding of the marvelous cycle of the salmon, but they also knew that if they offended the first, or chief fish—with whose spirit their own was interconnected—if they failed to thank him, by improper treatment, or crippled him by not carefully returning all of his bones to the river, the salmon might not return again.[8] To this day the life of Northwest fishing Indians gains strength and security from association with salmon and steelhead, and though the facts of the salmon's cycle are known, the ceremonies continue and have important religious meaning for all the fishing tribes. How sad, though, that the white man's history did not prepare us for a better present-day appreciation and understanding of people who still, deep down, dare not fail to honor and thank the spiritual life force of the fish to which they have for millennia been so closely attached.

After the fur trappers and traders came the missionaries. We are familiar with the white men's recorded histories of Daniel and Jason Lee, the Whitmans and the Spaldings, and all their contemporaries and successors among most of the tribes in the Pacific Northwest. But can we grasp, from the Indians' side, the enormity of what these representatives of the white men's religions were attempting to achieve? Far from simply bestowing on the tribes the beliefs and practices of white men, they tried, in truth, to *convert* the Indian peoples away from ancestral faith and trust in everything that held life together, that gave meaning to existence, that bound Indians to the seen and unseen world, that gave safety and security to the continuance of the group, and that ensured survival and well-being for their parents, wives, children, relatives, and friends. They were, indeed, asked to cut their links with the spirit world upon which their ancestors for untold generations had relied, and which they themselves had been instructed since childhood not to offend. Those links were as much of their being as their physical features and personality. In a sense, it was not only like asking them to shed their skin for a new one, but, in doing so, to imperil the universe of their people.

An appreciation of this perspective adds new breadth and depth to our understanding of the relations between missionaries and the tribes. From the point of view of the tribes, it is quite true that many Indians, including village, band, and tribal headmen and even the shamans with strong spiritual powers, eagerly sought knowledge of the white men's religion, welcomed the missionaries, and accepted what they taught. But what they were doing, or trying to do, was to acquire an understanding of additional — and seemingly very powerful — spiritual forces that could be added to their own systems to enhance their individual and collective existence. They did not intend to abandon their own spiritual life, only to enlarge and enrich it.

The missionaries seemed not to comprehend this and were doomed to frustration and heartsick defeat. Despite their years of labor from the 1830s to the 1850s, the missionaries of all denominations in the Northwest, including the Whitmans and Spaldings, did not make a single convert in the sense of weaning them away totally from still viable native religions. Spalding's most prominent converts, the Nez Perce headmen, Tamootsin and Tuekakas, known to whites as Timothy and Old Joseph, added Christian teachings to their spiritual inheritance, but in time Joseph found reason to abandon not the religious system of his ancestors, but the additions that Spalding had led him to accept.

Even individuals who had originally welcomed the missionaries with eagerness, like the Nez Perces Tackensuatis and Lawyer, the Yakima Kamiakin, and various Cayuse headmen, were not convinced to give up their ancestral understandings of their relations with the supernatural, which had guided them in their relations with their fellow humans and with nature and all creation. In March 1854, Gibbs's report to the government, transmitted through Washington Territorial Governor Isaac I. Stevens's subordinate, George B. McClellan, noted that Kamiakin possessed "the greatest influence" among the Yakima Indians, but that he, in turn, was "much under the influence of the missionaries, with whom he lives altogether."[9] Yet a year later, Kamiakin was in revolt against the whites. His decisions and actions still flowed from his native spirituality and continued to bind him to his land and his people.

Similarly, the Cayuses upon whom the Whitmans had worked so diligently—and who had learned much about Christianity from the fur traders and Iroquois trappers long before the Whitmans' arrival—by the 1850s had shown not a single sign of having shed the spiritual beliefs of their fathers. Even Lawyer, the steadfast Nez Perce friend of the missionaries and the whites, in supporting the acceptance of Christian teachings and the material goods and forces underlying the white men's power, could not and would not crusade for the abandonment of the Nez Perce spiritual system or religious beliefs. It was on materialistic grounds, in the matters that were Caesar's, so to speak, that the path he chose to follow separated most notably from that of the traditionalists, and it is significant that he himself was not baptized by Spalding and formally enrolled as a Christian convert until November 1871, by which time the original native spiritual foundation of Nez Perce life had been thoroughly undermined and the structure of Nez Perce society had gone through profound and fundamental changes.[10]

In the stormy period of treaties, hostilities, and dispossession of the tribes that followed the era of the missionaries, we see, perhaps more clearly than at any other time, the deep wounding of Indian religious sensibilities—not appreciated by the whites of those times and scarcely taken into account even today. At each of the treaty sessions conducted by Isaac I. Stevens in 1854 and 1855, first with the Puget Sound and coastal tribes and then with those in the interior, the tribes were cajoled, pressured, and threatened not merely into giving up the traditional economic base of their subsistence, but the very center of their spiritual universe. The white man saw it all in terms of dollars and cents—so many acres for so much goods, services, and annuities. The tribes saw it differently and said so.

At such treaty sessions as those conducted at Medicine Creek and Point Elliott, in December 1854 and January 1855, Nisquallies, Puyallups, Duwamish, and other tribes west of the Cascades were not only forced off their ancestral lands onto new, smaller plots or reservations, but were separated from their usual and accustomed fishing places—the sources of the fish which meant so much to their spiritual as well as economic existence. It caused so much turmoil that the treaties were soon amended so that, even though the tribes had originally demanded and been granted access to the fishing sites, their reservation boundaries were altered to include many of those sacred locations. Even so, interference with the necessities of their spiritual existence led to violence, the persecution and death of native spokesmen like Leschi, and the military destruction of these small, spiritually motivated tribes.

In the interior, Stevens, Oregon Indian Superintendent Joel Palmer, and other white negotiators had little or no understanding of the spiritually based objections raised at the Walla Walla and other treaty sessions by tribes that agonized over being forced to move away from lands and sites with which they were religiously interconnected. The minutes of the Walla Walla Council of 1855 overflow with the passionate spiritual pleas of the native spokesmen. "I wonder if this ground has anything to say?" asked the angry Tauitau, the Young Chief of the Umatilla Valley Cayuses. "I wonder if the ground is listening to what is said? . . . I hear what this earth says. The earth says, God has placed me here. The earth says that God tells me to take care of the Indians on this earth. . . . The water speaks the same way: God says, feed the Indians upon the earth. The grass says the same thing: feed the horses and cattle. . . . The earth says, God has placed me here to produce all that grows upon me . . . God on placing them on the earth . . . said, you Indians take care of the earth and do each other no harm . . ." And from Owhi, the Yakima: "God made our bodies from the earth. . . . What shall I do? Shall I give the lands that are a part of my body?"[11]

But Stevens and Palmer were impatient. Palmer could not understand what more information the Indians needed. He told them, they would get sawmills, gristmills, teachers, and annuities. "We don't come to steal your lands," he added. "We pay you more than it is worth." Howlish Wompoon, a Cayuse, glared at Palmer, and stated, "I cannot think of leaving this land. Your words since you came here have been crooked. That is all I have to say."[12]

Stevens and Palmer, of course, had their way, though it led to war and ultimate military enforcement of the Indians' loss of their lands. The same sort of confrontations, however, continued. When Smohalla arose to spread the so-called Dreamer Religion among many of the demoralized Northwest native bands and communities, white settlers, the military, and local and federal officials saw it as a plot to unite the Indians in renewed hostilities. Smohalla was giving voice to the traditional bonds between the Indians and all creation — bonds that white coercion and pressure were discrediting and stamping out:

> You ask me to plow the ground! Shall I take a knife and tear my mother's bosom? Then when I die she will not take me to her bosom to rest. You ask me to dig for stone! Shall I dig under her skin for her bones? Then when I die I cannot enter her body to be born again. You ask me to cut grass and make hay and sell it, and be rich like white men! But how dare I cut off my mother's hair?[13]

Such highly charged religious and emotional bonds with the earth increased the pain and agony of each loss of land. To understand the spiritual depth of the injury is to recognize why so many tribes refused to sell their homelands that the Creator spirit had given them and where their ancestors were buried, and why, like the Nez Perce bands of Chief Joseph, White Bird, Toohoolhoolzote, and others, they risked persecution and death in their struggles to stay where they were.

No meeting was more moving than that between General O. O. Howard and the non-treaty Nez Perces at Lapwai, Idaho, in May 1877, when Howard gave the Nez Perces their ultimatum to leave the Wallowa country and the other bands' homelands and come onto the reservation. Facing Howard, Toohoolhoolzote, a strong Nez Perce spiritual leader and headman of a Snake River band, spoke for all the non-treaty Indians, including Chief Joseph, who were at the meeting. "The earth is part of my body," Toohoolhoolzote told the general. "I belong to the land out of which I came. The earth is my mother."

Howard missed the whole point. "Toohoolhoolzote, the cross-grained growler," he wrote in his reminiscences, ". . . had the usual long preliminary discussion about the earth being his mother, that she should not be disturbed by hoe or plough, that men should subsist on what grows of itself, etc., etc. . . . He was answered: 'We do not wish to interfere with your religion, but you must talk about practicable things. Twenty times over you repeat that the earth is your mother. . . . Let us hear it no more, but come to business at once.' "[14]

The true climax of the great tragedy that followed — the so-called Chief Joseph war of 1877 — was not Joseph's speech of surrender at the Bear Paws in Montana, so often celebrated by whites, but Joseph's long struggle thereafter for his people's right to be returned to their sacred Wallowa homeland — a right never granted to them. In Washington, D.C., on January 14, 1879, Joseph, who had come from his Oklahoma place of exile to try to persuade the federal government to return his people to the Pacific Northwest, made his most eloquent plea: "Let me be a free man — free to travel, free to stop, free to work, free to trade, where I choose, free to choose my own teachers, free to follow the religion of my fathers, free to think and talk and act for myself — and I will obey every law, or submit to the penalty."[15]

The appeal was denied. Joseph's people were not returned to the Pacific Northwest until six years later — and then to further exile on the Colville Reservation in Washington where their descendants still live. Freedom of religion was banned among all American Indians by federal government regulations, vigorously enforced by agents, missionaries, and troops, until the passage of the Indian Reorganization Act in 1934 as part of Franklin D. Roosevelt's New Deal. When Joseph died on the Colville Reservation in 1904, the local physician reported that he had died of a broken heart. The spirits of the mountains, the meadows, the canyons, and the green grasslands of the beautiful Wallowa Valley, I am sure, understood and wept.

Following this brief historical appraisal, two points remain to be made. First, beyond any question, Indians, both individually and collectively, often did act in pursuit of political, economic, or materialistic goals, uninfluenced by spiritualistic considerations. To imply otherwise would be incorrect and misleading, and I have not meant to do so. But, at the same time, it has not been recognized adequately that such goals, in turn, very often did have religious motives, and even more importantly that goals considered to be entirely political or economic often sprang fully from adherence to native spiritual systems. The history of Indian-white relations, as the white man knows it, has placed too great a stress on equating the driving forces of Indian cultures with those of the whites. By taking into greater regard the native American spiritual impacts on the Indian side of what occurred in the past, we will acquire a fuller, truer, and often a different reading of history than we now have. No longer need we have a Nez Perce, Yakima, Coeur d'Alene, Klickitat, or Chinook history — or a biography of Leschi, Captain Jack, Kamiakin, Peopeo Moxmox, or Lawyer — written with blinders that preclude constant consideration of the influence of the natives' traditional spiritual system on every relevant event, action, and relationship that is discussed.

Secondly, we know that many Indians and even entire groups of them did, in the course of their histories, not only become practicing, as well as nominal Christians, but, in addition, abandoned their native religious systems. But in the Pacific Northwest, and elsewhere, this generally followed utter disasters to the Indians and their traditional systems of collective organization. In the case of the Chinooks and many of the tribes west of the Cascades, white men's diseases decimated their settlements in the early nineteenth century, killing most of their people, as well as their religious, civil, and war leaders, and leaving the handful of survivors demoralized and helpless. Other groups, including those in the interior, lost their leadership through warfare and execution, had their traditional structures of society undermined and destroyed by white missionaries, government agents, and the military, and were simply overrun and dispossessed. In both areas, there came a time for each tribe when the hold of native spirituality disintegrated or collapsed so thoroughly that, for many of the people, it was no longer valid, and Christianity or something else such as a mixture of Christian and native religious beliefs and practices replaced it.

These were all episodes of very deep human tragedies—periods when the long-taught meaning of life slipped away from peoples, when such foundations of tribal existence as identity, pride, hope, and motivation depended for continuance on people finding and accepting something else in which to believe. To recognize what the Native Americans experienced, let me again cite George Gibbs's 1854 report. In his reference to the once very numerous and strong Chinookan peoples of the lower Columbia River and the southern Washington coast—peoples who only a few decades earlier had played central roles in relations with the maritime fur traders, with Lewis and Clark, with the Astorians, the North West Company, and the Hudson's Bay Company, Gibbs wrote: "At present but few Indians remain here, the smallpox having nearly finished its work during the past year. . . . Some lodges upon the southern peninsula of Shoalwater bay were left without a survivor, and the dead were found by the whites lying wrapped in their blankets as if asleep. Quite extensive cemeteries are scattered along the bay, the canoes in which the bodies of former generations were deposited having outlasted the race itself."[16] Gone were the chiefs, the shamans, the grandparents, and their stories and teachings. Gone were the rich and intricate religions that had held the societies together. They were no longer needed, for the societies themselves were almost extinct.

And yet, across the country Indians and Indianness have both survived until today, and to a wondrous degree so have native American religions. In the 1960s and 1970s, it became evident that in many tribes, large numbers of traditionalists and their spiritual teachers still remained, keeping alive the beliefs and practices of their ancestors. Much had changed or taken on accommodating forms and ideas during the years, but even in the Pacific Northwest, among the fishing tribes of Puget Sound and the plateau peoples of the interior, Indian and tribal pride revived, fed in large measure by spiritual beliefs that had never died.

Many of the young Indians in the 1960s sparked the revival, looking to their elders to teach them what they knew or remembered of the beliefs and practices of their ancestors. By the 1970s, many of the elders who were also Christians joined this new interest in their own traditional religions. The strength of the revival is seen in the litigation of today. As with Chief Joseph and the tribes of the nineteenth century, native peoples with land and water claims now bitterly spurn money settlements. In New York State, a Seneca woman rebuffed congressional remuneration for reservation land wanted by the Army Corps of Engineers for a reservoir. "The White man views land for its money value," she said. "We Indians have a spiritual tie with the earth, a reverence for it that Whites don't share and can hardly understand."[17] In New Mexico, the Taos Indians, already mentioned, for years refused any money for their sacred Blue Lake; they needed the lake more than all the money the whites could give them. In South Dakota, the Sioux have refused in the 1980s to accept a money settlement for the Black Hills, the seat of their religion which whites took from them in the 1870s. And in the Pacific Northwest, land, fish, and water rights have been more important to many of the tribes than cash offerings.

The sacred circle between the spirits of the Native Americans and all of creation within their universe is now stronger and more vital than whites recognize, and is growing stronger and more meaningful all the time. And why not in these days when so much fear and insecurity is abroad for all mankind? Is there really so much difference between the traditional native systems and the white man's own growing realization that all of creation, including man and the ecological and biological systems of the earth, and even the universe, have a unity, bound interdependently together by the great spirit force above all others? "The earth is my mother," said Toohoolhoolzote. There are whites, as well as Indians now, who, if they think about it, will agree that his was, indeed, a valid religion.

The Great Raincoast of North America: Toward a New Regional History of the Pacific Northwest

EDITORS' NOTE

Regional consciousness in the Pacific Northwest perhaps goes back to the first white settlers and has often been expressed in historical literature. In this essay Richard Maxwell Brown offers a fresh view and status report. Indeed, he reaches beyond one region to propose that a new American historiography might well arise from a comparative study of the several regions of the nation. Brown argues that in the post-World War II generation a strong sense of regional vitality and creativity emerged in the Far West and, more particularly, in the Pacific Northwest. He documents the flowering of this regional thought with an impressive display of knowledge and a keenly critical appraisal of its pertinence to his theme. In sum, he gives to the historian, as well as other interested readers, an impressive guide to the study of regionalism and the Pacific Northwest.

Brown's interest in regionalism began during his boyhood in Mobridge, South Dakota, a small town ideally situated for casual inquiries into the past of western America because of its location on the Missouri River and the mainline of the Milwaukee Railroad. Historical sensitivity came naturally, he says, because "every time I saw the river I thought of Lewis and Clark and was very conscious of the history of my own locality — the Arikarees had a big camp near my town. . .[and] Sitting Bull was killed not too far from where my town would be founded. . . ." Upon graduation from high school, Brown took the train to Seattle on vacation and fell in love with the Pacific Northwest. Later, undergraduate study at Reed College in Portland reinforced his desire to live in the region.

For the next twenty-five years, however, he lived in the East, earning a Ph.D. degree at Harvard University (1959) and teaching in several institutions, principally Rutgers University (1960-67) and William and Mary (1967-77). His chance to return to Oregon came in 1977 when he went to the University of Oregon as the Beekman Professor of History. Brown characterizes his own maturation in historical sensitivity with this statement: "I have lived North, South, East, and West, which is to say that I have lived regionalism region-by-region and I have always been fascinated by various regional varieties and differences I have experienced." This diversity is also evidenced by his list of publications, which includes *The South Carolina Regulators* (1963), *Strain of Violence: Historical Studies of American Violence and Vigilantism* (1975), *Perspectives on the American South* (1981), and, as a contributor, entries in *Reader's Encyclopedia of the American West* (1977) and *Regionalism and the Pacific Northwest* (1983).

This photograph, showing the steam vessel *Melville Dollar* and the schooner-rigged *Espada* moored side by side, is a reminder of the way mechanical power displaced sails in the world of maritime transportation at the end of the nineteenth century. *Manuscripts, Archives, and Special Collections, Washington State University Library, Pullman, Washington*

The Great Raincoast of North America: Toward a New Regional History of the Pacific Northwest

RICHARD MAXWELL BROWN

Within the last fifteen to twenty years there has arisen a remarkable New American Historiography, and it is inevitable that in response there will also emerge a new historiography of the Pacific Northwest. This is not to suggest that the state of current Pacific Northwest historiography is poor. Far from it, for a number of landmark publications have occurred in recent decades: Norman Clark's incomparable historical trilogy for the state of Washington[1]; the incisive and comprehensive textbook by Johansen and Gates[2]; the five Bicentennial histories in the *States and Nation* series written by leading regional historians[3]; a revitalization of British Columbia history by our colleagues in that province[4]; the tendency to end the neglect of Alaska strengthened by the publications of Claus-M. Naske as well as two recently published, stunning works by John McPhee and Joe McGinnis[5]; exciting new scholarly monographs — among them, Carlos A. Schwantes on our radical labor heritage, Richard White on the ecological history of the Puget Sound area, and Michael P. Malone on the economic and political history of Montana.[6] There is a rich resource, too, of unpublished dissertations and theses such as those by Michael K. Green, Wesley Arden Dick, and Peter K. Simpson.[7] In our biographical literature there is Ivan Doig's highly original treatment of James G. Swan.[8] Also, there is the remarkable vitality of our state and provincial historical societies, archives, and historical journals with the latter being headed by the attractive, intellectually provocative *Pacific Northwest Quarterly*.

Yet we are in a transitional state from the old regional history of the Pacific Northwest to the new. Most assuredly the intellectual gains of the old regional history of the Northwest will not be lost, for they are indeed the foundation of our new emergent regional history.[9] Two national developments of the last couple of decades — the rise of the New Regionalism and the rise of the New American Historiography — suggest that a linkage of these developments will produce the New Regional History. The concluding half of this essay will be devoted to a discussion of the emergence of the New Regional History of the Pacific Northwest with specific attention to the concept of the Pacific Northwest as the Great Raincoast of North America.

The New Regionalism in America

One of the most vital intellectual forces in the nation in the 1930s and 1940s was the approach of regionalism.[10] The Institute for Social Research at the University of North Carolina in Chapel Hill directed by Howard Odum led a surge in interdisciplinary scholarship that had much to do with the creation of the rejuvenated New South of our own time while Vanderbilt University in Nashville, Tennessee, was a competing center of southern regionalism whose members expressed a conservative agrarian philosophy diametrically opposed to Odum's New South progressivism.[11] Other university centers of regionalism included Harvard for New England, Wisconsin for the Midwest, and California (Berkeley) for the Pacific Southwest. On the Great Plains three great regionalists worked to produce books that still inspire: Walter Prescott Webb and J. Frank Dobie at the University of Texas and James C. Malin at the University of Kansas.[12]

Regionalism has also been expressed in the fiction of such writers as William Faulkner, Thomas Wolfe, and John Steinbeck; in painting by the art of three midwesterners, Thomas Hart Benton, John Steuart Curry, and Grant Wood; and in documentary photography by Walker Evans and others.[13] There was also the remarkable output of the federally sponsored Writers' Project guidebooks to the states and cities of America and the local artistic work exemplified by the ubiquitous post office murals.[14] In our own region H. L. Davis, Stewart H. Holbook, and Richard L. Neuberger were among those contributing to the nationwide regional ferment.[15] Capping all of this was *Let Us Now Praise Famous Men*, a book by James Agee and Walker Evans that, although devoted to the South, perhaps best captured the combination of regional sensitivity and reform impulse that characterized the old regionalism of the 1930s and 1940s.[16]

By the 1950s the vibrant work of regionalism of the thirties and forties was all but gone and mostly forgotten — overwhelmed by the nationalizing tendencies of World War II and its Cold War aftermath. And as the 1950s merged into the 1960s, the technological developments that resulted in television, jet planes, and interstate highways seemed to homogenize America into one monolithic whole in which regional differences and distinctions were obliterated. The cutting edge of scholarship turned away from regionalism.[17]

In fact, regionalism and the regional identities upon which it thrives were eclipsed during the fifties and sixties. During the 1970s we entered a new era of regionalism. Sociologist John Shelton Reed and anthropologist Raymond D. Gastil, among others, have shown that regional cultural identities survived in the South, the West, and generally throughout our nation.[18] Individuals sought psychological refuge from the impersonal homogenizing tendencies of the age of television and jet airliners by a search for family roots and an increasing identification with the local community of residence.

A powerful contributor to the New Regionalism has been the movement for historical preservation. Its origins go back to such old colonial cities as Williamsburg and Charleston in the 1920s, but emerged during the 1970s as a coast-to-coast phenomenon commanding, on a locality-to-locality basis, millions of dollars, thousands of workers, and avid consumers without end.[19] Related to the historical preservation movement, too, has been the very new public history movement of the 1970s that often has a local orientation.[20]

The centralizing tendencies of the federal government, often seen as the foe of regionalism, has periodically been a major source of the New Regionalism of the 1970s. Federal funds, as well as federal legislation, energized the historical preservation movement, and the National Endowment for the Humanities (NEH) has, in many ways, fulfilled the same role that various federal agencies and programs filled in the 1930s in regard to the nurturing of regionalism.

One of the most striking and effective examples of the spur to the New Regionalism by the NEH has been *The States of the Nation* series of fifty Bicentennial state histories published in 1976 and later.[21] There is variation of quality and scope in these fifty state histories, but they form a rich historical and cultural heritage that is similar in impact to the forty-eight state guidebooks published by the Federal Writers' Project in the 1930s and 1940s.[22]

Two other vital contributions of the NEH to the growth of the New Regionalism need to be emphasized. One is the many national programs and grants subsidized by the endowment, and the other is, in a collective sense, the manifold programs of the state committees for the humanities. These state humanities programs have accomplished much in my own state of Oregon and throughout the rest of the nation. To grasp this point, one need only think, for example, of the film *Northern Lights*, a truly remarkable evocation of the cultural and historical heritage of the people of North Dakota that was sponsored by the North Dakota Committee for the Humanities.[23]

There has also been the emergence of new academic centers of regionalism. As the impact of Chapel Hill, Nashville, Cambridge, Madison, Austin, and Berkeley waned, their places were taken by such exciting new regional programs as the Center for Great Plains Studies at the University of Nebraska, the Center for the Study of Southern Culture at the University of Mississippi (1977), and the Appalachian Center of the University of Kentucky (1978).

Finally, during the 1970s, regionalism once again emerged as one of the most vital currents in the intellectual life of our nation. There are many signs of this close to home in our own American West and Northwest.

Americans and the California Dream: 1850-1915 (1973) by Kevin Starr[24] is the finest work of regional cultural history published in the last eleven years. Ivan Doig's *This House of Sky: Landscapes of a Western Mind* (1978)[25] is a touching memoir of a Montana boyhood that underscores the survival of timeless western (and generally human) characteristics of courage and endurance; while another work of fiction also focusing on Montana, *A River Runs Through It and Other Stories* by Norman MacLean (1976),[26] has the evocativeness of Hemingway's up-in-Michigan stories without the disturbing anxiety of the latter. In addition, Jane Kramer has vividly portrayed the mixing of the Old West values with modern western society, and Rob Schultheis has arrestingly treated the deep realities of surviving Indian cultures amidst the mystically appealing landscape of the desert backcountry of the American and Mexican West.[27] Aside from these works, some of the finest literature in America that draws upon but transcends the West in its human appeal has been written by such western authors as Wallace Stegner, Wright Morris, Ken Kesey, Larry McMurtry, John Nichols, Ivan Doig, and Joan Didion in fiction, and by William Stafford, Richard Hugo, and Gary Snyder in poetry.[28]

The New American Historiography, 1960 to the 1980s

Since 1960, and especially since 1970, a veritable revolution in American historiography has occurred. An explosion of knowledge has occurred simply in terms of the number of recently published significant books and articles. But even more striking than the huge increase in the quantity of new historical works has been the qualitative change in terms of the new approaches as well as the opening of new fields of inquiry. The adjective *new* has been repeatedly used and so we speak of "the new political history," "the new social history," "the new economic history," "the new urban history," and so on. This outburst of scholarship has produced enormous intellectual gains, but there is a pitfall. Much of the new work—being truly *avant garde* in character—is highly technical (especially in the more quantitative versions) and even esoteric. As such work became more technical, historians have stood in danger of losing their intellectual links to the nonprofessional audience who read and enjoyed the works of such older historians as Richard Hofstadter, Oscar Handlin, Arthur M. Schlesinger, Jr., David Potter, and C. Vann Woodward. In the last ten to fifteen years, historians have written more and more for each other, and so there has been a danger of intellectual isolation from the mainstream of American culture that has afflicted some other fields of scholarship even more than history. Even though the pluses of the New American Historiography are impressive, there remains the clear and present danger of historical obscurantism and obsessiveness which we all must guard against.

What is the New American Historiography? Its essence is best captured in a book published in 1980 by Cornell University Press for the American Historical Association entitled *The Past Before Us: Contemporary Historical Writing in the United States*. The book is edited by the Pulitzer Prize-winning historian Michael Kammen, and includes twenty essays by such distinguished older historians as William J. Bouwsma, William H. McNeil, Charles Bigson, and Carl N. Degler and by such rising younger historians as Peter N. Stearns, Kathleen Neils Conzen, Robert Darnton, Peter Loewenberg, and J. Morgan Kousser. The book's scope is as broad as possible; in chronological terms it ranges from the Middle Ages to the present, and its geographical scope includes Europe, Asia, Africa, and Latin America as well as the United States. *The Past Before Us* is as complete an intellectual inventory of contemporary historical scholarship in America as we are apt to have for many years.[29]

Kammen's work is, in effect, an intellectual benchmark for our own examination of the changing historiography of the Pacific Northwest. Thirteen of the chapters focus exclusively or largely on the historiography of United States history or what has been called the New American Historiography. Of these thirteen essays, four are concerned with new methods and sources of research, and the remaining eight essays deal with the favored new topical specialties of research.

In regard to the topical specialties, the following are especially germane to Pacific Northwest historiography:

1. The new political history
2. The new social history
3. The new community studies with their focus on urban and local history
4. The new history of women and the family
5. The new labor history
6. The new intellectual and cultural history

The above represent a sampling of the New American Historiography, but there are omissions. For example, there is no chapter on the new ecological or environmental history, or on the well-established new economic history.[30] The new ethnic history is treated under such headings as the new social history and new community studies, but there is, except for a chapter on "The Negro in American History," no separate treatment of ethnic history. A glaring omission is the absence of material on conflict and violence in American historiography. This particular omission has led to the partly correct charge that the book of essays represents an unduly homogenized treatment of American history.

Among the salient characteristics of the New American Historiography are an interdisciplinary orientation; frequent quantification of data by use of the computer; inspiration from such seminal European figures as Lewis B. Namier, E. P. Thompson, and the members of the French *Annales* school of historians; an emphasis upon the common people and innovative strategies to recapture their ways of life; strong attention, also, to such hitherto comparatively neglected groups as women, youth, the aged, and ethnic and racial minorities; an emphasis on the related aspects of popular culture and collective mentality; and an orientation to such key concepts as social and geographic mobility, class differentiation, modernization, and material culture. In pursuit of such themes, the four chapters in *The Past Before Us* that deal with new research methods and resources are also representative since they focus on oral history, psychohistory, quantitative social science history, and comparative history.

Toward the New Regional History of the Pacific Northwest

As elsewhere in America, regionalism in the Pacific Northwest has undergone a revival in recent years as indicated by the previously mentioned works of such writers of Northwest origin or residence as Doig, MacLean, Kesey, Stafford, Hugo, and Snyder. Other recent works of regional scholarship can be found in *Northwest Perspectives* (1979), edited by Edwin R. Bingham and Glen A. Love. Also of note is literary critic Roger Sale's brilliant historical account of *Seattle: Past to Present* (1976).[31] Don Berry's early 1960s fictional trilogy on early Oregon, *Trask, Moontrap*, and *To Build a Ship*, has taken on the mature status of a classic with its reprinting in the late 1970s.[32] In addition, several poets, some of whom were inspired by the genius of the late Theodore Roethke, form a significant Northwest group.[33]

The achievements of Mark Toby and other Northwest artists have received high praise beyond the borders of the Northwest,[34] while the distinctive Northwest style of architecture, exemplified by Pietro Belluschi and others, has been portrayed in historical and contemporary breadth and depth in the two-volume work *Space, Style, and Structure* (1974), edited by Thomas Vaughan and Virginia Guest Ferriday.[35] New writers of note, for example, Barry H. Lopez, author of the 1979 book, *Of Wolves and Men*,[36] continue to appear while the regional historical societies, historical and literary journals, art museums, and theatrical and musical endeavors flourish as never before.

The previously mentioned historical contributions of Norman H. Clark, Carlos A. Schwantes, Richard White, Michael P. Malone, and others are enriching our sense of the regional past in a way that is cognate with the exciting new achievements in fiction, poetry, art, and architecture, yet in *The Past Before Us* there is no chapter on regional history. The omission was a proper one, because in 1980 the New Regional History—as distinct from the New Regionalism—had not yet emerged. When the New Regional History does take shape and the process is under way now, it will represent a combination of the New Regionalism with the New American Historiography.

The most recent general treatments of Pacific Northwest regional history by Oscar Osburn Winther, Earl Pomeroy (in the Northwest portions of *Pacific Slope*), and Dorothy O. Johansen and Charles M. Gates have been highly skilled and represent sophisticated syntheses of social, economic, political, and cultural history.[37] They continue to be used with profit but one can foresee a trend by which the intellectual pioneering of the New American Historiography will, in combination with the sensitivity of the New American Regionalism, produce a New Regional History for the Pacific Northwest and elsewhere.

What will be the components of this New Regional History of the Pacific Northwest? What has been done and what remains to be done? To answer these questions, one needs to understand the thrust of the New American Historiography.

First, the new political history of the Pacific Northwest will include two very important quantitative and qualitative dimensions. The quantitative dimension will consist of an intensive analysis of state and local elections in the manner of studies done by Frederick Luebke on Nebraska, Ronald Formisano on Michigan, Richard Jensen and Paul Kleppner on the Midwest, and J. Morgan Kousser on the South.[38] The qualitative dimensions will focus on an elucidation of the political cultures of the localities, states, and the region of the Pacific Northwest. In regard to the quantitative dimension, little, as yet, has been done. However, the situation in the realm of political culture is better. A number of fine dissertations and theses on politics and government await synthesis for the production of a full-fledged portrait of the political culture of the early twentieth-century Pacific Northwest progressivism.[39] For Northwest political culture as a whole, the fine essays in this volume by Michael P. Malone and Dianne C. Dougherty and by R. H. Limbaugh give an idea of the future trend of research and writing.[40]

The new economic history, with its base in quantitative data and conceptual models of economic theory, still has vast stretches of uncharted territory. This comes as a surprise since our country's most influential proponent of the new economic history, Douglass C. North of the University of Washington, has spent most of his career in the Pacific Northwest. It is also surprising that the first truly distinguished regional application of the new economic history was by James N. Tattersall, who wrote a 1960 Ph.D. dissertation on the economic history of the Pacific Northwest to 1920.[41] Although Tattersall's work for the 1850-1920 period needs bolstering by more specialized new studies and although his orientation to the natural resources base needs to be carried on from 1921 to the present, the fact remains that Tattersall's neglected dissertation is a powerful resource for understanding Pacific Northwest history.

A special aspect of economic history is the approach of business history, which is far from being ignored in the Pacific Northwest. Business histories and biographies have understandably focused on the great regional railroad and lumber industries. Among railroad studies, two are devoted to the Great Northern: Robert C. Nesbit on Judge Thomas Burke of Seattle and Albro Martin's encyclopedic but flawed book on James J. Hill. The burgeoning lumber industry studies include older company histories of Weyerhaeuser and Pope & Talbot as well as newer books such as Robert E. Ficken's on the Simpson Lumber Company magnate, Mark E. Reed.[42] Among the small number of scholars who have dealt with the fishing industry is Gordon B. Dodds, while for new industries and companies *The Sporty Game* by John Newhouse contains an intriguing account of Boeing's rise to supremacy in the manufacture of jet airliners.[43]

In regard to the cluster of studies represented by such phrases as *the new social history, the new community studies, the new urban history,* and *the new local history*, the current situation is woefully thin. With Stephan Thernstrom's 1964 study of historical demography, property distribution, and social and geographic mobility in nineteenth-century Newburyport, Massachusetts, as the model for this cluster of quantitatively based new social, urban, community, and local history,[44] the question is: Who has emulated Thernstrom in work on our region? Regrettably, the list is short. It includes William Robbins's study of late nineteenth-century Roseburg, Oregon; Janice L. Reiff's dissertation on late nineteenth- and early twentieth-century Seattle; and a comparative study of San Francisco and Seattle in the early 1930s.[45] Yet, all is not barren, for there are two urban community studies that, while transitional in approach and thus not examples of the new social history movement, are nonetheless so original and provocative as to be truly inspiring examples of the possibilities of community study in the Northwest. This is in reference to Roger Sale's study of Seattle and to Norman H. Clark's book on early twentieth-century Everett, Washington, as a prototypical mill town.[46]

Another scholarly approach that is relatively neglected in *The Past Before Us* is historical geography. This is a topic which, in the hands of such authors as James Lemon with his study of late eighteenth-century southeastern Pennsylvania,[47] has much in common with the recent interpretation of American history. Indeed, there have been some notable recent contributions to the historical geography of the Northwest: William Bowen's treatment of white pioneer settlement in the Willamette Valley; Samuel and Emily Dicken's first volume of their historical geography of Oregon, and one of the finest scholarly works ever written on the Northwest, Donald W. Meinig's treatment of *The Great Columbia Plain* (1968).[48]

The new ethnic history is also a relatively neglected aspect of our regional history, but we can point at least to Paul George Hummasti's innovative work on the radical Finns of Astoria, to Kenneth Bjork's earlier study of nineteenth-century Norwegian migration to the Pacific Coast, and to

Erasmo Gamboa's recent article on Mexican migration into the state of Washington.[49]

The linked subjects of women and the family have been grossly neglected, but this situation is even now being alleviated by recent and ongoing works of scholarship. Ruth B. Moynihan's book on Abigail Scott Duniway, Margaret N. Haines's thesis of women in the late nineteenth-century Jackson County, Oregon, and an issue of *Montana: The Magazine of Western History* specifically devoted to frontier women in Montana and the Pacific Northwest spearhead research efforts that will inevitably increase.[50] Even less developed is research on the family *per se*, but that subject as well as the history of women will benefit significantly from the oral histories of the lives and achievements of Northwest women being collected by Susan Armitage at Washington State University.

The conflict-ridden and violent labor history of the Pacific Northwest before 1940 has been well treated in the works of Vernon Jensen, Harold Hyman, Robert L. Friedheim, Robert L. Tyler, Norman H. Clark, Carlos A. Schwantes, and others.[51] But the new labor history approach of E. P. Thompson, Herbert Gutman, David Montgomery, and David Brody[52] has been honored largely in abeyance. This situation is perceptively treated in an essay by Carlos A. Schwantes found in another chapter of this book.[53]

The new cultural history comprising a symbiosis of developments in social and intellectual history, literature, art, and architecture has been the subject of two suggestive recent works. One is the massive 1974 two-volume study of Northwest architecture and building style coedited by Thomas Vaughan and Virginia G. Ferriday, and the other is the 1979 collection of essays on the history, literature, and folklore of the Pacific Northwest coedited by Edwin R. Bingham and Glen A. Love.[54]

The ecological and environmental history of the Pacific Northwest has been slighted, although valuable perspectives appear in the standard monographs of forest and agricultural history. There is, however, a notable new book by Richard White—a study of land use, environment, and social change on Whidbey and Camano islands in Puget Sound—that successfully emulates the approach to ecological history developed by James C. Malin in his path-breaking grasslands studies for the Great Plains.[55]

In a special category are the studies of Northwest Indians, which are a rich resource of historical knowledge much influenced by the regnant approach of ethnohistory. Notable authors for these studies are Stephen Dow Beckham, Theodore Stern, Philip Drucker, and Keith A. Murray.[56]

The many gaps mentioned in this summary will inevitably be filled in as the years go by, but even so a major question has yet to be confronted. It is a simple, yet difficult question that is increasingly being asked of the New American Historiography: What does it all mean? Oral history, psychohistory, quantitative history, social science interdisciplinary history, and all the exciting new political, social, community, and other variants of the New American Historiography have not yet been transcended to produce the New American History of the late twentieth century. Bernard Bailyn and others insist there is now a need for a unified-field theory of American history that would synthesize the components of the New American Historiography into a unified interpretation of American history.[57] There is consensus that this is bound to come, but when and how? Possibly, it may come at the regional level where the work of synthesis could — region by region — form the basis for a new national synthesis of our history.

At the regional level, however, the process of synthesis will have to precede the national synthesis. Thus what is needed for the completion of the New Regional History of the Northwest is a unified-field theory of history for our own region. In this connection, I offer my concept of the Great Raincoast of North America — a historical unified-field concept as a basis for the synthesis of the production of the New Regionalism and the New American Historiography in the Northwest and also a basis for organizing and interpreting original research.

The Great Raincoast of North America

The concept of the Great Raincoast of North America is inspired partly by Walter Prescott Webb's classic study of *The Great Plains* published a half-century ago. Webb's book appeared long before the rise of the New American Historiography, but in its interdisciplinary approach and its exploration of hitherto unused research materials, Webb's book has much in common with the spirit of that concept.[58]

To recapitulate, Webb emphasized the structuring factor of semi-aridity and the level plains topography, noting such climatological and cultural concepts as the 20-inch rainfall line and the 98th meridian as a cultural fault line that separated the traditionalism of humid eastern America from the innovations provoked by the treeless, water-short environment of the Great Plains. In his remarkable survey Webb stressed the Plains Indians as a barrier to white pioneer settlement until an innovative cultural response — the six-shooting Colt revolver — enabled the pioneers to overcome Indian resistance. Webb also dealt with such cultural novelties as the rise of the cowboy, the long drive, the round-up, irrigation and the windmill, barbed wire, dry farming, and drought-resistant grains that all made possible the tandem penetration of the Great Plains by the cattle kingdom and the farming frontier. He also traced the emergence of new legal adaptations in the West that, in the form of enlarged land units and the innovative doctrine of prior appropriation of water rights, enabled settlers to adapt to the persistent aridity of the region.

In his conclusion, Webb assessed the literature of the Great Plains as a reflection of its history and confronted the question: What was the meaning of the Great Plains in American life? His book was an instant classic of the Old Regional History and one that still endures with a remarkably persistent intellectual vitality. To Webb's Great Plains, I want briefly to compare my hypothesis of the Great Raincoast of North America.

The Great Raincoast of North America extends from southwestern Alaska to northwestern California and lies to the west of the Cascade Mountains, encompassing as its core area the western portions of Oregon, Washington, and British Columbia. The chief regional identification is the gentle, yet steady rainfall during the long wet season from September to May. For this sector, as Norman H. Clark wrote in another context, the regional mystique has focused on a combination of "rain, rivers, forest, and sea."[59]

Essentially, the culture and history of the Great Raincoast embodies a reversal of what Webb found for the Great Plains. Thus, for the Great Raincoast we note not semi-aridity but abundant rainfall, and instead of the periodic threat of drought and crop failure we recall the old saying that "crops never fail in Oregon."[60] Instead of Webb's zone of semi-aridity we find along the Great Raincoast a salient of heavy precipitation reaching far into the interior to nurture such great stream flows as those of the Columbia, Snake, and Fraser and, closer to the coast, the Willamette, Chehalis, and Skagit. And instead of Webb's parallel climatological and cultural lines of 20-inch rainfall and 98th meridian we find the 60-inch rainfall line along the Cascade Mountains crest and the cultural fault line along the 122nd meridian that—running from Prince George, British Columbia, to Mt. Shasta, California—divides the dry interior plateau region from the rain-drenched coastal lowlands.[61] Instead, too, of the scarce-economy Plains Indians culture as a barrier to white pioneers, we find on the Great Raincoast the sophisticated cultural complex of the Northwest Indians (characterized by an economy of abundance) that presented no significant barrier to white settlement. And in British Columbia, at least, Indian culture survived with such persistent symbols and practices as the totem pole and the potlatch.[62]

Like the Indians, the ease of subsistence, rather than the challenge of environmental hardship, was the happy lot of the white settlers of the Great Raincoast. Two major industries that they developed were highly specific to the Great Raincoast's distinctive natural resources of towering Douglas fir forests and high-volume, swiftly flowing, steeply falling streams. The first was the Lumber Kingdom—an analogy to the Cattle Kingdom—which provided its own characteristic cultural adaptations that served to differentiate it from the lumber industry of the Great Lakes region. For example, on the Great Raincoast summertime logging replaced wintertime logging and the skid road replaced the white water log drives of the spring freshets.

New advances included bull-team, high-lead, and donkey-engine logging. The "high climber" and the individualistic I.W.W. logger were Great Raincoast variants of the lumberjack that were, in both workday function and romantic image, equivalents of the Great Plains cowboys just as the Lumber Kings of the Great Raincoast were analogous to the Cattle Kings of the Great Plains.[63]

The second industry was directly related to the abundance of streamflow in the Columbia and lesser rivers and has produced during the twentieth century what might be termed the Kilowatt Kingdom of hydroelectric power. Here, too, there have been distinctive regional adaptations in the form of the multi-purpose hydroelectric dam and the ultra high-voltage power line. Both helped to produce new industries such as aluminum and atomic energy and provided a social dividend of the lowest residential electric power rates in America.[64]

Analogous to the new legal adaptations that Webb depicted on the Great Plains were new institutional and legal responses to the Great Raincoast. In the Lumber Kingdom there arose the sustained-yield unit as a prototypical solution to the age-old problem of declining stumpage and poverty-stricken cutover lands.[65] New institutions that arose in the Kilowatt Kingdom were the municipally owned electric systems, the public (or people's) utility districts of Washington and Oregon, the two great governmental agencies of the Bonneville Power Administration and British Columbia Hydro, and the consortium of private and public power systems encompassed in the Northwest power pool.[66]

In regard to the cultural history of the Great Plains, Webb found that the cowboy life of the Great Plains gave rise to a colorful, romantic literature of the Cattle Kingdom while the harsh environmental challenge of drought, dust storm, incessant wind, searing heat, and freezing blizzard gave rise to the fatalistic, introspective literature of the farming frontier. In comparative terms the differing culture and history of the Great Raincoast has produced its own characteristic literature. For instance, there are the violence- and conflict-ridden stories of the Lumber Kingdom by such authors as James Stevens, Archie Binns, Robert Cantwell, and Ken Kesey.[67] In contrast to this literary outpouring of conflict and violence, the nurturing rainfall has encouraged a school of mystic Northwest painters,[68] a core of nature-oriented writers of fiction and poetry,[69] and a historically inspired group of architects practicing the Northwest architectural style that drew upon the rainlands folk-architectural style of the Oregon barn.[70]

Walter Prescott Webb addressed the meaning of his subject in his concluding chapter entitled "The Mysteries of the Great Plains in American Life." Here, Webb confronted such questions as: Why was the West considered to be spectacular and romantic? Why was the West considered to be lawless? Why was the West politically radical? And finally, what was the meaning of the Great Plains in American life?

For this issue—Great Raincoast regional culture in historical perspective—our questions and answers must constitute a reversal of those provided by Webb. While Webb plumbed the harsh life of the Great Plains, it remains for us to ponder the "good life" of the Great Raincoast. While Webb confronted in 1931 the Great Plains heritage of political radicalism, our task is to assess the meaning of the Great Raincoast's political heritage of moderation ("moderate conservatism" or "progressive anachronism").[71] A clue to our political and social heritage is found in a "calm moderation" that has, in the long run, "been the most distinguishing characteristic" of Great Raincoast history and life. Researching nineteenth-century pioneer diaries and letters and twentieth-century Northwest fiction leads one to the conclusion that "the supreme regularity of the calming, moderating psychological ambience" of the Great Raincoast's "climatic provenance of rainfall" is at the heart of what Webb might have called the "mysteries" of the Pacific Northwest life.[72]

Perhaps more so than anywhere else in the history of North America, the people of the Great Raincoast have enjoyed what Gordon B. Dodds, Norman H. Clark, and Oscar Osburn Winther have all referred to as the "good life."[73] The "good life" of the Great Raincoast has emerged from its unique heritage of nature, history, and culture. The individual prototype of this unique regional society measures up remarkably well to the norm of philosopher John Rawls's concept of the "self-respecting person"—an individual who finds personal fulfillment in the realization of a rational plan of life depending most crucially upon the respect of others as well as one's own self. The social result of the interaction of self-respecting persons, thus defined, is increasing cooperation and a rising sense of community.[74] This is an ideal, but it is an ideal that, more than any other, structures the successes and defines the failures of the society of the Great Raincoast of North America.

Alaska's Long and Sometimes Painful Relationship with the Lower Forty-Eight

EDITORS' NOTE

Until the discovery of oil on the North Slope in 1968, most Americans living in the "Lower Forty-Eight States" usually viewed Alaska only as a cold, faraway place of sparse population and spectacular natural beauty. The Japanese occupation of Kiska and Attu during World War II briefly dramatized the strategic location of that northern land, and Alaska's admission to the Union as the forty-ninth state in 1958 stimulated a short-lived national pride in bigness, giving rise to innumerable jokes about the relative size and diminished pretensions of Texas. Then the momentous development of petroleum irrevocably forced Alaska upon the nation's attention — something Alaskans had been trying to accomplish for a century. Yet most inhabitants of the Lower Forty-Eight still have little more understanding of Alaska's peculiar problems than they do of Canada's or any other foreign country's internal affairs. Not surprisingly, Alaskans have often been frustrated by these circumstances, and a rebellious frontier spirit has generally characterized their relationship with the federal government.

Following acquisition by the United States in 1867, Alaska chafed under a long and onerous apprenticeship, first as a district and then as a territory. In fact, Alaska suffered an unusual share of administrative and representational indignities during this colonial period. The main bone of contention with the federal establishment, however, has always been the development and disposition of natural resources. Long before the oil bonanza raised the stakes, Alaska was continually embroiled in controversy with distant Washington, D.C., over issues involving land, timber, coal, salmon, and other forms of natural wealth. With the federal government in control of a vast northern public domain, Alaskans have espoused decentralization and popular sovereignty. Thus, with a vengeance, Alaska joined other western states in the "Sagebrush" or, as it is called there, "Tundra" rebellion.

Claus-M. Naske first began studying Alaska when, as a youth in post-World War II Germany, he borrowed books on the subject from libraries of the American occupation forces. Becoming enamored of that northern land, he mailed an advertisement to an Alaskan newspaper in which he offered to work in exchange for payment of his passage to the United States. A Matanuska Valley farmer soon accepted this offer and paid his transatlantic fare to Alaska in 1954. After fulfilling his farm labor obligations, Naske completed a bachelor's degree (1961) at the University of Alaska, Fairbanks, and then a master's degree (1964) at the University of Michigan. In 1971 he received a Ph.D. in history at Washington State University, and then returned to teach at the University of Alaska, Fairbanks, where he is now a professor of history. A prolific author of Alaskan historical works, he has written *An Interpretive History of Alaskan Statehood* (1973), *Edward Lewis Bob Bartlett of Alaska: A Life in Politics* (1979), and, as coauthor, *Alaska: A History of the 49th State*, 2nd ed. (1987). He is also the author of several other books, numerous articles in journals, and many contract studies for various state and federal agencies. Naske has just completed a biography of the late Senator Ernest Gruening of Alaska.

Steamer, *Lavelle Young,* landing at Fairbanks, Alaska, circa 1905.
Manuscripts, Archives, and Special Collections, Washington State University Library,
Pullman, Washington

Alaska's Long and Sometimes Painful Relationship with the Lower Forty-Eight

CLAUS-M. NASKE

Several historians, including the ubiquitous Frederick Jackson Turner, have identified imperialism as a primary determinant in American history. Thus, as industrial America matured late in the nineteenth century, its quest for markets and influence abroad superseded the westward movement across the continent, and the expansionists adapted their rhetoric accordingly without altering the underlying rationale of imperialism. According to Jack E. Eblen, Alaska belonged to America's Oceanic Empire, which arose between the 1890s and about 1920 and which also included the Philippines, Hawaii, Puerto Rico, the Virgin Islands, and various other islands and concessions overseas. The principal island possessions of this new empire, although densely populated, did not share in the coveted Anglo-Saxon culture and were not likely to attract large numbers of American settlers. As a result, the federal government was not inclined to entrust the native peoples with republican institutions except under close supervision. In contrast, Alaska was sparsely populated, most conspicuously by transient and unruly white miners, and therefore also required a strong federal bureaucracy.[1]

Congress used the earlier Mississippi Valley model in organizing the Oceanic Empire, but with several changes that significantly altered the character of administration and permitted the federal government to exercise tight imperial control. Like the European nations during the era of the "White Man's Burden," the United States created a true administrative empire, with an elite cadre of imported administrators, often backed by the military, who governed and even exploited the colonial populations. This situation prevailed until the World War II period when world conditions and the demands by the colonial inhabitants for a different governmental relationship produced drastic changes in the Oceanic Empire. The Philippines gained independence, Congress extended home rule to Puerto Rico and the Virgin Islands, and Alaska and Hawaii attained statehood.

Not surprisingly, many Alaskans now feel, and have always felt, frustrated about Alaska's relationship with the "Lower Forty-Eight States," and in particular with the federal government. The core of disagreement with the federal establishment lies in the ownership, disposition, utilization, and management of renewable and nonrenewable natural resources. Most important has been the land itself, a not unexpected discovery, for to study Alaska's history, and, in fact, the nation's history as well, is to consider the problem of land and its use and control. It should be remembered, however, that more than half of the state's population is located in two urban centers, Anchorage and Fairbanks.

The fervor of feeling toward the federal bureaucracy can be illustrated by a recent event. In the primary election held on August 26, 1980, Alaskan voters approved, although by a narrow margin, this ballot question: "Shall the Alaska Statehood Commission be convened to study the status of the people of Alaska within the United States and to consider and recommend appropriate changes in the relationship of Alaska to the United States?" Seventeen months later, after numerous studies and formal hearings, the statehood commission issued its preliminary report. The document rejected secession as a solution, but recommended numerous steps Alaska should take, such as fighting aggressively with the state's legal, economic, and political powers to protect its resource income and control its resource development. Together with other states, it should also establish a legal defense fund and an organization to begin court action against coercive federal restrictions, burdensome regulations, and excessive use by Congress of the commerce power to override state law.[2]

No sooner had the Alaska Statehood Commission issued its preliminary report than the subsistence issue split the state in two. In 1978 the Alaska legislature had passed a measure requiring the Game and Fisheries boards to adopt regulations permitting state residents to take fish and game for subsistence purposes. When restrictions in the harvest of fish and game became necessary, the legislature decreed, subsistence use would have the top priority.

Congress was then considering a similar measure, and many northern residents hoped that passage of the state law would forestall action by Congress. It failed to do so, however, when advocates of the Alaskan native cause, explaining the state law as an indication of the subsistence issue's importance, prevailed on Congress to pass a federal law as well. Congress made this provision a part of the Alaska National Interest Lands Conservation Act (ANILCA), which President Jimmy Carter signed into law in December 1980. In declaring that the "nonwasteful subsistence uses of fish and wildlife and other renewable resources shall be the priority consumptive uses of all such resources on the public [federal] lands of Alaska," the measure went further than the state law. The federal act also stated that subsistence was the use of wild, renewable resources by rural Alaskans, both Native and nonnative. This definition upset a great many Alaskans, since it excluded about 85 percent of them from subsistence hunting and fishing rights simply because they lived in urban places.[3]

In Alaska the federal law was viewed as racist and divisive, pitting urban against rural citizens, setting whites against Natives, and establishing two classes of Alaskans. Most importantly, the measure violated the state's constitutional mandate that "wherever occurring in their natural state, fish, wildlife, and waters are reserved to the people for common use." Since statehood, Alaska's wildlife administrators had carefully observed that mandate.

Outraged citizens (mostly from Anchorage and Fairbanks), calling themselves Alaskans for Equal Fishing and Hunting Rights, prepared and obtained the necessary signatures on an initiative that would abolish the state subsistence law. The initiative appeared on the ballot in November 1982. Had it passed, it would have prohibited discrimination by state law in the allocation of fish and game based on race, sex, or residence, and fish and game would have been equally available to consumptive users. There no longer would have been any distinctions for reasons of economic status, land ownership, local residency, past utilization or dependence on the resource, or lack of alternative resources.

This initiative created a problem. For, if Alaska did not have a law establishing a rural subsistence priority, the federal act required the secretary of interior to take over management of fish and wildlife resources on federal lands within the state, which comprise about 60 percent of Alaska. No other state faced such a threat. No other state had a subsistence law, and Alaska's measure had nothing to do with scientific administration. It simply was a political scheme to allocate resources, an intrusion of politics into wildlife management. Alaskans had already learned that when politics rule fish and game administration, the resource can be destroyed. Federal management of Alaska's abundant salmon runs during territorial days had nearly destroyed the fish.[4]

Alaska's problems began after Secretary of State William H. Seward negotiated the purchase of that vast northern territory for the United States in 1867. Following Senate acceptance of the treaty of purchase, the secretary led his cabinet colleagues in planning three essential steps: the extension of customs authority over Alaska to bring revenues into the federal treasury and facilitate commerce; the formal transfer of the colony, together with its public lands, buildings, and archives; and the establishment of a military occupation to make American ownership known and to preserve order. Under Seward's guidance, the three steps were accomplished long before Congress approved the appropriation for the purchase. Seward's decisiveness initiated a pattern that prevailed for decades. The executive department planned, originated, and led, and Congress followed, accepted, and enacted.[5]

But what exactly the United States had purchased remained unclear for many decades. It only slowly dawned on Congress that it had bought a subarctic and arctic subcontinent, America's only far north possession, an enormous territory sweeping across four time zones and encompassing 586,112 square miles, fully one-fifth the size of the American contiguous land mass. From north to south, Alaska measures about 1,400 miles, and from east to west about 2,700 miles. The diversity of this sub-continent is just as incredible as its size. Alaska possesses arctic plains, great forests, swamps, glaciers, ice fields, broad valleys and deep fjords, the highest mountain of North America (Mount McKinley), active volcanoes, twelve major river systems, three million lakes, and countless islands. Alaska boasts 50 percent more seacoast than all of the contiguous forty-eight states—some 33,904 miles—and its coasts are washed by two oceans and three major seas. Geographically there are six regions, each with a distinctive topography and climate, ranging from temperate to frigid, and from desertic aridity to almost continuous rainfall and snowfall.[6]

There was no real understanding of Alaska's size and complexity when the United States Army arrived in 1867 and reluctantly provided the region's only government. The army left ten years later, in 1877, noting that it was too expensive to maintain troops in the north, and more importantly, "the Army had neither the machinery nor the authority for carrying on a civil government." Now, in addition to its duties of controlling commerce, fur trading, fishing, and sealing activities in the colony, the Treasury Department also assumed the army's duties. From 1877 till 1879 the collector of customs became the sole ruler of Alaska, supported by two cases of rifles and ammunition. This state of affairs continued until 1879, when the navy took over and administered the colony until 1884.[7]

American settlers had arrived at the same time the troops reached Sitka. By the end of 1867 Sitka residents impatiently requested that Congress establish a territorial government for Alaska. They went a step further and drafted a city charter, and then approved the document and elected municipal officers. The Sitka boom was short-lived, however, and frustrated residents soon blamed the damp climate and degenerate Indians for the lack of economic progress. They also added the Alaska Commercial Company, an American enterprise, to the list of impediments, accusing the business organization of monopolistic practices.[8]

Of the settlers' early protests, three stand out. First was the failure of Congress to provide an Organic Act, thereby blocking the district's civil progress. Second, the absence of homestead rights inhibited the growth of a permanent population. And third, the pioneer American residents complained about the federal government's failure to improve transportation and mail services with Seattle, Portland, and San Francisco—Alaska's supply centers.[9]

Finally, in 1884, Congress recognized the unsatisfactory conditions and passed the Organic Act, sponsored principally by Senator Benjamin Harrison of Indiana. Fifteen years had elapsed since the acquisition of Alaska before Congress seriously considered the question of organizing any government in the territory. Some twenty-five bills were introduced and died in committee, until Harrison's measure finally passed. When the senator became chairman of the Senate Committee on the Territories in 1884, he apologized for the severe shortcomings of the Organic Act. He conceded that "all of the provisions of the bill are inadequate. It is a mere shift; it is a mere expedient; it is a mere beginning in what we believe to be the right direction toward giving a civil government and education to Alaska." Senator Harrison concluded, in a tone of candor, "I hope more will follow, but the committee in this matter adjudged what they believed to be the probable limit of the generosity of the Senate."[10]

The Organic Act, although inadequate in many respects, was important because it established the foundation upon which Alaska's governmental structure could later be elaborated, refined, and expanded. In its restrictive aspects, the act prohibited both a legislative branch and a delegate to Congress. It made Alaska a "civil and judicial district," with a presidentially appointed governor, one statutory rather than constitutional district judge, four lesser judges, and other officials. All were given multiple responsibilities. The United States marshal, for example, was to act as surveyor general, despite the lack of legal provisions for a land system. Rather than draft a specific code of laws for Alaska, Congress decreed that judicial officials were to use the laws of Oregon, where applicable. In addition, the officials were required to administer any specific laws which Congress had provided for Alaska. Since the management of some territorial affairs would be carried out directly from Washington, the secretary of the interior would supervise education in the north.[11]

After many fruitless attempts, Congress finally passed a measure in 1906 providing for the election of a voteless delegate to Congress. The bill also stipulated that Alaska be referred to as a territory instead of a district, as it at first had been designated. Congress had taken some thirty-nine years to extend to Alaska that minimum of representation that had almost automatically been accorded every other territory. Hawaii and Puerto Rico, for example, had been given representation in the nation's capital in 1900, a mere two years after they had come under the flag.

James Wickersham, a colorful federal judge in the north, quit the bench and was elected as Alaska's third delegate to Congress in 1908. He took his seat in the House of Representatives in 1909, and wasted no time introducing a measure to create a legislative assembly for the territory. After a prolonged struggle and many alterations, Congress finally passed Alaska's second Organic Act in 1912. It gave the territory a legislature, but was more severely limited in its field of action than the legislature of any other territory. The act specified that the existing executive and judicial branches provided by the Organic Act of 1884 (as amended in 1900 and thereafter) could not be altered by the territorial legislature. Both of these branches were to remain appointed by and responsible to the president. The legislature was forbidden to deal with the laws relating to game, fish, and fur resources, since the federal government retained jurisdiction over these important resources. Nor could the legislature pass any law interfering with the primary disposal of the soil, thereby preventing it from changing land laws that were already unworkable. It could not alter the system of license taxes on business and trade imposed by Congress in the Alaska Criminal Code Act of 1899, nor could it change the Nelson Act of January 1905, together with its subsequent amendments, which provided for the allocation of the revenues from the aforementioned business and trade license taxes for roads, schools, and the care of the insane. And there were numerous other restrictions on the power of the legislature that caused northern residents to strive tirelessly to amend and change the act of 1912.[12]

Yet, after all was said and done, Alaska had finally become an organized territory and obtained a substantially increased, although limited, form of self-government, some forty-five years after acquisition by the United States. It took another forty-seven years before Alaska joined the Union as the forty-ninth state when, on January 3, 1959, President Dwight D. Eisenhower signed the formal declaration of admission.

Not surprisingly, many northern residents have complained about Alaska's colonial status, and quite a few historians have also examined the subject. Ernest Gruening, a former territorial governor, recounted these complaints when he addressed the Alaska Constitutional Convention on November 9, 1955. He reminded the delegates that they had assembled to validate the basic American principle of government by the consent of the governed. Since 1867, he said, Alaskan residents had protested against the federal restrictions, discriminations, and exclusions, but to little avail. Gruening then charged that the United States had held Alaska as a colony for its own selfish political, strategic, and economic advantages. Inherent in this colonialism was an inferior political and economic status. Alaskans had enjoyed no effective voting representation in Congress, Gruening declared, and absentee capitalists had exploited the natural resources for the benefit of outsiders.[13]

Jeannette Paddock Nichols, a noted historian, first voiced similar sentiments in a study published in 1924. She stated that geography, economics, and politics had conspired to subject Alaska to a series of misfortunes, foremost among them being the misguided administration of its affairs. For, Congress was located five thousand miles away, and the occasional pieces of legislation it hastily fashioned for Alaska almost never fit. Two scholars of American colonial administration, Earl S. Pomeroy and Jack E. Eblen, were even more severe in their judgment of the American administration of Alaska. Pomeroy stated that "Alaska stood in an outer political anteroom without the most rudimentary territorial status, governed (when governed at all) more like the Newfoundland fisheries of the seventeenth-century British empire than like a territory." Eblen observed that Alaska's first Organic Act of 1884 "provided a cruelly modified first-stage government and made no provision for eventual representative government."[14]

Alaskans could agree with these scholarly assessments. In fact, they were more specific with their many real or imagined complaints against Congress and the federal government. Although repeatedly requested to do so, Congress had refused to transfer the control and management of Alaska's game and fish resources to the territory. Yet the federal government had always given management responsibilities of the corresponding resources to all other territories in the past. Congress steadfastly refused to amend the Maritime Act of 1920, referred to in Alaska as the Jones Act after its sponsor, Senator Wesley L. Jones of Washington. This legislation contained a substantial modification of existing maritime law. It stated that goods shipped across the United States, destined either for the coastal ports of the Atlantic or Pacific or for shipment across those oceans to Europe or Asia, could use either American or foreign carriers. Alaska, however, had been excluded from this beneficial arrangement. So, instead of being able to take advantage of reasonably priced goods from midwestern markets shipped to Prince Rupert, British Columbia, and from there transshipped in Canadian vessels to Alaska, the Jones Act restricted the territory to the steamship services owned in Seattle, in Senator Jones's home state. That city soon gained a monopoly on the Alaska trade, as the senator had apparently intended. The Supreme Court upheld the discrimination of the Jones Act, on the basis that Alaska was a territory under the control of Congress.[15]

Alaskans have always hungered for land, and as early as 1872 scientist William H. Dall criticized Congress for its failure to aid immigration by extending the land laws of the United States to the territory. Twenty years later, Alaskan residents still remained without America's often liberalized homestead legislation. Congress apparently penalized the territory for land use illegalities practiced in the western states throughout the 1860s and 1870s when settlers had often violated the Homestead Act, the Timber Culture Act, and the Desert Land Act. Thus Congress was reluctant to add to these problems by extending the necessary legislation to the north. Alaskan residents continued to cite the absence of these incentives to settlement and complained about a neglectful Congress that denied them the historic right to land. As a special category, the Preemption Act of 1841 had legalized occupation of land in the western states, because pioneers were determined to extend settlement in spite of legal obstacles. Preemptive occupancy had democratized the American land system and put the actual settler on an equal basis with the speculator. The right of preemption, however, only applied to publicly surveyed lands, which did not exist in Alaska.[16]

In response to the influx of people during the Klondike gold rush, Congress passed several pieces of major legislation pertaining to the northern territory. One potentially important measure, enacted before the end of 1898, stipulated rules for the construction of railroads, extended the homestead laws to Alaska, and provided for the disposal of timber. The size of the claims was restricted to only eighty acres, and the burden of the survey had to be borne by the applicant. Prospective homesteaders were also allowed to use soldiers' scrip. Alaska Governor John G. Brady complained that the law was inoperative because homesteads could only be located upon surveyed lands. Yet Alaska remained without base or meridian lines or monuments.[17] Congress amended the law a few years later to permit entry on 160 acres of unsurveyed lands, but the amendment also included requirements for residency and cultivation in conformity with the national Homestead Act. These procedures were not designed for Alaska's unique physical, geographical, and economic conditions, and relatively few homesteaders were able to comply. Therefore, very little land was transferred from public to private ownership under this act.

Another piece of legislation, the Trade and Manufacturing Sites Act of 1898, enabled a citizen or corporation to purchase a small acreage of public land for the purpose of establishing a business enterprise. With the primary purpose of allowing corporations to obtain title to land for the construction of salmon canneries, it contained many safeguards to prevent its misuse for speculative endeavors. Thus the site for a proposed business could not be patented, but only land actually occupied could pass into fee simple ownership. The maximum acreage was set at eighty acres, and to protect public access, no claim could extend more than one-fourth of a mile along the shore of any navigable waters.[18]

For many years these two acts provided the only avenues for gaining title to public lands in Alaska. At various intervals in later years, Congress passed legislation making land available for recreational and residential uses, for grazing leases, and for the sale of timber and other materials from the public domain. All of these measures contained provisions discouraging the appropriation of public lands for speculative purposes.

The reserved era began in the western states only after large portions of the best public lands with known resource values had already passed into private ownership. In Alaska, however, Congress, the president, and the many new federal resource agencies freely withdrew and reserved large tracts of the best lands for permanent federal retention. Early in the twentieth century, the president withdrew all of the best forest lands in the Panhandle and along the coasts of south central Alaska to create the Tongass and Chugach national forests, while other areas characterized by unusual natural beauty were set aside as national parks and monuments. In the years that followed, executive withdrawals designated extensive tracts for wildlife refuges, Indian and military reserves, numerous small navigation sites, potential hydroelectric locations, public recreation areas, and various other government purposes. For the most part these reserved lands were closed to private entry and settlement.

The effect of these federal land policies was clearly revealed by the pattern of land ownership existing when Alaska joined the Union as the forty-ninth state in 1959. In that year the federal government still owned 99.8 percent of the land. Only a little over 500,000 acres had passed into private ownership. Lands withdrawn and reserved by various federal agencies for permanent public ownership and miscellaneous federal uses encompassed approximately 121,000,000 acres in 1944. By 1958 some of this land had been returned to the vacant, unappropriated federal public domain and federal withdrawals amounted to about 92,000,000 acres.[19]

Many Alaskans felt particularly aggrieved when contemplating the history of coal use in the territory. In the spring of 1906 federal coal land laws received special attention when Senator Robert M. La Follette of Wisconsin quoted statistics furnished by the United States Geological Survey on the value of coal lands being alienated from the Five Civilized Tribes in Oklahoma. On July 26, a withdrawal order closed approximately 50,000,000 acres of coal lands that the Geological Survey had listed. Then, on November 12, President Theodore Roosevelt shocked Alaskans when he directed Secretary of the Interior Ethan A. Hitchcock to withdraw from entry all valuable coal lands until an examination and proper classification could be made. A month later, the president explained the reasons for his action in Alaska: "The present laws put a premium on fraud because they forbid individuals and corporations from securing a sufficient quantity of land to warrant their going into the coal mining business, and yet render it easy for them to secure the extra quantity by evasion of the law."[20]

Alaskans were outraged at the president's orders and were not appeased even when Roosevelt appealed to Congress to pass a coal leasing act suitable for the territory's peculiar conditions. Congress, however, did not approve an Alaska coal leasing measure until 1914. By that time more than 1,200 claims had been filed, over 500 had been cancelled, and more than 560 were still pending, while only two had been patented. Territorial coal production in 1913 had amounted to approximately 1,200 tons, of which none came from the promising Bering River or Matanuska coal fields. Between 1899 and 1912 Alaskans burned 1,528,030 tons of coal. Of this total, a mere 36,669 tons had been mined in Alaska, while the rest had been imported at substantial expense.[21]

Congress intended the Alaska Coal Act of 1914 to be a complementary piece of legislation to the Alaska Railroad Act, which passed the same year. But the Department of the Interior did not issue regulations to implement the 1914 coal leasing law until 1916. Between 1906, the year the territory's coal lands were withdrawn, and 1916, when the new leasing regulations took effect, Alaska coal production increased by 19 percent and imports of coal decreased by 30 percent. The importation of heavy oils increased by 158 percent during the same time span. This was a harbinger of the future. It is true that coal production increased slowly during the 1920s, mostly to supply fuel to Anchorage and other communities along the railroad, as well as the Alaska Railroad's locomotives. An export market, however, never developed.[22] In 1983 Alaska still did not have an export market, and many Alaskans blame the federal government for not aiding Alaska's coal development in a timely fashion, and for blanketing Alaska with a crazy quilt of land withdrawals, reservations, and unworkable regulations.

Alaskans also complained long and loudly over the federal government's failure to provide an adequate transportation system, so necessary for economic advancement. The Klondike gold rush at the end of the nineteenth century increased steamboat traffic on the Yukon and, later, the Tanana rivers. There were hardly any roads or trails. Not until the establishment of the Board of Road Commissioners for Alaska in 1905 did road construction get under way. Yet, by 1930, a total of only 4,890 miles of trails and wagon roads had been constructed. The most notable link, the Richardson Road, named after the chairman of the Board of Road Commissioners for Alaska, Major Wilds P. Richardson, connected Valdez at tidewater with Fairbanks in the interior. Even this relatively short route of less than four hundred miles was open only during the few summer months for years after its completion.[23]

The situation with railroad construction was little better. Perhaps lured by the prospect of fabulous profits, some eleven companies reportedly petitioned for railroad right-of-ways in Alaska between the fall of 1897 and the spring of 1898. Several more applied later, but the panic of 1907, poor economic conditions, and restrictive federal legislation brought speculation to a halt. The 1898 transportation and homestead act in its final form, dealt more with settlers than with railroads. The railroad provisions were stingy in comparison with grants to railroads in the contiguous states. The right-of-ways measured a narrow one hundred feet on either side of the tracks. There were detailed regulations about the filing of locations, and entrepreneurs were to complete their lines within four years or forfeit the rights to the unbuilt segment. The license tax section of the Alaska Criminal Code of 1899 added another provision: a $100 tax per mile per year on each operating mile. Still, despite these handicaps, some railroads were constructed. In 1903 the Alaska Central Railroad began building from Seward toward the interior, but went bankrupt in 1908. It reorganized as the Alaskan Northern Railroad, and had finished seventy-one miles of track when it ceased operation. Several narrow-gauge railroads served local needs, such as one line on the Seward Peninsula and another in the Tanana Valley. Only two railroads made any money—the White Pass and Yukon Railroad built to connect Skagway with Whitehorse in the Yukon Territory, Canada, and the Copper River and Northwestern Railway completed by the Alaska Syndicate primarily to carry copper ore from its mines at Kennecott to the port of Cordova.[24]

The federal government finally realized that Alaska needed some help and authorized the building of a railroad in 1914. Construction began in April 1915 on the Alaska Railroad which ran from Seward on the coast to Fairbanks in the interior. It was not finished until 1923 and, although the line helped Alaska, Congress in subsequent years never appropriated quite enough money to maintain the railroad properly. Congress did not provide adequate funds until World War II, when military requirements made reconstruction necessary.[25]

If insufficient help with transportation was one of many sore points, Alaskans became even more outraged by federal mismanagement of Alaska's great salmon fishery. The first large-scale commercial utilization of salmon began in 1878 in southeastern Alaska with the construction of two canneries, followed by a period of unrestricted and ruthless exploitation of the resource. Entrepreneurs built hundreds of small processing plants, and each year imported fishermen, cannery workers, and supplies from San Francisco, Portland, and Seattle. Alaska's isolation and sparse population initially made this industrial structure necessary. As a result, the main outfitting, employment, and financial centers for the Alaska salmon industry were established from outside, and these three cities also became the storage and marketing centers for the canned salmon.[26]

In time, the industry consolidated its operations, and a handful of companies, headquartered in San Francisco and Seattle, organized the business. Alaska remained the principal source of supply, and despite the development and growth occurring in the north over the decades, the structure of the fishery remained relatively unchanged. While a much larger proportion of fishermen and cannery workers were local residents in later years, and the industry purchased more supplies locally, the centers of decision making for the operations still remained outside the region. Alaskans resented this classic pattern of absentee capitalism that gave rise to numerous problems, conflicts, disagreements, and misunderstandings, and compounded the problems of conservation.

Congress was slow to address the conservation of Alaska salmon, made imperative by the fierce competition of the firms bidding for control of the resource. In many instances entrepreneurs constructed stream barricades and fished out whole runs until they were completely destroyed. After several unsuccessful attempts at conservation, the United States Fish Commission appointed Dr. David Starr Jordan of Stanford University to conduct a thorough investigation of the Alaska salmon fishery. In 1904 Jordan submitted his final report to President Theodore Roosevelt in which he called attention to the appalling conditions existing in Alaska. Meanwhile, Congress abolished the Fish Commission and established the Department of Commerce and Labor, with a Bureau of Fisheries as one of its integral divisions. This new agency at last consolidated the many scattered fishery functions in the federal government and offered hope that fishery experts and scientists would handle such responsibilities.

The new arrangement was not perfect, and in time the department became a general service agency, primarily aiding American businessmen. In 1906 Congress considered a comprehensive Alaska fisheries bill. In hearings before the House Committee on Territories in March 1906, scientists and other officials of the Bureau of Fisheries and the Department of Commerce and Labor strongly supported the bill. C. W. Dorr, Vice President and General Counsel of the Alaska Packers Association, just as strongly objected to the proposed extension of the secretary's authority to regulate fishing in all Alaskan waters. He argued that such provisions would enable the Bureau of Fisheries to promulgate regulations that would put carriers out of business and prevent Congress from doing anything about it. Dorr had many other arguments, including the fanciful contention that the salmon were now coming up the rivers in such enormous schools that they were actually destroying each other in the spawning grounds.

The House committee was impressed with the industry's arguments, and instructed bureau officials to confer with packer representatives and devise an improved measure. The substitute eliminated almost all of the features to which the industry had objected, and the gutted bill became law on June 26, 1906. As a result of this close call, the industry in 1911 organized the Association of Alaska Salmon Canners to work cooperatively with the Puget Sound Salmon Canners Association. Shortly thereafter, a permanent legal staff was retained in Washington, D.C., to represent the cannerymen, and the packers pledged to share the expenses. This vigilance proved successful. When Congress enacted Alaska's second Organic Act in 1912, which granted the territory a legislature, the federal lawmakers, at the lobby's insistence, retained the authority to regulate and tax the fisheries. This action was unprecedented since all previous territories had been granted these powers denied to Alaska.

Increasingly Alaskans became agitated over outside control of the salmon fisheries, criticizing the industry for its opposition to community development and associated tax increases. Alaska received precious few benefits from the diminishing resource and suffered from unequal job opportunities. Despite these complaints, however, the Association of Alaska Salmon Canners and the Puget Sound Salmon Canners Association successfully maintained control over Alaska's salmon and minimized taxes. In fact, the canned salmon industry became one of the most effective lobbying groups in the United States. But what perhaps galled Alaskans most was the use of fish traps by the big processors, which assured them control over large supplies of salmon at low prices, and made it very difficult for non-trap operators to compete. The dissatisfaction with these conditions eventually led to a major fishermen's strike in 1912 in southeastern Alaska, and the demand of higher prices for fish sold to canneries. As a result, the canneries simply increased the number of traps and decreased their dependence on mobile gear.

By 1913 the canneries owned nearly all of the traps, and the proportion of trap-caught salmon totaled more than 30 percent and increased rapidly. Alaskan fishermen began to fear that the "Fish Trust" would soon control salmon harvests through the use of traps. They argued for the abolishment of such devices, but attempts at remedial legislation were frustrated by counterproposals from the processors to legalize ownership of the existing trap sites. For the time being, the lobby effectively defeated all attempts to abolish fish traps.

Faced with the certain passage of the Alaska Statehood Act in 1958, the lobby made one last attempt to preserve its property rights in fish traps and its control of the industry. Representative Jack Westland of Washington successfully offered an amendment providing that

> the administration and management of the fish and wildlife resources shall be retained by the Federal Government under existing laws until the first day of the first calendar year following the expiration of ninety legislative days after the Secretary of Interior certifies to the Congress that the Alaska State Legislature has made adequate provisions for the administration, management, and conservation of said resources in the broad national interest.

The lobby hoped that the last three words would provide a basis for arguing for an indefinite retention of federal control and a continuation of fish trap operations. To avoid obvious constitutional questions, the act further required that Alaskans specifically indicate their willingness to abide by this arrangement in a separate vote that became part of the "Compact with the United States." While campaigning for state and national Republican candidates in 1958, however, Secretary of Interior Fred R. Seaton effectively nullified the lobby's efforts. He announced the immediate abolition of all traps except those owned by Indian villages and promised the prompt certification of the transfer of all resource management functions to the new state.[27]

The fish trap had become the symbol of absentee control of Alaska's resources. It was not surprising that the delegates who wrote Alaska's constitution in 1955-56 had already attached an ordinance to their document which would, upon the effective date of the constitution, put the following policy into effect:

> As a matter of immediate public necessity, to relieve the economic distress among individual fishermen and those dependent upon them for a livelihood, to conserve the rapidly dwindling supply of salmon in Alaska, to insure fair competition among those engaged in commercial fishing, and to make manifest the will of the people of Alaska, the use of fish traps for the taking of salmon for commercial purposes is hereby prohibited in all the coastal waters of the state.[28]

The abolition of fish traps, which was enacted by the first state legislature, and the subsequent executive action in the administration of the newly transferred management responsibilities were both designed to break down the nonresident domination of the fishing industry. In fact, the 1961 session of the state legislature went one step further by passing a bill that permitted residents in areas where very small salmon runs were predicted to petition for priority fishing rights until they reached a minimum catch of one thousand fish per fisherman, the minimum considered necessary for a subsistence income.[29]

Thereupon, the governor of the state of Washington, threatening reprisals, sent a strongly worded protest against keeping out-of-state fishermen from using their "historic fishing areas in Alaska." Governor William A. Egan of Alaska undoubtedly expressed a widely held sentiment when he stated, in reply, that for decades Alaskans had struggled to attain statehood "to free themselves from outside controls largely centered in the state of Washington." This domination during Alaska's long period of territoriality had included the fisheries, shipping, labor organization, industry, and even "our political decisions." The governor continued that it had been "a long and sorry exploitation of Alaska by and for outside forces largely identified with the state of Washington." Maintaining that this external mastery had eventually united Alaskans in their desire for statehood and control of their own destiny, Egan concluded that "old habits are hard to break," and therefore the Alaska bills on fish traps and salmon runs had "resulted in a storm of protest unbecoming to the state of Washington and deeply resented by Alaskans."[30]

Not surprisingly, then, the vast majority of northern citizens applauded congressional passage of the Alaska Statehood Act in 1958. Congress determined to put the new state on a solid economic footing. As a result, it granted Alaska 103,350,000 acres of land, to be selected from the vacant, unappropriated, and unreserved public domain over a twenty-five-year period. Reflecting a new element of enlightenment on Alaska, the land grant, both in its magnitude and method of allocation, differed substantially from federal bequests to other states. Rather than forcing upon Alaska the traditional township-section pattern, Congress departed from precedent and allowed the new state to designate its acreage in large blocks. Due to a limited budget in the early 1960s, the state followed a conservative land policy in those years that focused on areas near the larger communities, primarily in south central Alaska, and numerous small tracts for specific purposes. Even so, Alaska Natives soon became concerned about threats to their own claims to lands and resources. They responded by forming local and regional organizations, which eventually united statewide. Thus the fear of losing their land aroused the Natives and radicalized them.[31] Finally, because of all the overlapping claims, Secretary of the Interior Stewart Udall imposed a land freeze in 1966, effectively stopping the transfer of any acreage until Congress had an opportunity to act on Native rights.

In the meantime, the state continued to make its selections, and by 1968 had designated 19,600,000 acres, of which some 8,500,000 acres had been tentatively approved and over 6,000,000 acres had been patented. In that same year Alaska Natives had clear ownership of fewer than 500 acres, and held in restricted title only 15,000 acres. About 900 native families lived on twenty-three reserves administered by the Bureau of Indian Affairs. These reserves, which included 1,250,000 acres of reindeer lands, totalled 4,000,000 acres. An estimated 270,000,000 acres of land remained in the public domain. Some 37,400 rural Alaska Natives lived on that land and the twenty-three reserves, while 15,600 of their kin had moved to Alaska's urban centers.[32]

Then a momentous event drastically accelerated change in the north and altered the relationship between Natives and Caucasians. On January 16, 1968, the Atlantic Richfield Company announced the discovery of substantial gas and oil deposits in the Prudhoe Bay geological structure, and on September 10, 1969, the state conducted its twenty-third competitive oil and gas lease sale. At the end of the day, the state had sold oil leases on less than .001 percent of Alaska's total land mass and raised more than $900 million.

It soon became obvious that the pipeline necessary for carrying crude oil from the Arctic to tidewater would not be built until the claims of Alaska Natives had been settled. After various proposals and many months of negotiations, Congress passed the Alaska Native Claims Settlement Act of 1971 (ANCSA), and President Richard M. Nixon signed the measure into law on December 18, 1971.[33] In exchange for 44,000,000 acres of land and $962.5 million, the Natives relinquished all aboriginal rights. But to gain conservationist support, Congress had included Section 17 (d) (2) in ANCSA, which instructed the secretary of interior to withdraw up to 80,000,000 acres for study and possible inclusion in conservation units such as national parks, forests, wildlife refuges, and wild and scenic river systems. Another provision of the legislation granted the Natives priority selection of lands over the state and its prerogatives under the statehood act. This stipulation effectively prevented the state from designating its statehood land grant. Soon the Natives and state officials clashed over acreages claimed by both, while the federal government dragged its feet in granting title to either side. Finally, in May and November 1978, the state identified a pool of state interest lands, thereby hoping to gain its remaining acreage. By November 30, 1978, the state had received patent to only 22,000,000 acres of its statehood entitlement and tentative approval for another 15,000,000 acres, and had selected another 144,000,000 acres—an overselection because nobody was certain how much land was available. Alaska Natives had gained title to less than 200,000 acres and tentative approval to another 5,000,000 acres.[34]

In the summer of 1978 the House of Representatives overwhelmingly passed an Alaskan land measure sponsored by Representative Morris K. Udall of Arizona, which proposed to set aside 124,000,000 acres of the state's land. Senator Ted Stevens of Alaska, a Republican, introduced a land bill of his own. By mid-October the Carter administration and congressional leaders had reached a compromise. But Senator Mike Gravel of Alaska, a Democrat, used a parliamentary maneuver to kill the compromise bill after failing to receive guarantees for seven transportation corridors across federal lands. Secretary of Interior Cecil Andrus then acted swiftly, and on November 16, withdrew 110,000,000 acres under Section 204-E of the Bureau of Land Management Organic Act. On December 1, President Jimmy Carter signed an executive order under the provisions of the Antiquities Act of 1906 creating seventeen national monuments containing 56,000,000 acres.[35]

Conservationists were elated and most Alaskans were outraged. Demonstrating in major Alaskan towns, dissatisfied residents burned or drowned, depending on the location, effigies of the president. The state government filed suit against the federal government, contending, in part, that the statehood act had been breached.[36]

The tumultuous uproar among Alaskans over the land did not then, and does not now, reverberate around the nation. For those directly involved in the struggle, both in Alaska and the nation's capital, the fighting has been intense, although its ramifications are only dimly perceived elsewhere. And the Alaskan interpretation of the land fight depends on individual images of that great land. Obviously there are views derived from regional orientation rather than from scholarly study or objective deliberation. Similar observations might be made about outsiders in the Lower Forty-Eight.

As seen from the East Coast, Alaska is cold and far away—a storehouse of natural resources to be utilized when the nation needs them. Seattle has claimed Alaska as its own ever since the gold rushes at the turn of the century. In fact, the wags said, it was the only American city to own a territory. Entrepreneurs doing business in the north but residing in Seattle have usually claimed that they understood Alaska's problems better than Alaskans did. In the nation's capital those favoring or opposing Alaska's development have waged bitter warfare for many years. In 1923, for example, President Warren G. Harding discovered that five cabinet officers and twenty-eight bureaus exercised authority over that northern territory. Many of these agencies quarreled over how best to preserve or, alternatively, develop the area's natural resources. Harding's secretary of the interior, Albert B. Fall, aggressively championed a plan to concentrate the administration of Alaska in one department, presumably Interior, thus allowing private enterprise to exploit its resources as speedily as possible. Secretary of Agriculture Henry C. Wallace, in whose department the conservation-minded Forest Service was located, objected to Fall's plan. President Harding went to Alaska in 1923 to take a firsthand look and concluded to make no major changes in Alaskan administration.[37]

Although outsiders usually made the major decisions affecting Alaskans, the northerners have long possessed definite views of their own role. They consider themselves hardy pioneers who scratch out a living from a harsh land. Much to their resentment, they feel that this already tough task is made even more difficult by the constant interference of the federal government in their lives. While most have probably never read a historical volume expressing the traditional, or "neglect," theme found in Ernest Gruening's *State of Alaska*, the popular press has constantly reminded them of federal shortcomings. Flailing the "feds" has developed into a favorite pastime of the press, which portrays Alaskans as hardy pioneers — sterling men and women who strive mightily to maintain their isolated communities in America's most hostile environment. According to popular mythology, these brave people have adapted admirably to a harsh land, to the vastness of Alaska, and to its remoteness from the rest of the country. In fact, scratch an urban Alaskan and he or she will turn out to be a subsistence hunter or would-be homesteader. But the "feds" have already abolished homesteading opportunities, and now also want to cut down hunting and fishing with restrictive land designations. So bumper stickers abound in the north with slogans like "Alaskans for Independence," and "Improve the Forest, Plant a Sierra Clubber." Many pickup trucks also race around the cities with full gunracks behind the driver's seat, apparently ready for any eventuality. It would be grossly inaccurate to say that there are no environmentalist organizations to be found in Alaska; but the "hardy pioneers" of urban Alaska have intuitively and wholeheartedly espoused the neglect theme, and are louder and "getting more press."

Under those circumstances, it should not be surprising that many northerners considered recent federal land actions as the most monumental and obscene land grab in history. The land battle, which raged throughout the 1970s, ended abruptly when Congress passed, and the president signed into law, a measure known as the Alaska National Interest Lands Conservation Act in December 1980. In November of that year American voters had chosen Republican Ronald Reagan as president. A conservative and a westerner, he aroused fears among conservationists that he would open the public domain to unbridled exploitation. Proponents and opponents of the Alaska lands measure, therefore, compromised in the waning days of Jimmy Carter's presidency and his conservationist secretary of interior, Cecil Andrus. A very complex act, it set aside an area larger than California for conservation. It placed more than 97,000,000 acres of Alaska in new or expanded national parks and refuges, doubling the size of both national programs. The measure also protected twenty-five free-flowing Alaskan rivers in their natural state, almost doubling the size of the wild and scenic rivers system. And by classifying 56,000,000 acres of these lands as wilderness, the law tripled the size of the National Wilderness Preservation System. The act broke new ground in a number

THE CHANGING PACIFIC NORTHWEST

of other ways. Congress deliberately included entire ecosystems in the protected status. For example, along the Alaska Peninsula an effective continuity of wildlife habitat lands has been created, utilizing a variety of land classifications.[38]

A desire to maintain the cultural integrity of native communities and life-styles within the newly created national parks led to provisions to continue subsistence activities, including hunting, fishing, and trapping by motorized vehicles such as snow machines and motorboats. Additionally, airplanes and motorboats are allowed as means of gaining access to wilderness areas. Congress excluded mineralized zones with known oil and gas potential from designated conservation areas to permit economic development when feasible. Cooperative management agreements between the state and federal agencies are also being negotiated for areas where such arrangements will provide better realization of management guidelines.[39]

With the passage of this legislation the final step in the allocation of lands in Alaska is nearly complete, except for minor adjustments. Distribution began in 1958 with passage of the Alaska Statehood Act, by which the new state was given the right to select 103,350,000 acres of land as its statehood entitlement. The Alaska Native Claims Settlement Act of 1971 settled outstanding native claims and awarded some 44,000,000 acres of land to twelve regional native corporations and more than two hundred village corporations. Finally, the 1980 Alaska National Interest Lands Conservation Act resulted in the inclusion within conservation units of 131,000,000 acres of land.

Now that the land issue is settled, it would seem that Alaskans should be developing a new attitude toward the federal government. But that is not the case. New dangers lurk. In 1981 the Alaska Statehood Commission concluded, and a majority of Alaskans probably agree, that there exists a new federal challenge to the rightful use of Alaska's lands and resources. Reportedly the heavily populated eastern and midwestern states, in a well-organized effort, were working through their congressional delegations to place a federal limit or tax on state resource revenues. These outsiders, "in their hunger for cheaper energy and for federal dollars, . . . would thus strike a killing blow to one of the last remnants of state sovereignty; the power to raise revenue."[40]

There are other issues as well. For example, as of 1981, the federal government has conveyed only about half of Alaska's statehood land entitlement. Moreover, with 74 percent of the nation's potentially energy-rich Outer Continental Shelf surrounding the state, the federal government has stated that the wishes of Alaska to cushion fisheries and coastal towns from the impacts of drilling must give way to the national interest in order to achieve the goal of energy self-sufficiency.

It seems clear that Alaska, the largest state but with a very small population, will continue to feel the heavy hand of the federal government in all walks of public life. And there is no doubt that northern citizens will continue to protest federal interference. Alaskans, by a margin of 72 percent of the ballots cast in the 1982 general election, approved an initiative claiming state ownership of federal lands. Thus Alaska officially joined the "Sagebrush" or, as it is called locally, "Tundra" rebellion. Together with other western states, it now would constitutionally challenge federal ownership of land within its boundaries. The configurations of this warfare are as yet only dimly seen, but the 1982 election issued the battle cry for Alaskan insurgency of the twenty-first century.

Territorial Elites and Political Power Struggles in the Far West, 1865-1890

EDITORS' NOTE

Even though American political history has traditionally received more than its fair share of attention, the story of territorial government in the Pacific Northwest has not been given this same degree of treatment. Indeed, that part of the region's development has often been interpreted as unique, if not parochial or merely episodic. The political leaders of territorial Washington, Oregon, and Idaho, with rare exceptions, have been presented as shadowy figures moving across a stage which itself seems insubstantial and fleeting. Ronald H. Limbaugh, on the other hand, attacks the issue of territorial political leadership on the broad basis of cultural roots and elitist power structures in Idaho and the Far West generally.

Limbaugh's interest in this subject arose from a strong family tradition as well as scholarly commitment, or as he has stated: "I am an Idaho native with an attachment for the Pacific Northwest and its history. With frontier pioneers on both sides of my family, and with strong memories of my early days on an Idaho farm, I took up the field as naturally as a duck takes to water." Drawing on Idaho's intriguing history, he develops the thesis that territorial elites existed there and in other far western territories in contradiction to Frederick Jackson Turner's frontier thesis as well as several more classical theories about American democracy. Moreover, those elites continued to thrive until the Populist era because they managed to accommodate the demands of diverse political elements in each area. Limbaugh has ranged widely over the literature of territorial development and political theory to support his case for Idaho and its applicability to the rest of the Pacific Northwest. Although historians studying Washington and Oregon must mark out their own paths, it is clear that Limbaugh offers them a thoughtful approach.

Ronald H. Limbaugh received his B.A. degree from the College of Idaho at Caldwell in 1960 and completed graduate study at the University of Idaho, earning his M.A. in 1962 and his Ph.D. in 1967. He began teaching at the University of the Pacific, Stockton, California, in 1966 where he was promoted to full professor in 1977. At UOP he also served three years as Director of the Holt-Atherton Center for Western Studies, and in addition is executive secretary of the Conference of California Historical Societies. From 1980 to 1986 he was project director and editor of the John Muir Papers Microfilm Project. Limbaugh is the author of several articles on western history and a book, *Rocky Mountain Carpetbaggers: Idaho's Territorial Governors, 1863-1890* (Moscow, ID: University Press of Idaho, 1982).

Inauguration of Elisha P. Ferry, first governor of the state of Washington,
November 18, 1889.
*Manuscripts, Archives, and Special Collections, Washington State University Library,
Pullman, Washington*

Territorial Elites and Political Power Struggles in the Far West, 1865-1890

Who rules America? For nearly two hundred years scholars of the western world have pondered this deceptively simple question. Discerning observers from Alexis de Tocqueville to Talcott Parsons have probed and poked the American body politic from every angle in an effort to identify the locus of power, yet there is still wide disagreement over how key decisions are made and by whom. By focusing on these issues from the perspective of late nineteenth-century territorial politics, it should be possible to generate new discussion and stimulate renewed scholarship in this challenging field.

In 1909 Carl Becker brought new insight to British colonial history by distinguishing between two levels of political conflict prior to the American Revolution. He arrived at this analysis by investigating two questions:

> The first was whether essential colonial rights should be maintained; the second was by whom and by what methods they should be maintained. The first was the question of home rule; the second was the question, if we may so put it, of who should rule at home.[1]

Students of late nineteenth-century territorial history can also profit from Becker's perceptive conundrum, for the American territorial system had its origins in British colonial practice and ever since has been subjected to comparisons, both friendly and invidious.

If viewed from a territorial perspective, Becker's epigram has the same two parts: one is a question of the relations between the territories and the federal government; the other is a question of internal struggles between competing factions and interest groups. Critics of the American territorial system after the Civil War directed all their attention to the first and virtually ignored the second part of the problem in their quest for home rule or political equality within the Union. Territorial editors filled their columns with vociferous attacks on nonresident federal appointees. Comparing themselves to medieval "wards or serfs," residents in frontier territories inundated Congress with petitions and resolutions demanding voting representation in Congress, participation in presidential elections and, above all, political autonomy in their territorial affairs.[2]

Echoing and interpolating these manifestations of frontier discontent, some historians have concluded that territorial home rule movements were essentially democratic and provided empirical evidence in support of Frederick Jackson Turner's oft-quoted hypothesis that "frontier individualism has from the beginning promoted democracy."[3] The contention here is that democracy, either in the classical sense of government by consent of the governed or in the modern sense of "power to the people," was not the real issue underlying territorial home rule movements. To understand the fundamental nature of territorial political conflict in the post-Civil War period we must cast aside the newspaper rhetoric and the Turnerian hyperbole in order to concentrate on the power struggles among competing interest groups. The central question is: Who held political power in the territorial system? Was it the federal government and its agents in the nation's capital, the holders of popularly elected office in the territories, the "people," or private interests accountable to no one? A corollary to these concerns is the question of who wanted political power and for what purpose. Did power struggles revolve primarily around economic issues or were they symptomatic of a broader conflict among competing cultures on the frontier? Finally, to what extent did those who held power satisfy or at least represent the needs of their various constituents? Unless we deal with these underlying issues, we are in danger of misinterpreting the real significance of political conflict in the territories.

Harold Lasswell pinpointed a key concept of democracy when he defined political power as "participation in the making of decisions."[4] Classical liberal theory presupposes a political system in which the will of the majority is effectively represented in the decision making process. Patriot opinion in 1776 mobilized over this very issue and overthrew the parliamentary doctrine of virtual representation, yet ironically the United States Constitution and the Northwest Ordinance of 1787 restored virtual representation by lodging ultimate power over the territories in Congress, where territorial residents had no voting representation. Thus at the federal level the home rule movement can be seen as an attempt to bring liberal theory and territorial practice into line. For a century following the Northwest Ordinance, liberalism marched triumphantly forward as Congress, either through neglect or by design, reduced federal supervision, expanded elective local government, and turned over federal patronage to local control. By 1885 territorial home rule, at least in the Pacific Northwest, was virtually completed.[5]

So much for the home rule side of Becker's coin. But the reverse is not so easily dispensed with, for home rule movements did not change the locus of power in the territories. Actual rule at home remained where it always had been, in the hands of elite power groups at the apex of the political, social, and economic structure.

It should be recognized at the outset that the concept of territorial elitism presumes a more sophisticated social order than could develop under the primitive conditions of a raw frontier. The initial frontier stage—the "meeting point between savagery and civilization," as Turner defined it — had passed when local communities began to agitate for home rule. The time it took for frontier territories to emerge out of a wilderness condition might vary from a few months to a few years, but by the 1870s and 1880s most western regions, even though still sparsely settled, had outgrown frontier adolescence and had acquired a matrix of social and political structures dominated and controlled by prominent business and professional leaders in the community.

To identify an elitist power structure in American society is nothing new, for generations of historians, political scientists, and sociologists have produced similar findings through studies that vary in both scope and historical dimension. It is now a commonplace observance that while the founding fathers accepted the concept of the people as the ultimate source of power, social practice placed power in the hands of controlling elites at every level of society and government.[6] To chronicle the rise of national political machines and interest groups is beyond the scope of this paper, but it is important to recognize that the pragmatic politics of the territorial system reflected the realities of the boss era rather than the ideals of democratic theory. Contrary to Turner's rhapsodic version of frontier democracy, the Mountain and Pacific states and territories exhibited the same pattern of elitist politics that could be found in the more developed metropolitan communities of the East.

By the late nineteenth century, political elitism characterized much of American life, especially in the larger cities in which political rings and cliques earned the opprobrium of a new generation of reformers like Samuel Tilden, E. L. Godkin, and Thomas Nast. While not exactly a mirror image, territories by and large followed national patterns of political behavior, differing more in degree than in kind. Regardless of the age or level of sophistication attained by the political infrastructure, elite power groups dominated most territories after the Civil War and held power no matter what their official status. They ruled the territories regardless of whether they were presidential appointees, elected local officials, or cloakroom lobbyists holding no political office whatsoever.

Recognizing the pervasive nature of elite rule in the West brings us back to the second half of the Beckeresque question: Were local power struggles in the territories actually efforts to expand democracy by overthrowing elites? The answer is an emphatic no, but to argue that democratic idealism was not the primary instigator is not to claim that territorial politics were inherently undemocratic. Before relegating the concept of territorial democracy to the scrapheap of worn-out platitudes, we must determine if elitism and democracy are somehow compatible.

Attempts to reconcile elitism and democratic theory have preoccupied a large number of social scientists in the twentieth century, especially those not comfortable with the apparent contradictions between the leaders and the followers in modern technocratic society. International conflict, the rise of totalitarianism, and the decline of western democracies in the first half of this century accelerated the study of political systems in a behavioral rather than a theoretical framework. Gaetano Mosca in *The Ruling Class* (1896) first formulated a pragmatic alternative to classical democratic theory by arguing that elite leadership is inevitable in any polity, but that modern electoral processes can ensure an open leadership system by allowing a continual renewal of leaders without revolution.[7] By World War II a new definition of democracy had emerged in the work of Joseph Schumpeter, who summed up his theory of elite rule in one sentence: "Democracy means only that the people have the opportunity of accepting or refusing the men who are to rule them."[8] Like a free economy, Schumpeter's political system functioned best when elites were forced to compete and not conspire, where civil rights were guaranteed and legality ensured through a sound court system, and where the body politic had free choices and alternatives for leaders. Hence in modern behavioral theory, democratic elitism is a functional system by which competing elites bring alternatives to the voter, who can then make effective choices. This is not to say that people share in decision making. Many political scientists agree that most "key political, economic and social decisions" of modern society are made by elites.[9]

For many political analysts, what counts in modern society is not shared decision making but accountability. Given the inevitability of elitism, defenders of a pragmatic view of modern democracy argue that democracy is assured so long as the leadership is accountable to its constituency.[10] But not all share this faith in the potential virtues of "democratic" elitism, especially those who believe societies are not truly democratic unless there is widespread sharing of power as well as the enhancement of individual dignity, education, and respect. These critics argue that elitism in any form is undemocratic because elites have an inbred distrust of mass opinion. An elitist oligarchy is in this view a one-dimensional political system that places power in the hands of a select few who believe they are most capable of defining and implementing the public good.[11]

The debate still continues over the implications of elite rule for American society, and indeed has accelerated since the 1950s with the publication of two countervailing hypotheses. One poses a growing authoritarianism by the "power elite,"[12] and the other sees a decline of centralized decision making because of the expanding pluralism of modern postwar society.[13] Regardless of the outcome of this confrontation, the analytical framework presented by social scientists can provide useful tools for dealing with the interpretive problems inherent in studying nineteenth-century territorial politics.

Thus we have at least two democratic models. The first is the classical model of a polity in which decision making is shared by all members of society, the public good is a product of the collective wisdom of the masses, and the representatives of the people act in the interests of their constituents and are accountable for their actions through frequent elections by which the citizenry exercise majority will. The second model is more pragmatic. It is based on the inevitability of emerging elites who make all key decisions of society and define the public good as the collective wisdom of the elites. This model is essentially democratic so long as access to leadership remains open to all members of society, no single elite dominates, and leaders are held accountable through frequent elections.

Having laid a theoretical foundation, can it be tested with evidence from the nineteenth-century territorial West? To answer conclusively presumes a more thorough study of territorial politics than this writer has yet undertaken. But based on primary research on Idaho, and secondary study of other western states and territories, there are sufficient grounds to reject both democratic models presented above. In short, even given the pragmatic model of process democracy offered by Schumpeter and the modern behavioralists, political elitism in the Far West was undemocratic. Territorial elites by and large were unaccountable, self-perpetuating coalitions composed of business and professional leaders primarily motivated by the desire to advance their own group interests.

Having set forth an elitist hypothesis, it is still necessary to distinguish between various modes of elite rule. William Kelso identifies three kinds of oligarchies: one characterized simply by an uneven but natural distribution of power between leaders and followers; the second in which power is uncontrolled or unchecked but not necessarily misused; and the third in which power is not only unevenly distributed but is also uncontrolled and abused.[14] The ideals of classical democracy are absent in all three of these modes, yet the public interest presumably is served in the first two. If tested by these standards, territorial elites can generally be categorized as uncontrolled and unaccountable but not abusive. In short, it would be difficult to concoct a conspiracy theory. Western elites did not arise out of a Machiavellian desire by conspiring power brokers to "fool the masses" and pick their pockets. On the contrary, elite leadership, even though largely insulated from public opinion, nevertheless arose naturally and accommodated significantly to the needs and desires of its constituents. As a result, elites in the Far West did not stir up massive outpourings of public criticism, at least until the Populist-Progressive uprising after 1890.

Numerous studies illustrate the pervasive nature of western elitism. In his perceptive overview of the Far Southwest, Howard R. Lamar found a characteristic pattern of elite rule in Arizona's Federal Ring, in Colorado's political machine, New Mexico's Santa Fe Ring, and even in Utah's Mormon hierarchy.[15] In Nevada, Territorial Governor James W. Nye built a strong Republican machine during the Civil War that helped perpetuate his power as United States senator after statehood.[16] Lord Bryce, with undisguised disdain, cited late nineteenth-century Nevada as a notorious example of western decadence, a rotten borough under control of the Silver Ring.[17] Wyoming's Francis Warren took charge of a Republican faction in the 1800s that went on to dominate post-statehood politics for nearly two decades.[18] In Washington, Elisha P. Ferry, a former territorial governor and a railroad attorney, organized a Republican coalition in the late 1800s and returned to political power as Washington's first state governor in 1889. He was called a "kind of political ringmaster" by one disgruntled Olympia preacher. Montana had a counterpart in Benjamin Potts, who served three terms as territorial governor by artfully developing a broad-based political coalition composed of both Republicans and Democrats but dominated by mining and cattle interests.[19] These late nineteenth-century patterns had a precedent in territorial Missouri, where "local government remained the prerogative of a select territorial elite" composed of large landholders and business interests that continued to dominate the legislature after statehood. [20]

Less well known, but still instructive, are the political elites that vied for power in Idaho Territory. Idaho's early political record is more chaotic than most territories, partly as a result of its adverse geographic circumstances and partly because of the extraordinary ineptitude of many of its political leaders. In addition, a clash of cultures between Mormons and Gentiles in the southeastern section, exacerbated in the 1880s by railroad construction which accelerated non-Mormon immigration patterns, contributed to the political fragmentation. This situation was not reversed until a non-partisan, anti-Mormon coalition stabilized territorial politics long enough to secure statehood.

The volatile nature of Idaho territorial politics does not invalidate the elitist hypothesis, even though one would expect heated elections and stormy legislative sessions to signify grass roots democracy at its best. Actually at the heart of most conflicts were factional fights among competing elites who sought political dominance to advance their own interests. Sectionalism also contributed to political instability in Idaho, as was apparent in the abortive divisionist efforts of north Idaho and in the confrontations between southeast Idaho's radical anti-Mormons and the moderate southwest Republican coalition, otherwise known as the Kelly-Pride Ring or Boise Ring.[21]

What is particularly striking about Idaho's sectional and factional fights is the elitist nature of their loose and shifting political combinations. Regardless of issue or outcome, political leadership passed back and forth among a relatively small circle of merchants, businessmen, mine owners, professional politicians, and attorneys, with an occasional addition from the ranching or farming interests. Power struggles within this circle were intense and disruptive, but even the most spirited conflict usually did not permanently or significantly dislocate enduring centers of local influence.

Power remained in the hands of elites, no matter whether they belonged to elected officials or behind-the-scenes kingmakers not directly accountable to the people. Such figures as Milton Kelly and Alonzo Leland, both journalists as well as politicians, and David Porter, Baker Pride, Fred Dubois, and E. J. Curtis, three federal appointees with good local and national connections, all rose to the highest orbit of territorial power without having to suffer the humbling indignity of voter approval.[22]

Thus in Idaho, and in other territories in the post-Civil War era, elite rule does not fit the pragmatic model of democratic elitism described earlier, and certainly was antithetical to the majoritarian principles of classical liberalism. Finding a lack of democracy in the territories will not surprise those who have studied the period and the home rule movements that accompanied the unrestrained criticism of the territorial system. But it is worthy of note that the most vocal critics of the territorial system were not arguing for democracy either in the pragmatic or the idealistic sense. They were, instead, trying to control important elements of political power that the federal territorial system placed outside local control. They were, in effect, members of competing elites trying to oust their rivals.

The real nature of these power struggles evidently escaped the perception of most contemporary observers whose vision was blurred by the rhetorical flourishes that accompanied home rule movements. Even the champion of popular sovereignty, Stephen A. Douglas, did not understand or at least ignored the true character of local factional fights in the territorial period. Robert W. Johannsen's probing biography shows how important Douglas was in influencing the seeds of home rule movements in the territories.[23] The argument that territorial residents should have political equality with the people of the states, of course, was an essential element of classical democracy, and Douglas proposed to speed up home rule by allowing territorial residents to decide what kind of domestic institutions they wanted even prior to statehood.

Evoking popular sovereignty, however, did not clarify the issue of who ruled at home. Actually, as George M. Dennison has observed,[24] popular sovereignty was already dead by 1850. By that time the federal courts had confirmed the ultimate sovereignty of the federal government under the Constitution, and local laws, regardless of territorial or state origin, were subordinate to federal law. Federal supremacy had to be imposed by force, but by the early 1860s popular sovereignty was little more than a worn-out cliché, the last refuge of a bankrupt theory of states rights. Unfortunately western territories never grasped the lessons of the Civil War era, for popular sovereignty as a states rights principle continued to be voiced by westerners who never accepted the doctrine of federal supremacy even though they had to live with the fact as embodied in the territorial system. Johannsen acknowledges this paradox by demonstrating that in the 1860 Oregon election campaign, resident Democrats interpreted popular sovereignty as local autonomy, which went farther than Douglas intended. Even Republicans in the Pacific Northwest distorted the issues of 1860 by claiming that Lincoln represented true popular sovereignty.[25] Westerners after the war still evoked the concept in the home rule debates, but no longer was egalitarian liberalism or grass roots democracy implied in its use.

Popular sovereignty, western-style, bore fruit in the home rule movements that ultimately brought all but three territories into the Union by 1900. To reiterate, democracy was not the real issue nor the consequence. Like southern states rights movements in the antebellum period, territorial statehood movements were led by political elites who often championed popular causes for self-serving ends. Under these circumstances, if the public interest was served it was more by coincidence than by design. As an antidote to unaccountable oligarchy, territorial policy sometimes wisely delayed statehood until true signs of government by consent appeared.[26] Utah is the best example of oligarchy forcefully opened up by imposing public education, open jury selection, and mass participation in the electoral process. But Utah's "peculiar institution" generated a public outcry that compelled Congress to take Draconian measures. Elsewhere politics rather than principle usually dictated territorial policy. As William Neil has noted, even the Northwest Ordinance, heralded as the great fundamental charter of territorial government and the harbinger of political equality, arose out of Congressional fears that outlying territories might seek independence if equality were denied or long delayed.[27]

Describing the extent and nature of undemocratic western elites still does not explain why they arose and why they lasted so long. Kenneth Owens has suggested that one reason was the lack of a two-party system in most western territories.[28] Only Colorado and Nebraska had well-developed two-party systems prior to statehood. The rest had systems that were either one-party, no-party, or a mixture of both. As a result, voters lacked clear choices among issues and personalities, and pragmatic coalitions avoided both issues and principles to soften criticism and perpetuate power. In Owens's view, the elitist nature of western politics developed because of the unique position of the interior territories of the Far West. They lacked economic diversification, were highly disrupted by sectional and ethnic clashes, and grew slowly because they lacked both a variety of resources and an adequate transportation network. Elites thus promised security, stability, and systematic development — fundamental economic goals desired by all members of the body politic regardless of party or class lines.

Owens's analysis is reinforced by the work of Howard R. Lamar, who found the "politics of development" a primary focus of territorial special interests.[29] Whether new territories were organized by commercial and business interests, as in Washington and Arizona, or whether the mercantile element emerged out of a sectional struggle that created a division movement, as in Idaho and Montana, new territories swiftly came into the hands of leading merchants and businessmen even if they differed in party membership. Actually, national party alliances, except for the Civil War era, made little difference in the politics of development. In most cases local political machines were bipartisan or nonpartisan in composition even while they might be partisan in outward appearance. The Santa Fe Ring is perhaps the best example of a successful and complex nonpartisan machine that controlled New Mexico from 1872 until 1900. On a lesser scale the Federal Ring in Arizona, the Carey-Warren machine in Wyoming, and the Boise Ring in Idaho all practiced the politics of development by organizing nonpartisan coalitions to control the exploitation of local economic resources such as land, mines, timber, and transportation systems and routes.

The lack of strong national party identities can also be seen as a result of territorial subordination. Local residents had no voice in national affairs, hence national issues were secondary to local affairs as a stimulus to public discussion and controversy. Furthermore, because they were geographically far distant from the nation's capital, western states and territories had less interest in national politics than did other regions farther east. Subordination and isolation also help explain the accommodationist attitudes that usually prevailed among local elites, political parties, and home residents. Unlike the intense and long-lasting eastern ethno-religious conflicts that produced deep-seated ideological cleavages in this Age of Political Confessionalism, as Paul Kleppner calls the period,[30] ideological battles in the Far West during the same period were less frequent and less divisive. In short, since everyone, at least in the territories, essentially wanted the same things, political battles usually hinged more on sectional and factional disputes and on personality conflicts than on substantive issues.

While economic and political success in a land of scarce resources called for nonpartisan coalitions to reduce political conflict and to prevent power fragmentation, power struggles among competing economic interest groups often disrupted the smooth operation of the politics of development. Outside Utah, whose Mormon hierarchy and social homogeneity helped reduce political friction at least before the 1880s, western territories were swept periodically by factional fights that dislocated local power structures.

Before 1885 a frequent source of factionalism was federal patronage practice, or the spoils system, which tossed territorial offices up for grabs to anyone with good connections in Washington. Often the focus of conflict centered on the office of governor, which was the most sought after, although probably not the most financially rewarding, position in territorial government.[31] Eastern appointees unfamiliar with local power elites or unwilling to accommodate local coalitions regularly found themselves embroiled in conflicts that invariably cost them either power, status, health, their job, or all four. Many of these struggles took place between the governor and the territorial legislature, especially if the two had divided partisan allegiances. Executive appointments to territorial office triggered many local wars; others emerged out of squabbling over printing contracts; still others over personality clashes.[32]

Obfuscating much of the internal conflict was the carpetbag smokescreen, which, like home rule platitudes, fogged the perception of residents, politicians, and even historians, at least until the mid-twentieth century.[33] No longer is it necessary to caution against taking anti-carpetbag rhetoric too literally, although some carpetbaggers were every bit as unworthy as their detractors claimed, and Idaho seemed to have more than its share of the likes of Caleb Lyon and Horace Gilson.[34] But aside from personalities, carpetbagging as a concept distorted the territorial picture. Often reported as primarily the reaction of "residents" to a system that imposed rule by "outsiders," the anti-carpetbag rhetoric, as William E. Foley and others have observed, contradicted the fact that most territorial residents were newcomers themselves. Place of origin was not nearly as important as residential intent once the carpetbaggers arrived. Those who took up permanent residence and were not frequently absent from office had little trouble finding a niche in the local political and social structure.[35]

The power struggles stirred up by carpetbag appointments died down quickly if new appointees adapted to local conditions and to the political status quo. Governor James W. Nye of Nevada is a good example of a pragmatic carpetbagger; Benjamin Potts of Montana is another. On the other hand, the most notorious battles involved inflexible carpetbag governors who disrupted the status quo and failed to accommodate local power structures. John C. Fremont's embattled years in Arizona and Mason Brayman's bitter experience in Idaho are both good examples. The pragmatists joined existing local elites and made the most of their opportunity; the moralists like Brayman or the exploiters like Fremont fought the local establishment and were destroyed by it.

State constitutional conventions can serve as one index to the importance of local power struggles in the home rule movement. New state constitutions often reflected the political conflicts of the territorial period by imposing new limits on executive or legislative power. In Idaho, for example, the members of a bipartisan constitutional convention restricted the spending power of the legislature, which had been in impecunious Democratic hands for most of the territorial period. The delegates also reduced the power of the governor over executive appointments, reflecting a lack of trust that had territorial antecedents.[36] Both the constitutions of Idaho and Washington set up executive boards and commissions under legislative rather than executive control, in effect transferring an important segment of executive power to the will of the legislature.[37]

Thus far we have analyzed western territorial politics largely from an economic perspective, since political interest groups in the territories can often be defined in economic terms. But the questions raised by the analysis of the power struggles either at the regional or the local level cannot be answered entirely by economic factors, as Frederick Jackson Turner implied. Many critics of Turner have demonstrated how he seemed to short-change the cultural dimension in his sectional studies that emphasized the physical and economic rather than the cultural antecedents of western development.[38]

The concept of political culture, which is an offshoot of the study of political behavior, has added vast new dimensions to American historiography. We owe a large debt to David Potter, whose *People of Plenty* was a landmark in the application of behavioral analysis to history. More recently the work of Daniel Elazar, Robert Kelley, Richard Jensen, and other behavioralists has opened new insights into political history.[39] In the Pacific Northwest, the behavioral studies of Idaho by Boyd Martin and Robert H. Blank have helped enlarge perspectives on regional history.[40] In studying the roots of political conflict in the territories we must therefore take cognizance of the cultural forces that have influenced political behavior. To what extent were political interest groups a product of ethnic and religious prejudice? How important were the cultural changes wrought by Far West migration patterns? What cultural values were most prevalent in the territorial period, and did value conflicts play a role in the political struggles of the era?

Behavioral studies have produced several different analytical models in recent years. Some behavioralists have analyzed American political history in terms of the conflict between traditional and modern cultures.[41] In this context, frontier territories, still in their earliest stages of settlement and development, are modern rather than traditional, for traditionalism never had a chance to take root in the formative frontier period, which was too unstable to provide a good breeding ground. During the California Gold Rush, for example, the cultural crosscurrents generated by the convergence of a transient population from all corners of the globe broke down traditions, placed values in flux, contributed to violence, and undermined family and social structures. But traditionalism soon surfaced once the formative period gave way to a more stable, pastoral, and emergent industrial era. Utah is perhaps an exception to this frontier pattern, for as a "convenanted community" it escaped some of the more volatile forces of modernism — at least under the authoritarian Mormon hierarchy. Brigham Young, for example, tried to keep Mormons insulated by importing Scandinavian farmers unfamiliar with American ways to colonize the fringes of Zion. But prescribed Mormon cultural isolation broke down quickly under the combined pressures of non-Mormon immigration and anti-Mormon reform efforts. By the 1890s the Saints had returned to the American cultural mainstream.[42]

Daniel Elazar has identified three dominant subcultures—moralistic, individualistic, and traditionalistic—that originated in the European and colonial cultural mainstreams and that spread westward along the major migratory routes. All three have influenced political behavior in the Far West, and, according to Elazar, still make up the predominant patterns of western political culture.[43] Thus in his analysis, Oregon, Utah, and Colorado have a predominantly moralistic subculture that evolved out of New England Puritan origins and that placed the social goals of the commonwealth over the private economic interests of the marketplace. Washington, Idaho, Montana, and California are strongly moralistic, but with an individualistic undercurrent that emphasizes commercial values, opposes government intervention, accepts the realities of a pluralistic society, and views politics as essentially a business. In Wyoming the individualistic pattern is predominant but with a strong moralistic undercurrent. Individualistic subculture is strongest in Nevada, where one-armed bandits still reflect the get-rich-quick psychology of the gold rush. Arizona and New Mexico have a moralistic undercurrent, but their predominant subculture is traditionalistic, a product of combined Hispanic and antebellum southern influences and geared to a hierarchical order of society with static ruling-class elites largely dependent on family or social status.[44]

In order to gauge more accurately the impact of cultural differences on political behavior in the Far West, we need many more regional empirical studies than are currently available. Few such studies have been undertaken for the territorial period, probably because of the scarcity and unreliability of the available data. Since territorial residents could not participate in national elections, only regional and local returns are available, and they must be used with caution.

For example, one analysis of reported Idaho territorial delegate election returns for 1870 shows a voter turnout of approximately 74 percent of all white male adults. Ten years later the rate was down to 55 percent and by the first state election in 1890, turnout had fallen to only 45.8 percent. Yet in 1892, according to Census Bureau tables, Idaho turned out 63.1 percent of its eligible voters at the state's first presidential election. The wide variance in these figures makes them highly suspect, especially considering the lack of registration procedures and the slipshod, often fraudulent, manner of counting ballots in that era. Even Paul Kleppner's monumental quantitative study of the Third Electoral System does not include the territories because of the presumed difficulty of "recovering large quantities of prestatehood data." He does acknowledge, however, that voter participation in the late nineteenth-century West was lower than in any other region—all the more reason to be wary of territorial voting statistics. Incidentally, perhaps as a commentary on the statistical reliability of western election returns, the Census Bureau's Bicentennial Abstract in 1976 reported that Nevada's first state election in 1864 yielded a voter turnout of 157.5 percent![45]

Despite the data-related problems of oversimplification and the super-ficiality of broad generalizations without extensive empirical testing, the Elazar studies provide valuable insights into western political culture. Our understanding of territorial politics, for example, can profit by consider-ing the impact of individualism. Individualistic subculture, brought westward by gold miners, small farmers, ranchers, businessmen, and politi-cians from middle-Atlantic, metropolitan, and border states' backgrounds formed a conducive climate for the politics of development. This system recognized politics as a process by which professional politicians served promotional ends and were rewarded for their efforts. But in the late nine-teenth century, the proponents of individualism clashed with Yankee moralists who attacked the self-serving business and commercial cliques and who fought to elevate the moral and social standards of the commu-nity. In Idaho in the early 1870s, for example, a fight arose between the Oregon Ring of Republican officeholders and the Democratic legislative majority. It was centered on the cultural clash between gold rush pioneer individualists, who viewed politics as a means of distributing favors to friends, and carpetbag radicals, who tried to impose Yankee Puritan values on what they deemed a degenerate frontier society. Eventually the issue of legitimacy of carpetbaggers in politics overshadowed the culture clash, and the locals won by organizing a regional bipartisan coalition against the radical outsiders. A similar clash of values animated the Brayman war in Idaho in the late 1870s. Governor Mason Brayman's Baptist pietism and post-abolitionist reform impulses contrasted sharply with accommoda-tionist attitudes of local business and professional leaders who formed a bipartisan coalition that prevented Brayman from securing a second term.[46]

Frontier social conditions also exacerbated culture clashes. In the gold rush era, the individualist culture stream crossed currents with various "ex-cluded" people from the Orient and from Hispanic America, which had some obviously adverse results. This phenomenon was reflected in the political arena by the passage of discriminatory legislation and in the social arena by various acts of violence.[47] Moralistic and traditionalistic cultures also came into juxtaposition in the Civil War era when large numbers of border residents escaped the war by moving farther west. For over a decade the aftermath of this migration reverberated in the legislative halls and in the newspaper columns, where "Copperheads" fought newspaper bat-tles with "Black Republicans."[48] Still another clash came in the 1880s with the anti-Mormon movement that ultimately came under the control of pragmatic individualists who used anti-Mormon rhetoric to win political power.

In a larger context, the vigilante movements that racked the territorial West also had cultural dimensions. Recent studies by Richard Maxwell Brown and others have singled out cultural and economic antagonisms that pitted merchant-business elites against outgroups.[49] In the Far West, therefore, political instability might be seen, in part, as a product of competing subcultures.

Political conflict arising out of the federal-territorial relationship also influenced regional attitudes. Robert F. Berkhofer has shown that the home rule movement arose partly from cultural conflict between East and West.[50] Condescending eastern attitudes toward western "backwoodsmen" became institutionalized in the territorial system. The presumption was that territorial residents had to be civilized through a colonial process before they could reach full equality with more sophisticated eastern cultures. Demands for immediate political equality therefore grew naturally out of western resentment against eastern snobbery.

As Robert Blank has pointed out, political culture can also be used to help explain popular territorial opposition to federal presence in the West, even though federal aid to underdeveloped western regions was essential. Western culture emphasized the values of individualism, private property, and the free marketplace. Thus, Blank claims, residents rejected federal regulation and control even while they demanded federal aid for mutual cooperation and development.[51]

If studies of political culture help explain popular attitudes and values in the territories, can they also shed light on the prevalence of western political elites? Recently Robert Kelley offered a tantalizing, if preliminary, response: "There is . . . a coherent relationship between elite ideologies and mass cultural attitudes. The ideas of the leadership and the cultural as well as economic interests of their followers do in fact align with each other, though not always easily."[52] Even if Kelley is correct, his theory has limited application. We must also recognize that elite power in the Far West depended more on pragmatics than ideology. Although elites had cultural as well as economic roots, successful elites transcended the taboos and parameters of culture by adapting to regional and local conditions regardless of cultural antecedents or values. Thus political success in the Far West ultimately depended not on goals but methods, not on ends but means, and not on values but process. Questions of cultural values, democracy, and the ends of society were not only abstract but irrelevant, for the real test was more pragmatically based on what worked, not how or to what end. From a pragmatic view of western politics, power elites arose in response to immediate demands for local services and rewards not available through regular channels of government. Elitist power structures were successful so long as they served the immediate interests of a majority of their constituents.

Nearly twenty years ago Ari Hoogenboom challenged historians to avoid moral stereotypes in assessing Gilded Age politics.[53] This caveat still applies as we evaluate the impact of political elites in the Far West. A number of recent studies have shown that political machines served useful ends, especially if they were flexible, pragmatic, and sufficiently stable to ward off chaotic factional fights for local control. This was especially true in the rapid social change in rising metropolitan areas such as New York and San Francisco, where recent immigrants ameliorated the hardships of adjustment by turning to boss rule.[54] To a lesser but still significant extent, regional and local elites outside metropolitan areas played the same role. Thus the Santa Fe Ring, the Warren machine, the Mormon hierarchy, the Boise Ring, and a number of other elitist coalitions served productive ends in a developing western society.

To conclude, however, that western elites produced beneficial social results still does not meet the democratic standards by which we are accustomed to judge the American political tradition. Regardless of their geopolitical base, in either the industrial East or the frontier West, political elites operated outside the framework of classical democratic idealism. And they did not meet the behavioral test of accountability, for even the most successful nineteenth-century rings and bosses remained largely independent of mass opinion. By demanding a larger voice in the political process, and by attacking large concentrations of political and economic power, the Populists led the first major challenge to elite rule since the Jacksonian era. The Populist response still echoes in modern American politics, particularly at election time. Yet the primary goal of most twentieth-century politicians has not been to reaffirm the values and standards of classical democracy. It has been to make elite rule more competitive, more open, more accountable, and more palatable by organizing counter elites and interest groups, and by politicizing larger segments of the population than had an effective and an independent voice in the nineteenth-century political system.[55]

Montana's Political Culture:
A Century of Evolution

E D I T O R S ' N O T E

The most striking characteristic of Montana politics has been the liberalism of the state's elected officials in Washington, D.C., and the conservatism of the people back home. In comparison with the conservative proclivities of neighboring Idaho and Wyoming, Montana's strong strain of liberalism stands out in bold relief. For much of the twentieth century "the Company," otherwise known as the "Montana Twins" (the Anaconda Copper Mining Company and the Montana Power Company), held sway in the Treasure State's economic life as well as in its politics. Now a more complex corporate and financial power structure has arisen to wield its influence in Montana affairs. Actually the state has a delicately balanced spectrum of interest groups that usually shifts to reflect changing national conditions. Elections are often close and vigorously contested. As a result, according to a recent assessment, "Montana's political battles sometimes discourage us, but they seldom bore us."*

This system might possibly be attributed to a unique political culture. The authors of this essay, avoiding broad-brush conclusions such as those advanced by political scientist Daniel Elazar, seek to explain Montana politics by studying historical forces in the Treasure State during the past one hundred years. Oversimplification of the struggle between the Company and the reform element must be eschewed as well. The resulting inquiry for the true situation, which the authors state "is more subtle, more complex, more deserving of close analysis," provides a valuable overview of political evolution in one state of the Northwest. In the broader context of regional history, this perceptive discussion of Montana politics should give direction to similar investigations in neighboring states.

A native northwesterner, Michael P. Malone was born and began his schooling in Pomeroy, Washington. He received a B.A. degree in history (1962) at Gonzaga University and a Ph.D. in American studies (1966) at Washington State University. After teaching a year at Texas A&M University, he joined the history faculty at Montana State University where he is now dean of the College of Graduate Studies. Malone is the author of *C. Ben Ross and the New Deal in Idaho* (1970) and *The Battle for Butte: Mining and Politics on the Northern Frontier, 1864-1906* (1981), coeditor of *The Montana Past: An Anthology* (1969), coauthor of *Montana: A History of Two Centuries* (1976), and editor of *Historians and the American West* (1983). In addition, he has written several articles on Montana history for scholarly journals and serves as the book review editor for *Montana: The Magazine of Western History*. Dianne G. Dougherty, previously a graduate student in history at Montana State University, recently earned a law degree at Gonzaga University.

---

*Michael P. Malone and Richard B. Roeder, *Montana: A History of Two Centuries* (Seattle: University of Washington Press, 1976), 289.

Ore cars ready to be unloaded at the ore bin just above the Iron Mountain Mill in the 1890s.
Photograph courtesy of Bill Pike, Superior, Montana

Montana's Political Culture: A Century of Evolution

MICHAEL P. MALONE AND
DIANNE G. DOUGHERTY

Students of regional history seldom write explicitly about the concept of *political culture*. Yet they often seem to work on the tacit assumption that such a thing does exist. For what is political culture? It is, simply, the configuration of ideas, attitudes, biases, and emotional attachments that characterize a political community, whether that community is a city, a state, or a nation. If this general definition is accepted, then it follows that each of the fifty states should exhibit a political culture that is somewhat uniquely its own. In each case, that culture is a product of several long-term factors: geography, history, economics, demography, and social developments. In the following essay, we propose to examine the evolution of a changing political culture in Montana over the course of one hundred years, from the late territorial period to the present.

Remote, sprawling, and thinly populated, Montana is in no real sense a "natural" community. Neither its boundaries nor its history and politics follows the patterns of any particular logic. Rather, like most, if not all its sister states, Montana is the product of a long succession of historic occurrences, many of which have been random and undirected. The Treasure State spreads endlessly across three variously defined regions: the eastern reaches of the Pacific Northwest, the cross-cutting mountain ranges of the "Northern Intermountain" area, and the northwestern expanses of the Great Plains. Western Montana looks westward toward the Columbia Basin, toward the cities of Spokane, Portland, and Seattle, and southward toward Salt Lake City, while the eastern plains face eastward toward Minneapolis-St. Paul and southward toward Denver. Despite these centrifugal forces, however, the state's disparate parts are also drawn closely together, most strongly by Montana's political boundaries and by its political culture.

How should the study of the complex, multifaceted political cultures of the individual states be approached? Probably the best known interpretation is that of political scientist Daniel Elazar in his book *American Federalism: A View from the States*. Painting with broad strokes, Elazar identifies three fundamental American cultures, each of them radiating westward from the Atlantic settlements of the colonial and early national periods. Extending westward from Puritan-Yankee New England, the culture he describes as "moralistic," later enriched by Scandinavian immigration, favors an activist government, and welcomes social and political reform. Elazar sees an "individualistic" culture stemming primarily from the Middle Atlantic region. The individualistic culture is essentially utilitarian, preferring minimal government to deliver only basic services. Finally, he finds a "traditionalistic" culture based in the deep South and favoring a planter-style elitist system. In Montana and the Northwest, Elazar judges the Yankee-Scandinavian moralistic culture to be dominant, but he also finds a heavy influx of the individualistic impulse.[1]

How valid are these sweeping generalities? Although they seem facile and simplistic, at least they raise the right questions. So do other regional studies by social scientists such as Ira Sharkansky and Raymond Gastil.[2] In the following pages, we choose to avoid such broadly gauged conclusions and to look instead more closely and carefully into the fascinating political evolution of this one state. In the past, Montana's political history, especially that of the last sixty years, has been too often oversimplified and too often viewed as a clear-cut struggle between corporate titans and heroic but beleaguered reformers. The truth is more subtle, more complex, and more deserving of close analysis.

The Nineteenth-Century Heritage

Like most other western states, Montana experienced a long and unhappy period of political gestation as a territory of the federal government, with only limited powers of self-government. Again like most of its neighbors, Montana Territory (1864-89) evolved from an early, unsettled period of what Kenneth Owens describes as "chaotic factionalism" into a more settled commonwealth in which local economic interests found their political identity. At first, the territory's population centered almost wholly upon the remote mining camps of its southwestern corner, and it seemed convulsed by the heated animosities carried over from the Civil War and Reconstruction. The Democratic party, brought in especially by Irish miners and immigrants from the border states of the Confederacy, took quick and lasting root as Montana's majority party. Locally elected Democratic legislatures fought angrily with governors, judges, and other territorial administrators appointed by Unionist-Republican governments in Washington.[3]

Gradually, as the passions of Civil War faded, the thinly settled territory began to show signs of political maturity during the long tenure of capable Governor Benjamin F. Potts (1870-83). The boom of the 1880s and the arrival of railroads brought a burgeoning silver-copper industry to western Montana and a scattering of open-range ranches to the eastern plains. A logical development then surfaced as the two dominant economic groups — freewheeling mining barons of the west and cattle barons of the east — took control of territorial government and politics. The mining men usually predominated. They normally maneuvered the large voting majorities of Butte-Anaconda, Missoula, Helena, and Great Falls, majorities that were all the more imposing since they were concentrated in the Democratic party and spoke increasingly with the Gaelic accent of Marcus Daly's Irish miners. By the late 1880s Montanans talked commonly of baronial rule by the "Big Four" — Butte mining kings Marcus Daly and William A. Clark, and Helena capitalists C. A. Broadwater and Samuel T. Hauser. These men clearly dominated politics in the Treasure State, as Montana styled itself when it became the forty-first star on the American flag in 1889.[4]

From the perspective of ninety years, the tumultuous decade of the 1890s seems a critical period in the development of Montana and the Mountain West. The Panic of 1893 and the resultant hard depression gripped the region; two powerful and unsettling forces, the Populist party and the notorious Clark-Daly feud, shook Montana's newly formed state government. The Populist party emerged in 1892 as a farmers' protest party mainly based in the South and Midwest, but in the silver producing intermountain states, such as Idaho, Nevada, and Montana, it thrived as a miners' protest party. For, in addition to radical calls for reforms to aid distressed farmers, the Populists also demanded currency inflation by means of the free and unlimited coinage of silver dollars. This, of course, promised much to the depressed mining industry of the West.

The Populist silver crusade took Montana by storm. In 1896 a fusion ticket of Populists, majority Democrats, and Silver Republicans swept the state for William Jennings Bryan and "free silver," and Butte's Marcus Daly was reportedly Bryan's greatest single campaign contributor. The Populist tide ebbed after 1896, but by then it had already worked profound changes. Populism scrambled party lines in the state and left an enduring legacy of party irregularity and anti-corporate, anti-eastern radicalism on the left. Although the Populist party died, Populist ideology and rhetoric lived on in future farmer-labor attacks upon banks, railroads, and corporate "exploitation" in general. Montana liberals such as Burton K. Wheeler and Lee Metcalf echoed the neo-Populist outcry against the economic "colonization" of their region for many years into the future.[5]

Even more unsettling than Populism was the epic feud between mining moguls Marcus Daly and W. A. Clark, which raged from the election of 1888 until Daly's death in 1900. The details of this story are familiar enough and are too complex to repeat here, but it must be noted that the feud left deep and lasting scars upon the body politic. First Clark and then Daly bought up newspapers and blatantly used them for their own partisan ends. Both men spent freely to manipulate legislators and other public "servants," and Clark seems clearly to have bribed certain members of the 1893 legislature in his quest for a Senate seat. His wholesale bribery of the 1899 assembly was attested to by the fact that, of the fifteen Republican members of that august body, eleven voted for Clark the Democrat. The feud ended in 1900-01 when Clark, after being forced to resign from the Senate due to charges of bribery, managed to win reelection, this time serving out a full six-year term (1901-07).[6] Montana's reputation suffered as these antics gained national attention.

The marathon political-economic struggle to control the great Butte mining district climaxed and subsided during the years 1899-1906. In 1899 a tough and ruthless group of Standard Oil executives led by Henry Rogers and William Rockefeller bought control of the mighty Anaconda Copper Mining Company and made it the foundation of their newly created holding company, Amalgamated Copper. Rogers and his cohorts aimed to "consolidate" ownership of the Butte Hill by buying up the major holdings there and gathering them into Amalgamated. Control of Butte, they assumed, would bring control of American copper production, which would allow them to corner world copper just as they had earlier cornered oil.

The "Standard Oil Gang" ran into unforeseen problems in their Butte escapade. In the frenzied political campaign of 1900, Butte's two major independent mine owners, Clark and the brilliant and brash young F. Augustus Heinze, pilloried the Amalgamated men as out-of-state robber barons. Following Daly's death in 1900, the mercenary Clark quickly dropped his antitrust posture and joined forces with Amalgamated. This left Heinze struggling alone against the Standard Oil-Amalgamated colossus. He fought ruthlessly and ingeniously, portraying himself as Montana's champion against the "Kerosene Crowd." His friends occupied two of the three judgeships of Butte's Second Montana Judicial District and, with this weapon, Heinze tied up the trust in endless litigation while his cronies ruled the government of Silver Bow County.

Imperiously, the lords of Amalgamated fought back with their own lawsuits, their own dirty political tricks, and a campaign to buy up newspapers across the state to bend a hostile public opinion in their favor. They finally won. With a dramatic shutdown of its mines, mills, smelters, and refineries late in 1903, Amalgamated forced the governor to convene the legislature in special session to pass a judge disqualification law that was drafted by the company and effectively neutralized Heinze's control of the courts. Heinze and his allies continued the fight for a while, but in 1906 he sold the majority of his family's Butte holdings to the copper trust for a reported price of $10,500,000 to $12,000,000.[7]

Heinze's sellout and subsequent departure paved the way for the corporate consolidation of the Butte Hill. In 1910 Amalgamated organized all of its once independent Butte companies into one, Anaconda. And in 1915, the now unnecessary Amalgamated holding company was dissolved, which meant that the enlarged Anaconda Copper Mining Company was once again an independent corporation. The world's greatest nonferrous metal mining company, the mighty Anaconda, controlled much more than Butte. In addition to properties beyond Montana, it held mines at Butte, reduction works, smelters, and refineries at Anaconda and Great Falls, vast timber acreages and mills in western Montana, and coal properties in Carbon, Cascade, and Gallatin counties. In short, it was one of America's greatest giant and well-integrated corporations, which ruled supreme in a remote and thinly populated state. In 1912 Anaconda executives took steps to extend that rule by creating the Montana Power Company through a merger of small scattered plants already in operation. Closely tied to Anaconda at the executive level, Montana Power eventually carried the Company's presence far into the hinterlands of west-central Montana.[8]

Thus the "War of the Copper Kings" left behind a heavy political residue. Dominated by Marcus Daly's lieutenants, John D. Ryan (until 1933) and Cornelius F. Kelly (until 1955), the Company held sternly to the tough and ruthless practices it had acquired in the battles of its youth. By 1910 roughly 65,000 of Montana's 376,000 people lived in the firm's two "company towns" of Butte and Anaconda. Thousands more depended upon it, either directly or indirectly, for a livelihood. Its lobbyists, pet legislators, and allies seemed ubiquitous in the halls of state government at Helena. Perhaps most ominously, its growing network of newspapers soon included all of the major urban dailies of Montana except the *Great Falls Tribune*, for the Company used these papers unflinchingly to pursue its interests. In sum, as University of Montana professor Arthur Fisher wrote in 1922:

> On the one hand, firmly entrenched, stand the ramifying and inter-linked corporate interests centering in the copper industry, now under the leadership of the Anaconda Copper Mining Company. On the other stands the rest of the population which feels it has no stake in the Company's prosperity but suffers from the Company's exploitation of every natural resource and profitable privilege, its avoidance of taxation, and its dominance of the political and educational life of the State.[9]

New Arrivals and New Politics

Even as the Company consolidated its economic and political power during the years after Heinze's defeat, the political profile of Montana was being drastically altered by new demographic and ideological forces. In a peculiar coincidence of historical events, the homesteading frontier and the Progressive Movement occurred simultaneously here, and each had a sizable impact upon the political development of the state.

The northwestern Great Plains, covering eastern Montana and the western Dakotas, witnessed the last great land-taking in the United States. During the period 1909-18, thousands of families followed the siren call of railroad advertising into the vast expanses of east-central Montana, especially into the Highline plains lying north of the Milk and Missouri rivers. The homesteaders, or "honyockers" as they were sometimes disparagingly called, came mainly from the upper and central Midwest. Many were first and second generation Scandinavian and German immigrants. Their scattered farms and ambitious little towns quickly challenged the monopolistic hold that the stockmen had on eastern Montana and planted there the moralistic political culture that Elazar sees extending in a Yankee-Scandinavian amalgam from Wisconsin and Minnesota to the Dakotas and Montana. Largely Lutheran in faith and activist-moralistic in politics, the agrarians immediately began agitating against the mining-based power structure. They demanded that the mining interests pay a heavier share of the tax burden, for instance, and voted in a state dry law in 1916. Many of them, especially the Norwegians and Germans, embraced an advanced liberalism and in some cases leaned toward socialism. Like their political relatives, the Robert La Follette Progressives of Wisconsin and the Farmer-Laborites of Minnesota, thousands of North Dakota and Montana farmers joined the radical Nonpartisan League, which advocated an anti-corporate program of state-owned banks, grain elevators, and utilities.[10]

These politically active homesteaders had much to do with Montana's Progressive Movement. As Richard Roeder has convincingly demonstrated, Montana produced a hearty and rather typically western variety of state progressivism during the years after 1902. Like their counterparts around the country, the Montana progressives aimed, with a good deal of moralistic and highblown rhetoric, to counter corporate political power and malfeasance by fostering direct democracy and direct political action. They succeeded in passing into law an impressive amount of direct democracy and regulatory legislation: the initiative and referendum in 1906, the direct primary in 1912, direct election of United States senators in 1911-13, women's suffrage in 1914, workmen's compensation in 1915, and statewide prohibition in 1916.[11]

In Montana as elsewhere, the progressives produced an impressive and colorful group of leading personalities. On the Republican side, there was the handsome and capable young Missoula lawyer, Joseph M. Dixon, who during his long career served as a United States congressman (1903-07), senator (1907-13), manager of Theodore Roosevelt's national Bull Moose Progressive presidential campaign of 1912, and governor (1921-25). Jeannette Rankin combined a peculiar blend of pacifism, feminism, radicalism, and practicality and became America's first congresswoman. She served terms in 1917-19 and 1941-43 and, remarkably, cast votes against American entry into both World War I and World War II. The progressive Democrats also had their notables, like Thomas J. Walsh, the taciturn and accomplished Helena attorney who represented Montana in the Senate from 1913 until 1933 and won national fame in unearthing the Teapot Dome scandal. Walsh became the only Montanan ever appointed to a presidential cabinet when Franklin Roosevelt named him attorney general, but he died in 1933 before assuming his duties. Also another outstanding younger progressive, Democrat Burton K. Wheeler, served in the Senate from 1923 until 1947 and gained national headlines as an outspoken isolationist and as the leader of the Senate coalition that defeated Roosevelt's "court-packing" bill in 1937.[12]

Montana's progressives did well in their efforts to broaden public participation in politics, but fared badly in their attempts to curb corporate power in government. Logically enough, the reformers viewed the bare-knuckled might of Amalgamated-Anaconda as the very epitome of political abuse. In the heated election campaign of 1912, Republican-Progressive Senator Joseph Dixon carried the battle directly to the Company, which responded in kind. Dixon's Progressive Party stationery carried the forthright letterhead: "Put the Amalgamated Out of Montana Politics." The senator made his point, but lost his seat to Democrat Thomas Walsh.[13]

In the Treasure State, as in the nation at large, the liberal momentum of the Progressive Movement halted abruptly with the tidal wave of reaction and xenophobia that accompanied America's entry into World War I. Montana and the other states of the Northwest held large German and Scandinavian populations, and these groups, as well as the anti-British Irish and the anti-capitalist radicals of the far left, greeted the war effort either with a lack of enthusiasm or outright criticism. The radicals of the left were numerous and powerful in Montana. A healthy Socialist party thrived in working class cities like Butte, Anaconda, and Livingston; at Butte, the Socialists garnered enough support to elect Lewis Duncan as mayor. The leftist-syndicalist Industrial Workers of the World (I.W.W.) grew rapidly by recruiting the lumber workers and miners of western Montana. A radical faction of the Butte Miners' Union, sympathetic to the I.W.W., battled openly for control of the organization, leading to riots and dynamitings in 1914. Meanwhile, on the eastern Montana plains, the outspokenly radical—and sometimes anti-war—organizers of the Nonpartisan League (NPL) swept in from North Dakota, winning thousands of new members.[14]

By taking an antiwar stand, the radicals of the left placed themselves in a vulnerable position, facing the wrath of super patriots, many of whom were led by right-wing leaders of the corporate community. I.W.W. organizer Frank Little was lynched at Butte after delivering fiery anti-war speeches there in July 1917. Butte, gripped by a near class war, was repeatedly occupied by the army and national guardsmen in order to insure maximum copper output and to stifle dissent. Spokesmen for striking lumber workers and for the Nonpartisan League frequently faced similar repression, sometimes even beatings. An atmosphere of near hysteria gripped the state. Led by the state-sanctioned Montana Council of Defense, flag-waving super patriots crushed any free speech they found offensive. Early in 1918, the legislature enacted a repressive criminal syndicalism law, a gun registration law, and the notorious Montana Sedition Act, which actually made it illegal to criticize the government. This latter measure served as a model for the federal 1918 Sedition Act, one of the most severe restrictions of civil liberties in the history of the United States.[15]

Thus the war ended in an atmosphere of unreality and incredible tension. Hitherto powerful, the far left was shattered, and it never fully recovered its lost strength. Radical politicians such as United States District Attorney Burton D. Wheeler, who courageously resisted demands that he prosecute anti-war critics, and Congresswoman Jeannette Rankin were temporarily driven from public life. Yet, paradoxically, progressive and radical fortunes momentarily revived after the war, given new life by the unrest generated by a severe drought and recession. Hard-pressed farmers, in particular, took up the old Nonpartisan League demand for a tax reform that would force the mining companies to bear their fair share of the property tax burden. The tax revolt dominated the heated gubernatorial race of 1920, which pitted two foes of Anaconda, progressive Republican Joseph Dixon and radical Democrat Burton Wheeler, against one another. A tough, outspoken, and brilliant campaigner, Wheeler mustered a hard-hitting campaign against the Company. But in 1920 the country was in an anti-radical mood and the corporate press, faced with a choice between disagreeable alternatives, chose to vilify Wheeler as a dangerous "Bolshevik." The result, in what probably ranks as the toughest campaign in the state's history, was a sweeping victory for Dixon.[16]

In his single-term administration (1921-25), Governor Dixon faced a myriad of perplexing problems. The dominant right wing of his own Republican party distrusted him as an old Bull Moose Progressive; the Company mobilized against his program to equalize taxation; and Dixon had to shoulder the burdens of a severe agricultural depression. Despite some limited successes, Dixon failed to win support for his programs in the conservative legislatures of 1921 and 1923. Running for reelection in 1924, he went down to defeat under a barrage of corporate criticism, even as his Initiative 28, which instituted a higher and more equitable rate of taxation on mines, passed. Some observers, such as K. Ross Toole, view Dixon as a heroic figure battling the corporate Goliath. In his defeat they also see the collapse of progressivism in Montana. Dixon was an honest and able public servant, perhaps the state's best chief executive, and his defeat did end the old-style Progressive Movement in Montana. But it did not end liberalism as such. Temporarily set back, liberalism would burst forth again with the New Deal of the 1930s.[17]

A Mature Political Culture

During the years following Dixon's defeat in 1924, a period of political calm set in across the Treasure State. In part, the tranquility simply reflected the national mood of Calvin Coolidge-Herbert Hoover conservatism, and, in part, it resulted from the end of the drought and the momentary return of a measure of prosperity. Democratic Governor John E. "Honest John" Erickson, a conservative favorite of the Company, typified the standpat mood of the time, as did the Republican-dominated legislatures of 1925-31. Montana's sole liberal manifestation of the time was in Washington, D.C., where its prestigious team of Democratic senators, Thomas Walsh and Burton Wheeler, caused a sensation with their exposures of wrongdoing in the Harding Administration. Both men rose to the front ranks of prominence in the Democratic party. In 1924 Wheeler ran for the vice presidency on the Progressive party ticket with Robert M. La Follette of Wisconsin. Walsh chaired the national Democratic party conventions of 1924 and 1932 and mounted a short-lived race for the presidency in 1928.[18]

The peculiarly schizoid posture of conservatism in state government and liberalism on the national stage, which first surfaced when Wheeler joined Walsh in the Senate in 1923, is puzzling and has never been fully explained. Liberals have sometimes argued that conservative interest groups work to keep friendly politicians in key state offices while pragmatically relegating dangerous reformers to faraway national offices. Conservatives frequently counter with the argument that an intelligent electorate simply votes its own interests by choosing frugal conservatives for state offices while sending big-spending liberals to "fetch" federal dollars in Washington. Certainly, the fact that senators and congressmen are elected by broader based constituencies has given liberal candidates for these offices an edge over those liberals who run legislative races in smaller, rural-conservative districts. One must also agree with Clark Spence's judgment that Montana's small, wide-open, and highly personalized political order enables popular politicians like Wheeler and Mike Mansfield to draw votes freely from across weakly defined party lines. In any case, Montana's preference for liberal-Democratic senators is indisputable. Since the popular election of United States senators began in 1913, the state has elected only one Republican to that body, and he was by and large a political accident.[19]

In this and in other ways, Montana had struck its "classic" political profile by the 1920s. The frontier settlement process had truly closed with the collapse of homesteading agriculture after World War I, and the state had by now entered the modern era. On the right side of the political spectrum, Montana conservatives drew strong support, of course, from the Company—Anaconda-Montana Power. And, contrary to the stereotype of Montana as a "one-company" state, conservatives also garnered support from other economic interest groups. Corporations such as the five major railroads of the state as well as smaller lumber, coal, and oil interests usually lined up behind Anaconda on major statewide issues. Often they were joined by the conservative stockmen, organized mainly in the Montana Stockgrowers Association, and by the closely related large-acreage grain farmers, who were by now gathering under the flag of the Montana Farm Bureau Federation. Frequently overlooked by those who saw Montana as a corporate bailiwick, this alliance between western Montana corporations and eastern Montana ranchers and large farmers is critically important to understanding the state's political development. The "cowboys" sometimes wielded greater strength than the businessmen, especially in the legislature. Of course, the conservatives also drew ample support from the small middle class, and from the main street business communities of the towns and cities.[20]

The progressives, who by the 1920s were beginning more frequently to call themselves "liberals," also drew considerable middle-class support. The stereotypic image of Montana as a corporate colony of Anaconda, which was obviously inaccurate in accounting for conservative strength, was even more misleading in that it ignored the strength of Treasure State liberalism. The essence of this liberalism was an alliance — sometimes more dream than reality — between small farmers and union labor that was somewhat similar to the formalized Farmer-Labor movement in Minnesota. During the 1920s, the agrarian reformers moved *en masse* from the dying Nonpartisan League into the less radical, but still outspokenly liberal National Farmers Union. Especially along the Highline, the Farmers Union was a potent political force. It frequently aligned with the mine-mill union men who were now organized by the International Union of Mine, Mill and Smelter Workers, and with the numerous locals of the Railroad Brotherhoods scattered along the main lines of the Great Northern and Northern Pacific railroads. The mining unions lay dormant during the twenties under an "open shop" arrangement instituted by the Company in 1914, but they would soon regain the "closed shop" with New Deal encouragement in the big strikes of 1934.[21]

The Montana political culture that had coalesced by the post-frontier 1920s was a more complex and closely balanced alignment of interests and populations than is usually believed. Despite a continuing Democratic majority, the two parties competed on quite even terms. And despite a sometimes imposing conservative bias in Montana politics, the opposing forces of the political left and right competed on even terms, too. Prior to Dixon's debacle in the early twenties, Montana's Republican party held a stronger progressive wing than did the Bourbon-style Democracy, but this situation began to change as the conservatives now gained clear control of the GOP with Dixon's defeat. It would soon change even further as the New Deal drew Montana's progressive community overwhelmingly into the Democratic party. These changes, which mirrored a national trend, have persisted to this day. Like the other Mountain states, Montana seems to accommodate few liberal Republicans. Its Republican party is strongly rightist, and its Democratic party is usually visibly divided into liberal and conservative wings.

Depression and Political Turmoil

The onset of the Great Depression, accompanied by another terrible drought cycle, ended the political calm of the late 1920s and ushered in an era of political turbulence and change comparable to those of the 1890s and World War I. By 1931, the Depression had devastated every sector of Montana's economy, from the parched eastern plains where farm commodities were at rock-bottom prices, to the dormant mining and lumber regions of the West. Governor John Erickson and the conservative legislators tried to meet the problem simply by cutting costs and payrolls in an effort to cope with the falling yields of the property tax. In 1931 the legislature adopted a limited income tax to broaden the bases but refused to follow the Depression trend of imposing a state sales tax. Like most states, Montana lacked the financial resources to combat what was in reality a national calamity.[22]

As the Depression steadily deepened, it naturally carried down in its wake the fortunes of President Herbert Hoover and the Republican party. In Montana the election of 1932, which brought Franklin D. Roosevelt and his New Deal to Washington, was an epochal event. The election ushered out the conservative Republican legislative majorities and brought in Democrats who followed the lead of the White House. Even before the election, Montanans played the most conspicuous national role in the state's history, as Senator Walsh chaired the 1932 Democratic convention in Chicago. Senator Wheeler brought key supporters such as Huey Long of Louisiana aboard the Roosevelt bandwagon, and longtime Democratic national committeeman J. Bruce Kremer chaired the powerful convention Rules Committee. Partly as a reward for such service, no doubt, Walsh was appointed attorney general in FDR's cabinet, although he died before he assumed the post.[23]

The New Deal reform program of 1933-38, which had an enormous influence everywhere, had a giant impact upon Montana. Its spending-regulatory programs brought millions into the state, dramatically increasing the federal role in Montana. By 1935, relief agencies like the Public Works Administration and the Works Progress Administration offered some kind of support to nearly one in every four Montanans, and the Agricultural Adjustment Administration paid up to $10,000,000 annually to Treasure State farmers. Federal agencies, like the Civilian Conservation Corps and the Rural Electrification Administration, brought in valuable and highly popular new services. Montana boasted one of the New Deal's greatest projects, the giant earth-filled Fort Peck Dam on the Missouri River. In all, Montana ranked second among the forty-eight states in federal spending per capita, a fact largely explained by its small population and broad acreages as well as by the political effectiveness of its politicians in Washington.[24]

Such far-reaching measures had a sizable impact upon state politics. The popularity of Roosevelt and the New Deal, reflected in FDR's four landslide victories in Montana, naturally raised the political fortunes of Treasure State Democrats. In fact, the period 1933-40 marks the single greatest era of one-party domination in the history of a state that is normally characterized by intense interparty competition. Republicans barely figured in political contests, and then only because of Democratic feuds. The most important battle occurred when Senator Burton K. Wheeler, now the state's dominant political figure, broke with President Roosevelt over his controversial 1937 effort to "pack" the Supreme Court. Indeed, Wheeler actually led the Senate coalition that handed the president the most stinging defeat of his presidency by defeating the court-packing plan.[25]

Wheeler, who had entered Montana politics twenty years earlier as a young radical, was becoming an elderly, anti-statist conservative. His break with the administration sped the polarization of the Montana Democratic party into a conservative, pro-Wheeler faction and a liberal New Deal majority led by the steadfast liberal Senator James E. Murray (1935-61) and the fiery radical Congressman Jerry O'Connell (1937-39). In the heated 1938 campaign, Democratic infighting broke into the open. Congressman O'Connell boldly announced that with administration support he planned to challenge Senator Wheeler in 1940, but O'Connell got a lesson in practical politics when Wheeler Democrats joined Republicans and voted for O'Connell's Republican opponent in the House contest of 1938.[26]

The chasm between liberal and conservative Democrats steadily widened. Senators Murray and Wheeler feuded openly, and in 1940-41 Wheeler again enraged the Roosevelt men by launching a vigorous isolationist attack against the president's pro-Allied foreign policy. Showing a deft political maneuverability, Wheeler faced off his liberal Democratic enemies and won reelection in 1940 by gathering thousands of votes from his newfound Republican admirers. By the end of the Depression decade, the great New Deal Democratic majority vessel had thus run aground on the reefs of factional discord. This allowed the Republicans to regain a measure of power, most notably by electing Sam Ford to the governor's chair in 1940. Nonetheless, the New Deal undeniably cast a long shadow into Montana's future. It heralded a massive, new federal role in the state, began the growth of the modern governmental bureaucracy in Helena, and organized a liberal coalition in the Democratic party that is still in place today.[27]

World War II coincided with a period of confused, labyrinthine politics in Montana. Party lines once again disintegrated as angry liberal Democrats fumed at what they called the "Wheeler-Ford-Rankin Axis," an informal marriage of convenience between Wheeler Democrats and moderate Republicans led by Wheeler and his GOP pals, Sam C. "Model T" Ford and land developer-politician Wellington Rankin. All three of the principals, Wheeler, Ford, and Rankin, were not inappropriately referred to as "tired radicals." All three had started out years earlier on the left, but now stood to the right of center. While they failed in their effort to place Rankin in Jim Murray's Senate seat in 1942, they succeeded in holding control of the state government through the war years. In 1944 Ford won reelection in an angry campaign against liberal Democrat Leif Erickson, who championed the idea of a TVA-style Missouri Valley Authority. The end of this strange interlude of bipartisan politics came in 1946 when the old warhorse Burton Wheeler failed in the Democratic primary, a victim of angry internationalists and union liberals who retaliated against him for his isolationist and conservative leanings. Wheeler's defeat was significant, for it "allowed the Montana political parties to regroup along ideological lines and to function once again as legitimate opponents in the political arena."[28]

Montana Politics Reshaped

After a decade and a half of political turmoil and change, the postwar period began in Montana as a new era in which long-term social and economic forces, already long at work, were fundamentally recasting the state's political culture. Agriculture, for instance, had ranked as the state's key industry since the early years of the century. But by now, the national trend toward fewer and larger, more heavily mechanized and capitalized units was having a heavy impact upon Montana. From a total of 46,904 farms and ranches in 1925, the Montana total sank to 35,085 in 1950 and to 23,324 in 1974.[29] Subsistence farmers left the land, and larger operators gathered up their holdings. The demographic hemorrhage of rural population caused most of the counties of northern and eastern Montana to lose sizable percentages of their people, and this trend fostered a conservative attitude that tended to view change as threatening. Naturally enough, the remaining, highly capitalized farmer-businessmen leaned to the right, while the Farmers Union, that traditional bastion of liberalism, saw much of its support base crumbling away.

Just as the old progressive "family farmers" were being reduced in numbers by national economic forces, so were their long-time liberal allies of the Butte-Anaconda-Great Falls miners' and smeltermen's unions. By the forties and fifties, the old, labor-intensive deep mines of Butte could barely compete with the mass production, open pit mines of Arizona and Utah. Anaconda finally gave in and began open pit mining at Butte. In the years that followed, the company eventually closed all of its deep mines, terminating thousands of jobs. So the miners' unions lost much of their membership, even as other, less ideological unions such as the Teamsters expanded. A similar loss of membership afflicted the declining rail brotherhoods of cities such as Livingston and Missoula. This amounted to a serious erosion of the proletarian base of the Democratic Party and Montana progressivism.

The losses of these farmer-labor constituencies, it must be remembered, were gradual and long-term occurrences, which were partly offset by an inflow of middle-class liberals to Montana's small but growing cities. Long into the postwar era, therefore, Montana continued to manifest a strong liberal presence, consisting of a farmer-labor brand of progressivism that contrasted sharply with such neighboring states as Wyoming and Idaho, where conservative cultures were less alloyed by strains of liberal tradition. For instance, the *People's Voice*, the outspoken advocate of farmer-labor liberalism, continued publication until 1969. Thus the old Montana pattern of liberalism in Washington, D.C., and conservatism in Helena persisted even through the 1970s.

Postwar liberalism in Montana found special embodiment in three liberal Democratic United States senators: James Murray, Mike Mansfield, and Lee Metcalf. One of the most devoted of New Deal-Fair Deal liberals, low-keyed old Jim Murray, heir to a Butte mining fortune, closely resembled such urban liberals of the time as Robert Wagner of New York in his voting record. He played a significant role in promoting such progressive legislation as the United Nations, national health insurance, a Missouri Valley Authority, and the Employment Act of 1946. Mike Mansfield, the soft-spoken history professor from Missoula, served ten years (1943-53) as a workmanlike congressman before winning a Senate seat from conservative Republican Zales Ecton in the bruising election campaign of 1952. During his long and distinguished Senate career, Mansfield won respect from both sides of the aisle as a moderate progressive with special expertise in foreign affairs; he served longer as Senate majority leader than any other man in history. Probably no public servant ever won more federal plums for Montana than did Mansfield. Lee Metcalf, an outspoken liberal who often antagonized the right, resembled Murray more than Mansfield in his reliance upon the old farmer-labor coalition for support. During both his congressional (1953-61) and his senatorial (1961-78) careers, Metcalf consistently held to his progressive and environmental ideals and commanded a devoted liberal following.[30]

Of course, in time there were shifts not only on the left, but also on the right. The most fundamental change was the decline of Anaconda's political role in Montana. This decline can be traced back to the 1920s, when Anaconda expanded by purchasing the country's foremost brass fabricator, American Brass, and then bought up the great Guggenheim mines in Chile. Gradually, as the firm came to rely overwhelmingly upon its Latin American mines, its obsession with Montana politics waned. The loosening of its political grip was barely discernible until the fifties, but then changes came rapidly. Following the retirement of Cornelius Kelley, Marcus Daly's aging successor, the Anaconda giant seemed to shrink appreciably. The Company sold its newspapers in 1959 and moved away from its age-old alliance with Montana Power, allegedly because of corporate rivalries and disagreements over the benefits of public power generated at Hungry Horse Dam. By the mid-1960s, Anaconda seemed to differ little in its political tactics from other western resource companies. Its offspring, Montana Power, appeared to be much more politically potent. Atlantic Richfield absorbed the ailing Anaconda in the mid-1970s, and as that decade closed, Montanans worried less about Company political power than about the calamitous repercussions of the closure of the Arco-Anaconda smelter and Great Falls refinery, which the Company announced in September 1980.[31] In 1983, Arco closed the last of its Butte operations, signalling the end of a century of copper mining in Montana and the end of a remarkable era of political domination.

As Anaconda's power waned, other corporations such as the railroads and Montana Power maintained their grip, while new lumber, oil and coal, and banking companies arrived on the scene. All of this amounted to a healthy broadening and diversifying of the corporate community in the state. The business interests continued to lobby and politic as always, but the heavy-handed old Gilded Age approach faded into memory. Still frequently allying with the plains ranchers and dryland farmers, business and industrial interests continued to form the backbone of Treasure State conservatism.

Thus, as the old farmer-labor alliance of the left and the seemingly monolithic Anaconda behemoth of the right both faded with time, the political spectrum seemed to narrow toward convergence upon the center. Montana's small but growing urban middle classes, which concentrated in the expanding cities of Billings, Great Falls, Missoula, and Helena, came to play an increasingly larger role in politics. And the role they preferred, whether Republicans or Democrats, seemed to be middle-of-the-road, poised between the union-led Democrats to the left and the rural conservatives to the right. The overall tilt in voter preference appeared to be generally rightward, for Montana was drifting along with the general Rocky Mountain region toward a more conservative political culture. Commenting upon this regional edging to the political right, away from the northeastern-dominated welfare-liberalism of the postwar era, Kevin Phillips stated appropriately:

> Liberalism was turning away from the popular economic progressivism with which Mountain states support had been forged—the Norris-Borah-Wheeler era was over and done with—and was shifting into a welfare establishmentarianism lacking in appeal to the old radical Mountain states (where Northeastern causes are suspect whether liberal or conservative). . . .So long as the Democrats remain oriented towards the Northeast, their presidential nominees are not likely to carry the old populist Rocky Mountain states. . . . Sparsely settled though they may be, the Rocky Mountains have become pillars of the new national Republicanism.[32]

Liberal Democrats, it is true, kept their grip upon the Senate seats, and usually upon the western congressional district, which has traditionally been dominated by Butte-Anaconda and Missoula. But conservative Republicans and Democrats normally held sway over state government and over the plains-oriented eastern congressional district. Following the single term of moderate Democratic Governor John Bonner (1949-53), a long succession of conservatives presided over the government of Montana: Republicans J.Hugo ("the Galloping Swede") Aronson, who genially held office during the Eisenhower years (1953-61); Donald Nutter (1961-62), the arch conservative who perished in a winter plane crash before being able to complete his retrenchment programs; Tim Babcock (1962-69); and the veteran conservative Democrat Forrest Anderson (1969-73). Only with the 1973-81 tenure of moderate liberal Democrat Tom Judge did this conservative gubernatorial pattern show any sign of breaking, and the current incumbent, Democrat Ted Schwinden (1981-), is more in the traditional conservative mold.[33]

This same rightist coloration can be found in the various key agencies of state government, especially those like the Montana Supreme Court and the Public Service Commission that become focal points in struggles between corporations and their adversaries. In a penetrating series of articles in 1972 the Billings *Gazette*, an ex-Company paper, estimated that during the preceding fifteen-year period the Supreme Court had ruled in favor of Montana Power-Anaconda-Burlington Northern thirty-two times and against them only twelve.[34] Conservatism also ruled supreme, generally speaking, in the legislature. Rural traditionalists, especially stockmen, often visibly dominated the assembly through seniority and the chairmanship of key committees, even after the court-ordered reapportionment of 1965.

The two houses of the legislature reflect an irregularity in party control that attests to the close partisan competition in the Treasure State. Since the hamstrung first session of 1889-90, the Republicans have controlled both houses of the legislature seventeen times and the Democrats thirteen times; on seventeen occasions control of the two houses has been divided. Admittedly, the liberals have more than held their own on some legislative issues over the years, for instance in their long-standing opposition to the "regressive" sales tax and to "right-to-work" laws, and in their more recent tough stands for protection of the environment. Generally, though, bipartisan conservative coalitions have prevailed on the big issues of restraining taxation, spending, and bureaucratization. This tight-fisted conservatism is usually popular at election time and it is sometimes justified by pointing to the state's slipping per capita income (ranking approximately thirty-fifth in the nation). But it has also taken its toll in the quality and quantity of state services funded; even on a per capita income scale of measurement, Montana ranks thirty-seventh among the states in welfare funding.[35]

Montana's Political Culture

Montana entered the 1970s in an activist mood. In a pivotal special election in November 1971, the voters chose delegates to a constitutional convention that met the following year. In the same election, they overwhelmingly rejected a Republican-sponsored 2 percent sales tax, laying that issue to rest for the foreseeable future and leaving Montana among the five remaining states (along with Alaska, Delaware, New Hampshire, and Oregon) that still do not tap this lucrative source of revenue. The voters ratified the new constitution by a razor-thin 50.55 percent margin in the 1972 election, which measured a progressive victory of urban over rural areas. Progressivism surfaced in other ways too, particularly in the environmental protection laws that the legislature began enacting in 1971. Montana's environmental statutes are today among the toughest in the Union; the current energy crisis is surrounding them — especially the 30 percent coal severance tax — with controversy.[36]

The liberal surge of the early 1970s seems, however, to have brought few enduring changes. In fact, Montana liberals suffered major setbacks when Senator Mike Mansfield retired in 1977 and when Senator Lee Metcalf died suddenly in early 1978. The passing of these prestigious and powerful lawmakers, heirs to the earlier Walsh-Wheeler-Murray tradition, cost Montana dearly in federal influence, while raising questions for the future about the state's traditional liberal posture in Washington. Although two Democratic congressmen, John Melcher and Max Baucus, gained election to the Senate seats, many liberals judged Melcher to be well to the right of themselves. As Montana voters revealed in their heavy votes for Ronald Reagan in 1980 and 1984, they seem to be moving ever closer to the western states' mainstream of Republican-conservative preference. The Democratic hammerlock on the state's two Senate seats may soon be broken. Nonetheless, the persistence of its liberal Democratic tradition still makes Montana more a swaying political weathervane than are its immediate neighbors.

So we must conclude that the political culture that had bloomed in its classical flowering by the 1920s has, during the past half-century, changed markedly. Montana's classic political culture grew naturally, as we have seen, out of its narrowly based economic order. Stockmen and large-scale farmers joined the business community, led by Anaconda-Montana Power, on the right in opposition to a coalition of small farmers and unionized workers on the left. The state's small middle class therefore wielded little influence. But then the passing years took their toll. The attrition of small farmers and blue-collar workers at one end of the body politic matched the ebbing of nineteenth-century baronial rule by Anaconda at the other. At the same time, the growth of service industries, tourism, and especially government employment expanded the middle-class population of the cities and towns.

As a result, Montana shed its older, colorful, combative political culture like a snake molting its skin. The newly evolved culture, although streaked with colorations of heredity, is really more homogenous, more broadly regional and national in tone, with fewer local peculiarities. Even as they enter fully into the national mainstream, though, Montanans show many signs of the lingering influence of their past: in their strong attachment to environmentalism, their "gut" suspicions of corporations and of a distant federal government, their proud individualism and low regard for party regularity, their lingering fondness for ethnic politics, and their impassioned attacks upon and defenses of extractive corporations and tough-minded unions. That is Montana; that is the political reflection of its history.

The Pacific Northwest Working Class and its Institutions
An Historiographical Essay

EDITORS' NOTE

Many aspects of labor history in the Pacific Northwest are poorly charted, a condition that exists nationally as well. Carlos A. Schwantes summarizes the different kinds of research that have been done in this region's labor history, compares regional and national trends, and makes suggestions about the investigations left to be accomplished. "My primary theme—the role of violence—," he has explained, "occurred to me while I was a student in Richard Maxwell Brown's NEH-sponsored summer seminar on Violence in American History, taught [at the University of Oregon] in Eugene in 1980." Labor and violence, together with a heavy emphasis on the rise of trade unionism, are the familiar ingredients of labor history. Schwantes here expresses his dissatisfaction with this conventional approach when he points out that the study of violence has not been pursued to its logical conclusions. Actually workingmen were often the victims of these bloody actions and subject to debilitating industrial accidents, with serious consequences for families, communities, and society as a whole. He does see some promising signs in recent writings that stress working-class culture, the workplace, and the dictates of the work processes.

Not surprisingly, then, a major problem for those interested in Pacific Northwest studies has been the great popularity of the many narratives that capitalize on the violence of radical unionism. To help offset this difficulty, Schwantes provides an enlightening bibliography, much of it in the form of overlooked theses and dissertations. In addition, he describes the Pacific Northwest Labor History Association, an organization of scholars, union leaders, and interested citizens, which offers a forum for a variety of new topics and interpretations and has started publishing a series of labor studies.

A prolific scholar, Schwantes is at present Professor and Acting Chair of the Department of History at the University of Idaho. He was born in North Carolina in 1945 and did all his collegiate studies in Michigan, earning his B.A. degree at Andrews University in 1967 and M.A. and Ph.D. degrees at the University of Michigan, in 1968 and 1976 respectively. His doctoral dissertation, completed under the direction of the noted labor historian Sidney Fine, was published as *Radical Heritage: Labor, Socialism, and Reform in Washington and British Columbia* (1979). This book won the Emil and Kathleen Sick Prize in Western History and Biography, awarded by the University of Washington in 1979. Besides many scholarly papers and articles, Schwantes is also the author of *Coxey's Army: An American Odyssey* (1985) and a forthcoming new textbook on Pacific Northwest history.

A union exhibit booth at one of the early twentieth-century Interstate Fairs held in Spokane, Washington.
Eastern Washington State Historical Society, Spokane, Washington

The Pacific Northwest Working Class and
its Institutions:
An Historiographical Essay

CARLOS A. SCHWANTES

Zane Grey wrote only one novel about the Palouse country of eastern Washington. He aptly titled it *The Desert of Wheat*, first serialized in the *Country Gentleman* in the spring and summer of 1918, and eventually saw it made into a movie. *The Desert of Wheat* was about Wobblies. The best-selling western writer recognized and exploited their dramatic appeal even as he deprecated them as tools of imperial Germany and approved their violent suppression. Grey's piece of World War I propaganda remains today largely forgotten, though the writing of Pacific Northwest regionalists and labor historians testifies to the Wobblies' enduring appeal. In fact, radicalism, as exemplified by the Wobblies, and two topics generally related to it, strikes and violence, serve as focal points for the bulk of published writing about the Pacific Northwest working class and its institutions. As a consequence, the labor history of the region resembles, in effect, three islands of *terra cognita* surrounded by a vast and still relatively unexplored sea.[1]

A rough quantification of the labor studies published by four major Pacific Northwest history journals from 1960 through 1983 confirms the peculiar configuration of the region's labor history. Approximately eighty articles relating in some way to labor history appeared in these publications during that time: five in the *Oregon Historical Quarterly*; twelve in *Montana: The Magazine of Western History;* eighteen in *Idaho Yesterdays*; and forty-two in the *Pacific Northwest Quarterly*. If general studies of ethnic groups — Portland's Italians, Washington's Scandinavians, and Montana's Chinese, for example — were included, the list would grow slightly longer. Articles about the Industrial Workers of the World (Wobblies) constituted about one-sixth of the total, while studies of females or children as special classes of workers did not appear. Rare was the article dealing with a subject such as minimum wage legislation. Approximately one-third of the articles dealt primarily with left-leaning individuals and organizations. Perhaps most notable was that at least one-half of the total focused on strikes and/or violence — especially violence. In the Pacific Northwest the two were frequently related. Articles on violence appeared in all four journals. A similar classification of books about the region's labor history would no doubt underscore the preoccupation with violence.[2]

Violence is a theme prominent in Pacific Northwest labor history for a number of reasons. Quite obviously, there are several notable episodes for historians to write about. Examples that can be classified as vigilante violence include the Knights of Labor-sponsored crusades to rid the area of Chinese in the mid-1880s and the lynching of Wobblies Frank Little and Wesley Everest during the World War I era. Anti-radical disturbances, a category that often overlaps vigilantism, broke out during Seattle's Potlatch Days in 1913 and was later epidemic during World War I. The well-known Everett Massacre and Centralia Conspiracy are examples of this type of violence. Industrial warfare occurred in Idaho's Coeur d'Alenes, Washington's Cascade coal fields, and the fishing grounds of the lower Columbia River during the late nineteenth century. In a special category is the assassination of former Idaho Governor Frank Stuenenberg in 1905 and the subsequent sensational trial of William D. Haywood, Charles Moyer, and George Pettibone. Even with the addition of the periodic episodes of industrial violence in Butte, the labor-supported anti-Hindu riot in Bellingham in 1907, the Wobblies' free speech fights, Coxeyite train stealing in Montana and Oregon, and riot and property destruction occasioned by the Pullman Strike in 1894, the list remains far from complete. Not only have almost all of these episodes of labor-related violence been the subject of serious historical inquiry, but several have also been sensationalized in Sunday supplements of the region's major newspapers.[3]

A second reason for the prominence of violence in Pacific Northwest labor studies is that tales of labor-related disturbances constitute a major part of the region's folklore. Popular accounts of the *Verona's* ill-fated voyage to Everett or the miners' dynamiting of the Bunker Hill concentrator in north Idaho are the region's equivalent to the shoot-out at the O.K. Corral or the James gang's Great Northfield Raid. Or, it is as if recounting the epic David and Goliath struggles between workers and grasping railroad, mineral, and timber barons performs the same soul-stirring function for some Pacific northwesterners that myths surrounding Pickett's charge or resistance to Sherman's march do for many southerners. In the nation's far corner, America's frontier past and its industrial future abruptly intersected in a way that frequently saw the folklore of the former era recycled to encompass labor-related violence in the latter era. Zane Grey's vigilantes in *The Desert of Wheat*, to cite an outrageous example, lynched a Wobbly organizer and affixed to him a placard bearing the cryptic message, "Last Warning. 3-7-77," the numbers representing the dimensions of a grave and being a pointed reference to the Virginia City, Montana, vigilante movement fifty years earlier. In fact, Butte vigilantes attached that same message to the body of Frank Little in 1917.

Grey was not the only popular writer to treat the violent side of Pacific Northwest labor history as an up-to-date version of Old West melodrama. Both types of folklore appealed to people for many of the same reasons: they recalled the excitement and drama that was supposedly the frontier, and they portrayed virtue and villainy in simple, easily understood terms. Because accounts of labor-related violence remained popular with both editors and readers, labor historians could hardly be faulted for concentrating their scholarly efforts in an area that generated much interest, even if they sought only to debunk the many myths.[4]

The third and perhaps most significant reason for preoccupation with the violent side of Pacific Northwest labor is that these outbursts profoundly shaped both popular and scholarly awareness of wage workers as a distinct class. Violence was often the only window through which contemporaries viewed labor. The region's first real introduction to what newspapers called "the labor question" was the disconcerting anti-Chinese crusade of the mid-1880s. Fundamentally, it was a struggle over jobs during a brief period of hard times that followed completion of the first transcontinental railroads to the north Pacific slope. Its importance lies in its consciousness-raising effect on people who had previously been uninterested in or unaware of the Pacific Northwest's new and growing class of wage workers and their struggle with periodic unemployment. The anti-Chinese agitation not only plunged frightened residents of a hitherto geographically isolated region into the mainstream of the nation's social and economic controversies, but it also stimulated in America's far corner the first widespread, sustained interest in a radical social and economic critique.[5]

Much of the early discussion of "the labor question" was ill-informed and sensationalistic, and conducted to win converts, sell newspapers, or gain political power. Sylvester Pennoyer, who served as governor of Oregon from 1887 to 1895, was one of the first prominent public officials to call attention to the special needs of the region's wage workers. He did so in spectacular fashion in an 1893 Christmas letter publicly criticizing President Grover Cleveland's inaction during hard times: "Today is the first Christmas in the history of Oregon when more than two-thirds of the people were without employment and more than one-third are without sufficient means of support." Detractors denounced Pennoyer's statistics as absurd but could produce no better ones. The need to move beyond impressionistic treatment of "the labor question" led governments to establish bureaus of labor, but such agencies were late in coming to the north Pacific slope. Twenty-nine other states and the federal government founded labor bureaus before Montana became in 1893 the first Pacific Northwest state to do so. Washington followed in 1897, Idaho in 1900, and Oregon in 1903. Their early compilations of labor reports and statistics attracted few readers because they tended to be uneven and dull. Violent episodes that grabbed newspaper headlines, and later the historian, continued to stimulate most of the interest in labor in the Pacific Northwest.[6]

A pattern of outbursts followed by publication of popular accounts of the incidents began with the Coeur d'Alene trouble in the 1890s. People appalled by the violence published what were probably the first book-length treatments of Pacific Northwest labor: Mary Hallock Foote, *Coeur d'Alene* (1894); May Arkwright Hutton, *The Coeur d'Alenes, or, A Tale of the Modern Inquisition in Idaho* (1900); and Job Harriman, *The Class War in Idaho: The Horrors of the Bull Pen* (1900). Foote, a novelist, wrote a piece of anti-union fiction. Hutton and Harriman, both radicals motivated by a sense of outrage against the mine owners and their allies, initiated the treatment of labor-related violence in the region as folklore — although when Hutton later became wealthy, she tried to buy up all copies of her embarrassingly amateurish novel. The bloodlettings in Everett and Centralia encouraged other authors to add to the literature of outrage.[7]

The Coeur d'Alene trouble also prompted Congressional investigations that resulted in early documentary accounts of workers in northern Rocky Mountain mining camps and towns. Such government-sponsored studies were perhaps more common north of the border in British Columbia, where labor turbulence in 1903, an anti-Japanese riot in 1907, and tumult caused by a lengthy coal strike that began in 1912 prompted formation of royal commissions to investigate and publish their findings. Once again, though, it was violence that spurred these investigations. If violence was not present, government researchers usually paid scant attention to the working-class experience on the north Pacific slope. When the United States government studied female and child labor, immigrants, or working-class housing, it devoted relatively little attention to conditions in the nation's far Northwest as compared with those elsewhere.[8]

The emphasis on violence that is prominent in traditional primary sources of information about Pacific Northwest labor — newspaper accounts, special government studies, and recollections of participants — has fostered a distorted view of working-class life that labor historians need to correct. For one thing, workers were often the victims and not the initiators of violence. The amount of writing devoted to labor-related trouble might also mislead unwary readers to conclude that industrial relations in this part of the nation were more antagonistic than elsewhere. No scholar, however, has yet devised the yardstick necessary to make meaningful comparisons between labor-related outbursts in the Pacific Northwest and that in other regions such as the Midwest or New England. Furthermore, if violence is defined broadly as physically reckless, aggressive, or destructive behavior, as some scholars have done, the labor historian needs to study mine, mill, and logging accidents as a form of it. Scholars, incidentally, have not yet attempted a general investigation of Pacific Northwest labor-related violence, nor have they analyzed it as a variety of political action or examined in detail its relationship to radicalism, with which it often appears intertwined.[9]

Radicalism, as noted earlier, has attracted almost as much attention from writers on Pacific Northwest labor as violence, for perhaps many of the same reasons. Not only was there a great deal of radicalism about which to write, but much of it easily passed into folklore, as when the Seattle General Strike, which was neither long nor unusually bloody, became "The Revolution in Seattle." Like violence, radicalism shaped popular and scholarly perceptions of the region's working class. Finally, labor-related bloodshed and radicalism were, in fact, closely linked in everyday life.[10]

The interplay between violence and radicalism in working-class life occurred in several ways. Certain forms of outbursts stimulated popular discussion of contemporary social and economic issues, as happened when anti-Chinese agitation of the 1880s gave rise to an ideology of disinheritance. This ideology, a body of ideas that explained the relationship between the fortunate few and the impoverished many and provided a program of corrective action, flowed like a subterranean stream to link the region's many radical movements, agrarian as well as industrial. In addition, periodic episodes of industrial warfare coupled with widespread economic misery tended to heighten public awareness of the educational work conducted by street corner agitators and radical journalists and thereby encouraged producers — workers and farmers — to side either with labor or capital. That division occurred clearly in a conversation between two antagonists in Zane Grey's *The Desert of Wheat*, Chris Dorn, a struggling farmer, and his son, Kurt:

> "Anderson is a capitalist," said Chris Dorn, deep in his beard. "He seeks control of farmers and wheat in the Northwest. Ranch after ranch he's gained by taking up and foreclosing mortgages. He's against labor. He grinds down the poor. He cheated Newman out of a hundred thousand bushels of wheat. He bought up my debt. He meant to ruin me. He. . . ."
>
> "You're talking I.W.W. rot," whispered Kurt, shaking with the effort to subdue his feelings. "Anderson is fine, big, square — a developer of the Northwest. Not an enemy! He's our friend."[11]

Not only did radicals encourage people to take sides, their opponents did, too. In fiction as in fact, especially during the World War I era when the two were not always distinguishable from one another, conservatives drew the battle lines in ways that legitimated the use of anti-radical violence. Thus, in the folklore created by supporters, workers caught up in a struggle with massed capital assumed heroic proportions and became the vanguard of the cooperative commonwealth. At the same time, another group of observers treated labor as a kind of social pathology, literally the "dangerous class," volatile and easily manipulated by traitorous radical agitators, who, for the safety of society, had to be intimidated into silence. The two contrasting views fed on each other, as when a Seattle commercial journal, *The Flour and Grain World*, declared in 1918, "No other place in the world sizzles more with insolent labor ideas than is daily vomited forth in the sadly pestered city of Seattle." Likewise, the declamations of a parade of anti-Wobbly businessmen before the Spokane Chamber of Commerce foreshadows vigilantism in Grey's *The Desert of Wheat*. Grey, who visited the Pacific Northwest to research his novel, accurately recorded the mood of the region's businessmen. About the time the novel appeared in book form in 1919, *The Manufacturer and Industrial News Bureau* of Portland advised workers: "If you have the backbone of a jelly fish you will bean the next loafer who calls you a 'wage slave'. Thrash your troubles out with your employers but first thrash the agitator who lives by creating trouble for you."[12]

The mere imputation of unconventional action might also be used to undercut and destroy radicals, as Joseph Conlin notes in his revisionist essay "The IWW and the Question of Violence." Though Wobblies often talked and sang about violence, they seldom practiced it. Conlin finds that Wobblies were usually its victims, tagged with an undeserved reputation for initiating bloodshed by their numerous enemies: employers, rival unionists, reform socialists, and anti-labor politicians.[13]

Like the writing on labor-related violence, that on radicalism encompasses a remarkable variety of subtopics. These include Wobblies, socialist and anarchist utopias on Puget Sound, Astoria's Finns, Portland's sawmill workers, metal miners in the northern Rockies, agricultural workers on the Pacific coast, socialist parties in Washington and Oregon, the various cooperative commonwealth federations of the 1930s, farmer-labor parties, left-wing journalism, and individual rebels like Portland's John Reed and Charles Erskine Scott Wood. There is an equally rich body of literature on radicalism in British Columbia. My book, *Radical Heritage: Labor, Socialism, and Reform in Washington and British Columbia, 1885-1917* (1979), attempts to bridge the international and scholarly boundaries that too often separate the study of radicalism in the United States from that in Canada, and calls attention to the variety of unpublished material on the subject. Much more study on Pacific Northwest radicalism remains to be done. One finds, for instance, intriguing similarities between sentiments voiced in Alliance, Socialist party, and Wobbly songbooks that might support the notion of a common ideology of disinheritance derived from the unhappy experience of producers in turn-of-the-century America.[14]

On the other hand, the nonviolent, nonradical aspect of working-class life in the Pacific Northwest remains one of the least explored frontiers in American history. One obvious reason is the enduring popularity of studies of violence and radicalism discussed in the first half of this essay. Another major reason is that American labor history evolved in a way that ignored major aspects of the working-class experience until comparatively recent times. The chronological development of Pacific

Northwest labor history since World War I is the subject of the second part of this essay.

Pacific Northwest workers have never been the subject of the kind of intensive study that Paul Kellogg and associates conducted in Pittsburgh, but perhaps they would have been if Carleton H. Parker had survived the World War I influenza pandemic. Parker, forty years old at the time of his death, was a pathbreaker in the scholarly treatment of Pacific Northwest labor. As the head of the Department of Economics and dean of the College of Business Administration at the University of Washington, he spent much time studying the attitudes and living conditions of Wobblies prior to and during the Great War. His firsthand observations, published as *The Casual Laborer and Other Essays* two years after his untimely death in 1918, stand in refreshing contrast to the era's characteristic pro- and anti-Wobbly declamations. Parker treated Wobblies neither as dangerous subversives nor as pioneers of a promising economic order. In a similar vein, another book that appeared just prior to publication of Parker's study — Paul Brissenden, *The I.W.W.: A Study of American Syndicalism* (1919) — was the first scholarly historical treatment of the organization. Neither of these fine accounts, however, signaled attempts by scholars to enter a regional publishing field dominated by either radical pamphleteers or right-wing propagandists like Ole Hanson, the Seattle mayor who authored *Americanism versus Bolshevism* (1920).[15]

Scholarly treatment of Pacific Northwest labor remained at best sporadic until the early 1960s. During the forty-year interval between Parker's *The Casual Laborer and Other Essays* and Robert Wayne Smith's 1961 study of industrial violence, *The Coeur d'Alene Mining War of 1892*, only a handful of scholarly books appeared that related even in passing to Pacific Northwest labor other than Wobblies. Among those were Donald L. McMurry's *Coxey's Army* (1929) and Vernon Jensen's *Lumber and Labor* (1945) and *Heritage of Conflict: Labor Relations in the Nonferrous Metals Industry up to 1930* (1950). Treatment of the topic in scholarly journals was equally infrequent.[16]

Behind the scenes, in the cloistered halls and libraries of the region's major colleges and universities — and occasionally at schools outside the region — scholars, primarily candidates for the master's or doctoral degrees, made forays into the field of Pacific Northwest labor history. Some even ventured off campus and into Hoovervilles and hiring halls to conduct interviews and surveys. But their studies seldom generated any historiographical controversy and almost all remained unpublished, forgotten even by academics. That is unfortunate because the research done during the 1930s contains material that is today a primary source for the study of unemployment and labor and radical organizations during the New Deal era, to cite but one example. Typically, the first and second generations of academics who were interested in labor were trained in business or economics and consequently concerned themselves primarily with the labor union as an economic institution. Political scientists and historians whose scholarly interests turned to the Pacific Northwest wrote extensively on its notable infatuation with political and economic reform—especially the Populist and Progressive movements—but not many were interested in the general history of labor or its involvement in the region's politics.[17]

That changed during the 1960s—a decade that was a watershed in the scholarly treatment of American labor and a time when interest in the subject among scholars surged. The journal *Labor History*, established in the late 1950s, served as a clearinghouse of information as well as an outlet for serious writing about labor. In the Pacific Northwest, likewise, interest in labor history grew, though largely in the subcategories that had dominated the field since before World War I. Wobblies remained a favorite subject, with the appearance of Robert L. Tyler's *Rebels of the Woods: The I.W.W. in the Pacific Northwest* (1967) and Melvyn Dubofsky's encyclopedic *We Shall Be All: A History of the Industrial Workers of the World* (1969), which contained much information about industrial labor in the Pacific Northwest. The number of books in print increased with publication of such varied works as Harold M. Hyman's *Soldiers and Spruce: Origins of the Loyal Legion of Loggers and Lumbermen* (1963), Robert Friedheim's *The Seattle General Strike* (1964), Charles Pierce LeWarne's *Utopias on Puget Sound* (1975), and Roger Buchanan's *Dock Strike: A History of the 1934 Waterfront Strike in Portland, Oregon* (1975). Many of the books were based on research for advanced degrees and published by university or local presses—a reflection, no doubt, of the fairly limited market for regional labor studies and a primary reason why many good but specialized studies remain unpublished.[18]

Toward the end of the 1960s an important event occurred with the formation of the Pacific Northwest Labor History Association. Meeting first on an informal basis in 1968 and 1969, members established a more permanent organization in 1970 and elected as their first president, Robert E. Burke of the University of Washington. The Pacific Northwest Labor History Association was from the beginning a mixed body, with its membership divided almost evenly among academics, trade unionists, and local history buffs. Ross Rieder, a leader in the Washington state labor movement, was the group's first secretary-treasurer and later its president. One of the main purposes of the association was to facilitate "a closer dialogue between those actively involved in labor-management relations in the Pacific Northwest and the academic community." Its annual meeting not only served as a forum for the presentation of papers on a variety of topics but also afforded members the opportunity to enjoy the films and songs of the labor movement and the recollections of its former leaders such as Dave Beck. In addition, the association published *Unionism or Hearst* (1978), the William Ames and Roger Simpson study of Seattle's

1936 *Post-Intelligencer* strike, and the first in the association's ongoing series of labor studies.[19]

It is, of course, an overstatement to say that one organization or individual was responsible for the surge of interest in the history of labor in the Pacific Northwest; nonetheless, no one deserves more credit for this accomplishment than Robert E. Burke. As noted earlier, he was a founding father of the Pacific Northwest Labor History Association. As professor of history at the University of Washington, he directed a number of master's and doctoral candidates through the intricacies of labor history. He opened the pages of *Pacific Northwest Quarterly*, which he edited, to a variety of labor studies ranging from a documentary account of the Everett Massacre and a bibliography of Washington's early labor newspapers to numerous monographs. As editor of the University of Washington Press's Americana Library series, he fostered republication of several history classics, including two that relate to Pacific Northwest labor: Carleton Parker's *The Casual Laborer and Other Essays* and Donald McMurry's *Coxey's Army*. He facilitated publication of Friedheim's *The Seattle General Strike* and a revised version of my University of Michigan doctoral dissertation, *Radical Heritage*. Finally, together with Richard C. Berner and Karyl Wynn of the University of Washington Library's Archives and Manuscripts division, he helped amass what is probably the largest collection of materials on the region's labor history.

Like stones cast into a calm pond, Burke's multiple activities have created many ripples, even waves. One of his recent doctoral students, Jonathan Dembo, not only produced a detailed account of the Washington state labor movement but also published a comprehensive bibliography of Washington's labor history that is now a starting point for anyone interested in the subject. Another of Burke's students, W. Thomas White, completed a study in 1981 of the region's railway workers that bridges the gap between the so-called "old" and "new" labor history.[20]

The basic premise of the new labor history—as stated by one of its foremost practitioners, Herbert Gutman—is that the history of workers encompasses more than the study of labor unions, which were the primary concern of the institutional economist who long dominated the field. It should include the whole network of community relationships, work habits, and the aspirations and expectations that gave meaning to workers' lives—in other words, the working-class culture. The stimuli to the new labor history came from many sources, including the general increase of interest in labor studies noticeable in the 1960s and publication of several seminal works, especially E. P. Thompson's *The Making of the English Working Class* (1963) and Gutman's 1973 essay in the *American Historical Review*, "Work, Culture, and Society in Industrializing America." The result was research and writing on topics almost totally ignored by earlier generations of labor scholars. David Montgomery's collection of essays,

Worker's Control in America (1979), for instance, presents labor's efforts to protect its prerogatives and values on the shop floor as a central issue of the modern industrial age. Several overviews and critical assessments of the new labor history have already been published, and they need not be reiterated here. The question is, what impact has the dramatic expansion of the horizons of American labor history had on studies in the Pacific Northwest? To provide an answer is deceptively difficult.[21]

From one perspective the new labor history has had very little impact in this region. Few of the thesis and dissertation writers interested in Pacific Northwest labor history have consciously attempted to utilize the conceptual insights offered by Thompson, Gutman, Montgomery, and others. By the same token, there have appeared almost no articles on the subject along the lines of those that Milton Cantor included in his *American Workingclass Culture* (1979), which samples several scholars' writings on labor primarily in the nation's northeast quadrant. A time lag between the development of important new interpretations and their assimilation by students of Pacific Northwest history was perhaps inevitable: whether labeled old or new labor history—or something in between—there has long been too much for them to do and too few to do it.

The number of professional historians who claim Pacific Northwest labor history as their primary field of research and writing has never been great. Some of the most avid students of the subject are trade unionists and local history buffs such as those who comprise much of the membership of the Pacific Northwest Labor History Association and whose interests tend to lie along traditional lines of inquiry. Some of the methods used to do history from the bottom up—to concentrate on the workers themselves—are not likely to be utilized by other than specially trained academic researchers. One popular technique involves combing through city directories and the federal manuscript census to obtain numerical data on a variety of items: a worker's age, sex, occupation, ethnicity, education, and so on. The historian then uses a computer program to transform the raw data into sometimes arcane statistics that must be interpreted with care. The whole process seems formidable and intimidating to many. Nonetheless, scholars combining a variety of concepts and techniques, both old and new, have written a number of exciting social histories. A lucid method of presentation undoubtedly remains the key to generating interest in any kind of serious study of Pacific Northwest labor.[22]

An example of the successful presentation of history that analyzes working-class institutions within the context of the larger community and antedated the vogue of the new labor history is Norman Clark's *Mill Town* (1970), a social history of Everett, Washington. A graceful style of writing combined with a refreshing approach to a popular old subject, the Everett Massacre, earned the book widespread recognition. In some ways, though, *Mill Town's* influence, like that of the new labor history, remains yet to be seen in the writing on the region's working class. No one has published a similar study of Centralia, an obvious candidate, or some of the communities in which workers in a single industry predominated, such as the railroad towns of Sprague and Auburn, Washington; Huntington, Oregon; and Livingston, Montana. *Mill Town* also demonstrates the importance of probing the attitudes and concerns of a community's businessmen in order to understand their reaction to labor. As the influence of the new labor history increases in the region, *Mill Town*'s place as an important landmark in the scholarly treatment of the Pacific Northwest working class will stand out ever more clearly. It is a prototype for the kind of study that draws inspiration from both the old and new labor history and presents its findings in a clear manner that appeals to a broad spectrum of readers.

What does the future hold for Pacific Northwest labor history? The subject has achieved a degree of maturity, but it still seems to lack a central theme. Only geographical proximity links many of the disparate historical studies. In short, further exploration into its many neglected aspects must be accompanied by some responsible reductionism to interpret and give unity to what has hitherto been a very eclectic matter. Foremost, then, is the need to identify those regional characteristics that supposedly set workers in the nation's far corner apart from those elsewhere — if, indeed, they can be. Were they more violent or radical than counterparts in other regions? Perhaps an "index of insurgency" applied to various regions of the United States would give an answer. Would some of the studies of working-class culture in New England communities yield similar results if done in the Pacific Northwest? If not, why? Asking that question helps to focus attention on those aspects of the region's labor history that most need exploration: the working-class family, workers on the shop floor, the working class in the larger community, female workers, and working-class institutions in general.

To be sure, one working-class institution, the labor union, has been studied extensively, but usually from the top down. And only a minority of the region's workers ever belonged to labor unions. What about other working-class institutions: churches, clubs and lodges, and schools? The formal and informal education of the region's early working class encompassed not only public schools but also labor colleges and lyceums, reading rooms in union halls, and labor and radical newspapers. These topics deserve study. And what about scabs? No one has yet produced a general study of scabs, a group that played a very prominent role in the region's labor-management conflict. In the eyes of organized labor a scab was a loathsome being. Walter Lippmann called the scab a "traitor to the economic foundations of democracy." In their own eyes, though, they served a positive purpose, as one scab noted during a Portland strike about 1918. To the tune of "Yankee Doodle" he argued:

A scab's a substance on a sore
That keeps us pure and healthy;
So we will work and try to make
Our country grand and wealthy.

The strikers quit their work,
Their family's on starvation;
They walk the streets and howl and shriek,
They cause their own damnation.

In most histories damnation falls on the scabs. The point is, the subject has for so long been obscured by prejudice that historians do not know much about that aspect of Pacific Northwest labor. But labor history has now reached a degree of maturity that permits vigorous reexamination of the folklore, myths, and impressionistic assertions that have colored treatment of the region's workers.[23]

Within the Pacific Northwest, in another instance, labor studies have tended to focus on workers in certain geographical areas to the exclusion of others. Oregon's labor has received far less scholarly attention than Washington's. The same disparity marks the treatment of the working class east and west of the Cascades. The first step that must be taken to encourage scholarly exploration into neglected areas—labor in eastern Washington, for example,—is better identification of the sources of labor history. Jonathan Dembo's bibliography for Washington labor is an example of the kind of work that needs to be done for the region's other states. I have begun to compile a list of the region's labor and radical papers that indicates where they are available. The July 1980 issue of *Pacific Northwest Quarterly* contained the first installment. Researchers need also a guide to the relevant manuscript materials, some of which are tucked away in places easily overlooked by students of Pacific Northwest history. Whitman College has a large collection of records relevant to union activity in Walla Walla and southeastern Washington. The Northern Pacific and Great Northern railroad collections of the Minnesota Historical Society contain files relating to several aspects of working-class life in the Pacific Northwest: migratory labor, Japanese railroad workers, Wobblies, and the role of railroad police in Everett prior to the 1916 massacre. Photographic collections, such as those compiled by Darius Kinsey and Asahel Curtis, give many details of the workers' world in the turn-of-the-century Pacific Northwest.[24]

This essay attempts to chart the territory that is Pacific Northwest labor history, to identify its salient features. Like early maps of the New World, some parts appear sketchy, tentative, and incomplete; others—possibly the suggestions for further exploration—seem fanciful, even utopian. That, however, is the nature of the subject and explains why in the coming years it will likely remain an exciting frontier to explore.

The Challenge of Women's History

Women's history is one of the newest of several subfields in Pacific Northwest history. Many standard accounts about this region are heroic chronicles, tales of adventure, and reports of exploration and war in which women are usually left out. Still other well-known historical works emphasize the tribulations of homesteaders and pioneer townspeople, the daring ventures of early merchant princes, and the development of a regional identity and culture. Although women were full participants in all these important events, they seldom receive adequate credit or attention.

In her essay, Susan Armitage surveys the state of the art for women's history and considers the work already done as well as topics still to be explored. Central to her argument is the belief that women's history means more than adding "a few female faces to existing history." Instead, she contends, scholars need "to introduce new kinds of evidence, new issues, new perspectives," and thus contribute to a reconceptualization of the region's heritage. Armitage suggests a number of areas — women's work and community activities, in particular — where new research is beginning to modify older interpretations. For instance, the conventional view of the northwest frontier as a predominantly masculine culture is faulty at best because recent investigation indicates that the settlement of the Willamette Valley, the regional "Cradle of American Civilization," was accomplished largely by families. She also predicts that future scholarship will prove equally fruitful and revealing for topics such as the lives of women missionaries and teachers (as told from their own viewpoint), the supportive networks pioneer women created among themselves, and the political and social significance of women's clubs. In fact, Armitage maintains, historians must never fail to ask this question: "What were women doing while men were doing the things they deemed important?"

Susan Armitage received her B.A. degree in philosophy (1959) from Wellesley College, an M.A. in history (1965) from San Jose State College, and her Ph.D. in history (1968) from the London School of Economics and Political Science. She taught at the University of Colorado at Boulder before coming to Washington State University as director of Women Studies in 1978. Armitage has written a number of articles on western women's history dealing with topics such as oral history as a research tool, black women, housework and childbearing, women's diaries, and attitudes of white women toward American Indians. Among her most recent publications are the theme article "Becoming to Come into Focus: Western Women," for a special frontier women's issue of *Montana, the Magazine of Western History* (Summer 1982), and an introduction for the reprint edition, *Phoebe Judson, A Pioneer's Search for an Ideal Home*, issued by the University of Nebraska Press in 1984 and coedited *The Women's West* (1987). In 1983 Armitage served as the project director and keynote speaker of "The Women's West," the first national conference devoted exclusively to the role of women in western history, held at Sun Valley, Idaho. Her current research concerns the family roles of women in the rise of specific eastern Washington communities.

Women on a 1920s assembly line packing raisins for the Sun Maid Raisin Growers Association.
Eastern Washington State Historical Society, Spokane, Washington

The Challenge of Women's History

What is women's history? The occasional mention of an extraordinary woman is not enough, nor is a sentimental paragraph eulogizing the woman in the sunbonnet as the true pioneer. Women's history seeks to explain the significance of the daily lives, activities, and values of ordinary women. This explanation is not easily achieved. The idea of seriously and comprehensively treating women as historical subjects is still novel and requires detailed research in unfamiliar topics. This, then, is the first challenge, and for the researcher, a new perspective is required. Then, too, findings in women's history inevitably challenge earlier interpretations of historical events. This second challenge affects all historians whatever their own research specialties, for it concerns how they teach history to their students.

Viewed from the perspective of women's history, present Pacific Northwest history is incomplete. The history of the women of the region is largely unexplored. In this respect, the Pacific Northwest is not unique – in all regions of the country, women's history has been neglected. Furthermore, state and regional historians are generally quite ill-informed about women's history at both the theoretical and the national levels because it has not seemed relevant to their interests. This essay provides information on those aspects of women's history that are relevant to the history of the Pacific Northwest, points out some omissions in regional studies, and suggests some insights that may prove useful in future investigations.[1]

Women's history is generally considered to have begun as a contemporary specialty with the publication in 1968 of Gerda Lerner's article "New Approaches to the Study of Women in American History."[2] Since then, there has been an explosion of historical research on women and a very rapid refining of insights. Like all developing academic specialties, women's history has changed as it has grown. Yet Lerner's categorization of the stages in that development provides us with a useful framework within which to consider Pacific Northwest studies of women.[3]

The first works were biographical studies of "women worthies" – those unusual women whose extraordinary achievements could not be ignored. Clifford Drury's accounts of the "First White Women Over the Rockies" – Narcissa Whitman, Eliza Spalding, and the other missionary women who followed shortly after – fall into this category.[4] Other regional "women worthies" have not been ignored. The best known are Abigail Scott

Duniway, journalist and leader of the suffrage movement in Oregon; Jeannette Rankin, Montana's first female U.S. Representative; and suffragist May Arkwright Hutton of Spokane.[5] Bethinia Owens-Adair, M.D., historian Frances Fuller Victor, suffragists Eva Emery Dye and Emma DeVoe, and more recent figures such as Bertha Landes and Anna Louise Strong of Seattle have also received some attention.[6]

Lerner termed the second stage of historical writing about women as "contribution history." What have women done that can be considered significant by the accepted historical criteria? Apparently, the answer for the Pacific Northwest is Sacajawea and suffrage. About Sacajawea, there is embarrassingly little to say. Rarely has such a large heroine been created out of so little historical fact.[7] For all practical purposes Sacajawea has passed into American folklore and beyond the reach of historians. She should be consigned to American mythology, henceforth to keep company with Paul Bunyan, Mike Fink, Pecos Bill, and friends.

Suffrage is a different story. T. A. Larson's articles on suffrage in the western states have made a good start, and recent studies of politically active regional women are adding detail. However, there is as yet no link between studies of western suffrage and the most recent interpretations of the eastern suffrage movement.[8]

Lerner's third stage, which she terms "transitional" history, incorporates the current scholarship. Historians in this third stage share a perspective that is openly and honestly woman-centered. A serious effort has been made by these historians to view women's historical experience through women's eyes. Some of the results of this reinterpretation are controversial. Two articles in particular, Faragher and Stansell, "Women and Their Families on the Overland Trail,"[9] and Lillian Schlissel, "Women's Diaries on the Western Frontier,"[10] aroused the wrath of historians who do not share their feminist perspective. One critic accused the authors of taking women's experience out of context; furthermore, they are accused of creating a dreadful new stereotype, that of the "downtrodden drudge."[11] In fact, the initial portrait was too limited in those two early articles, as the authors themselves implicitly admit in their subsequent monographs.[12] But their final conclusion is even more radical than that of the earlier articles. Faragher concludes that there were *two* Overland Trail experiences, one male, one female:

> For men the trip west was an active test of competition, strength, and manliness. It meant measuring themselves against the already romanticized images of their heroic fathers and grandfathers traversing the Wilderness Road and the Cumberland Gap. For women the trip west was a test of their inner strength. They did their part and more; they were comforting wives and attentive mothers, to the many single men of the trail as well as their husbands. They did all this, because of, not in spite of, their not wanting to leave home in the first place.[13]

This point is important. The evidence that men and women experienced the Overland Trail differently is fully in accord with recent research in eastern nineteenth-century women's and family history. The two sexes inhabited separate spheres. What women did was dramatically different from what men did, and their perceptions were shaped accordingly. David Potter saw all this years ago, and he also saw clearly the implications for historical interpretation. As he said, an explanation that does not apply to women cannot be considered comprehensive. Looking at the West, Potter observed, "In cold fact, the opportunities offered by the West were opportunities for men and not, in any direct sense, opportunities for women."[14] This is serious, indeed, for it means that Frederick Jackson Turner was, at best, half right.

Turner's thesis—that the frontier liberated the individual from social, class, and psychological restraints—is apparently not true for women (and perhaps untrue for all men). We are so accustomed to thinking of the frontier as an area of freedom and of choice that this conclusion is unwelcome. Yet the most substantial book so far published on women in the West, Julie Roy Jeffrey's *Frontier Women*, argues convincingly that most women did not view the frontier as an opportunity to liberate themselves from conventional sex roles. Indeed, they resisted changes that would have caused them to deviate from traditional woman's work and a womanly role.[15]

How shall historians respond to the challenge that female frontier experience poses to the traditional norm? The rationalization that because the West was largely settled by men, the prevailing culture was masculine in tone, does not fit the northwest reality. The initial Willamette Valley settlement was made largely by families. A recent study shows that in rural areas (although not in towns) the sex ratio was roughly equal from the beginning of the settlement.[16]

There is another very simple way to justify the historical omission of women, and that is to say that whatever women did, their activities were never as important as those of men. As T. A. Larson has said, "Women, after all, did not lead expeditions, command troops, build railroads, drive cattle, or ride Pony Express."[17] But some women did indeed participate in these events. For example, the writings of Elizabeth Custer and other Army wives are a valuable source of information on many aspects of western army life. A Pacific Northwest example, Frances Fitzgerald's *Letters of An Army Doctor's Wife*, conveys a vivid sense of the tension and confusion at Fort Lapwai in the days before and during the Nez Perce war of 1877.[18]

Yet another, and better, explanation is that earlier historians simply did not ask the basic women's history question: "What were women doing while men were doing the things that they deemed important?"[19] This is the question that can and must now be answered. Historians can indeed discover the actual, historical roles that women played in the development of the Pacific Northwest. Information to document women's activities exists. Much of it is readily available in archival collections; much has recently been catalogued. Sometimes more persistence is required; information about women must be pieced together or "teased out" of the documents.[20] More frequently, it is simply a matter of not taking women's activities for granted.

The following example illustrates how taken-for-grantedness has affected the writing of history. Among the early settlers in Thurston County was the Bush family, whose members were black. Their presence is frequently mentioned in Washington state histories, which usually refer to the "George Bush family." A careful search in sources such as county histories provides valuable information for this case. One report on the Bush family, which is largely based on an oral history with Lewis Bush, the youngest son, describes the active role of his mother Isabella Bush in the family's survival.

Hudson's Bay Company officials were not pleased when a pioneer group of thirty Americans, including the Bushes, settled a part of Thurston County in 1845. The local factor at Fort Nisqually, Dr. William Fraser Tolmie, had orders not to sell food to American settlers. Consequently, life for the new arrivals was hard, indeed frightening, for the first few years. Lewis Bush recounted how his family found a solution:

> Mother made friends with Dr. Tolmie and it was through him that she got her first start in poultry and sheep. She had traded for a few hens from a French family who were connected with the Hudson's Bay Company, and when one of these hens showed her willingness to set, mother got a setting of turkey eggs from Dr. Tolmie. She was very successful with this hatching and by coddling those young turks soon had a nice flock. Dr. Tolmie had not been so lucky with his turkeys so he told mother he would trade her a fine ewe for every turkey she would let him have. She was glad to do so and in that way she got the first start of the large flock of sheep which was one of the greatest sources of profit in a few years. From Dr. Tolmie also, we got the first start of hogs. Well, so we lived for years, always getting ahead a little and I am glad to say, always having a little to share with our poorer neighbors. Neither father nor mother could bear to deny anyone who applied to them for assistance.[21]

Isabella Bush provided food for her family at a difficult time; most other women in the Pacific Northwest did the same as a matter of course, but in much less dramatic circumstances. Throughout the region, whenever possible, women grew and preserved the family food supply; and the lower the family's cash income, the more important this female provider role became. Accumulating evidence tells us that this provider role was the basic female responsibility throughout the West, even after eastern urban women had been fully incorporated into a cash and consumer economy. The domestic activity of women made a direct contribution to the household economy. To overlook this role, or to take it for granted, falsifies the reality of how early settler families survived and functioned as economic units.[22]

Unfortunately, evidence to document the economic contributions of women within the household is often difficult to find. Census records contain only those parts of women's work that fall within the wage economy. Even such a widespread female economic activity as taking in boarders escapes specific mention, and its existence in each particular case has to be a supposition based on household size and the number of unrelated persons recorded by the manuscript census. Furthermore, census data is unavailable for the period after 1910. Historians have turned, therefore, to two other sources for documentation of women's household activities: personal documents (diaries and letters) and personal testimony (oral history).

A recent book, Mary Beth Norton's *Liberty's Daughters*, is a useful model. Based mainly on women's personal documents, the study links changes in the attitudes and household activities of women with ideological and economic changes in the Revolutionary and early National periods.[23]

We need regional studies that will do the same. For instance, women's wage work is still a neglected topic in Pacific Northwest history. The one exception is research on women shipyard workers in World War II, which has produced two excellent recent studies.[24] However, it may be that the very novelty of wartime employment has distracted attention from the ways in which more traditional women's labor, particularly as service workers, has contributed to regional industries such as agriculture, logging, mining, and fishing.[25]

Moving from the family to the community level, the same pattern of omission of women's activities persists. Most community histories mention only men; it often seems that women had only a minor part in the founding and shaping of community institutions. In this case, appearances are deceiving. All over the country, historians of women are now documenting a forgotten range of female community activities.[26] Recent research shows a strong pattern of informal female activities in which many community projects are begun, lobbied, and arranged. But when the moment of formal organization comes, the women seem to step back. Men are elected as officials, and often given public credit for the entire enterprise.[27] Newspapers report this final, formal stage and thus overlook women's activities. To fill out the record, other less customary sources must be consulted as well as newspapers. In many areas of the West, women's clubs were deeply involved in community affairs.[28] Where club records exist, they should be examined. Oral history is another important tool in community history, when used to explore the "unofficial" story of the founding and development of community organizations. Often there are family stories about the mother's role in community building. In this recently settled region, interviews with (now aged) children of pioneers can frequently carry us back nearly *to* the point of white arrival.[29]

These few brief examples illustrate the ways in which women's history challenges earlier interpretations. Women's history means more than adding a few female names to existing history. New kinds of evidence, new issues, and new perspectives inevitably arise. Consideration of the historical activities of women in the Pacific Northwest will change our regional history. The challenge for historians of women in the Pacific Northwest is to put together a coherent narrative that is simultaneously true to the personal and emotional experience of women and integrally connected to the developing social and political realities of the region.

Some examples will illustrate the possibility of illuminations and connections. The lives of the missionary women have yet to be explored on their own terms. What do their diaries and letters tell us that we cannot learn from the writings of their husbands? Myra Eells, shocked at the grime and discomfort of the Overland Trail, wrote emphatically to her female relatives that *only* dark-colored undergarments could be considered suitable for the trip. Mary Walker, overwhelmed by childrearing and housekeeping, repeatedly filled her diary with her sense of failure because of the frustration of her own missionary activities. With increasing urgency, Narcissa Whitman's letters express her longings to be reunited with her parents.[30] These three examples are not trivial. They are some of the clues we need to reimagine the missionary experience through women's eyes. There are many other unasked questions about the first women missionaries and about the lesser-known female missionaries who followed them west. What was the relationship of the pioneer missionary women to the newly founded Mt. Holyoke College and other institutions intended to train women for Christian teaching in the West? Hundreds, perhaps thousands, of single eastern women traveled west to teach school. Some of the best known of these women were motivated by missionary zeal.[31] What can we discover about the more numerous teachers who ventured to the Pacific Northwest?

Once in the West, on what resources did the pioneer women draw for their psychological survival? Narcissa Whitman and Eliza Spalding formed a Maternal Association almost as soon as they arrived in the Oregon country. In the East maternal associations provided important emotional support to mothers in the early nineteenth century.[32] The Oregon organization was therefore an effort to recreate eastern conditions on the frontier. But what kinds of supportive bonds did single women create among themselves in the West? These and other questions about female companionship and support networks have been asked about eastern women. Research in western sources is needed to fill out the picture.

The same kinds of questions need to be asked about our regional "women worthies." Why was Abigail Scott Duniway, for example, such a radical? To answer that question fully, we need to know about the lives of ordinary women of her time and place, about the supports that women derived from remaining within the conventional female sphere, and the possible rewards for breaking out of that sphere. Duniway herself answers some, but not all, of these questions.[33] As an undergraduate at the

University of Washington, Montana's Jeannette Rankin was active in the women's suffrage movement, and then in its culminating drive in Washington. Many women originally found their own voice within supportive women's political groups, subsequently moving into mainstream politics. Was Rankin's Washington activity such an experience for her?

There are other questions to ask about women's groups and clubs. Historians of women are interested in understanding the formation, development, and growth of women's groups. A clear pattern has emerged in national research—from conventionally social beginnings, many women's groups evolved into vehemently activist reform groups.[34] The strong support that the General Federation of Women's Clubs gave to the suffrage movement is just one example of this trend. How did women's clubs develop in the Pacific Northwest? What role did women play in local reform movements? How and why did women join the suffrage struggle, and what did work within that movement mean to them? These questions, which seek to understand the activism of women's groups within the context of women's lives, have not yet been explored in our region.[35]

Beyond these topics are some other, more personal questions. Sexual behavior and attitudes, marriage and divorce, birth control, childbirth, childrearing, and widowhood are among the personal items that historians of women have helped us to view as historical questions. These questions are not gender-specific; the answers can shed new light on the lives of men as well as women. Nevertheless, historians ought not to overlook the fact that some or all of these matters have been central, overriding concerns in the lives of women. Yet in some recently published women's primary sources, the editors *do* overlook these concerns. Commentary that focuses only on landmarks and political events does not adequately illuminate the lives of women. Sensitive reading, alert to personal concerns, is essential.[36]

The considerable agenda outlined in the preceding pages is far from being achieved. Regional historians of women are still deeply engaged in discovering what women actually did and how they felt about it. We are beginning to make strong connections between our materials and the wider social context. Finally, however, the challenge of developing good women's history for our region is everyone's. If women's history is regarded as a narrow subspecialty, of interest only to women, then the connections between women's activities and regional political and economic history will be slow to develop. If, on the other hand, historians work together to consider sources in the light of the concerns mentioned above, our regional history will change quite dramatically.[37] Pacific Northwest history will be larger, more complete, more representative than it could be when the women were missing.

The Role of the Editor:
Watchful Waiting and/or Purposeful Searching

E D I T O R S '   N O T E

Editors of historical journals provide an opportunity for airing new topics and interpretations, as well as for introducing neophyte authors. Yet few historiographical works explore the complex responsibilities of these editors or the significance of their role in reshaping historical writing. In an exception to this rule, one noted editor asserted that historical periodicals deserve special attention because of their great numbers, "and because of the medium they afford historians to breathe and proliferate and become articulate from issue to issue." The prominent editor then outlined the failings and potential strengths of his colleagues. Unfortunately, many never attain the professional standards required for nurturing and presenting the best historical research. If the backlog of articles runs thin, an editor may become guilty of reducing the journal "to a reflection of his own poor self." For "the creative editor," however, the possibilities are unlimited. It is true that he must be a paragon, that is, an able historian with the superb diplomatic skill to satisfy authors, readers, and the sponsoring agency. With these attributes, together with tact and forbearance, an editor can publish a distinguished journal and become *primus inter pares*, "first among equals."*

Robert E. Burke, managing editor of the *Pacific Northwest Quarterly*, earned this distinction and similar accolades for the premier regional periodical he has helped direct since 1959. His astute essay explains the standards that undergird a successful editor's ideals and strategy. The subtitle, "Watchful Waiting and/or Purposeful Searching," suggests the dilemma in editorial tasks and also the necessity for a pragmatic approach. He concedes the importance of trusted associates who do the "real editing," as well as of those who labored before him to build the reputation of *PNQ*. Nor does he fail to point out advantages bestowed on editors by a backlog of articles, which, in the words of Mark Twain, gives one "the calm confidence of a Christian with four aces."

A professor of history at the University of Washington, since 1957, Burke specializes in recent U. S. history, recent social movements, and western history. Born in Chico, California, in 1921, he received his B.A. degree (1946) from Chico State College and his M.A. (1947) and Ph.D. (1950) from the University of California, Berkeley. He served as director of the Bancroft Library's Research Program in England (1950-51) and head of the Manuscripts Division at the Bancroft Library (1951-56), and then taught at the University of Hawaii (1956-57). He has been associated with the *Pacific Northwest Quarterly,* published by the University of Washington, since 1959, became managing editor in 1966, and retired from that position in 1987.

---

*Lester J. Cappon, "The Historian as Editor," in William B. Hesseltine and Donald R. McNeil, eds., *In Support of Clio: Essays in Memory of Herbert A. Kellar* (Madison: State Historical Society of Wisconsin, 1958), 186-88.

Sawmill and loggers convention on the deck of the *Skookum.*
*Manuscripts, Archives, and Special Collections, Washington State University Library
Pullman, Washington*

The Role of the Editor:
Watchful Waiting and/or Purposeful Searching

ROBERT E. BURKE

When I was asked to speak informally about "an editor's perspective," I agreed without knowing exactly what to say. While I was determined to be frank, I also wanted to be discreet, since I would still be editing the *Pacific Northwest Quarterly*. I decided not to be scholarly, in a historiographical or bibliographic sense, for it is up to others to judge the quality of *PNQ*. And, above all, I was determined to remember that I was talking to a general audience of people deeply interested in the history of the Pacific Northwest, not in the day-to-day routine problems of the editor of a scholarly journal.

"Editors' roundtables," informal and usually unstructured chit-chats about practical problems of journal editing, are now a regular feature of several of our history meetings. Formal sessions dealing with journal editing occasionally show up on conference programs, although they appear far less often than sessions about large-scale editorial projects. These, as well as editorial internships, have often been sponsored by the National Historical Publications and Records Commission, with generous grants from the Andrew W. Mellon Foundation.

I do not know how other journal editors feel, but the several roundtables I have taken part in have rarely led to any significant changes in the way we operate *PNQ*. The editors' roundtables are often essentially recitals of "how we do it in our shop." This, of course, necessarily involves responding to the situation editors find themselves in when they take charge of their journals. It is at least mildly interesting to compare problems: sources of funding, how to handle printers, pricing, selection and duties of advisory editors, relations with constituencies, salaries (if any) of helpers, supplementary salaries (if any) of editors. But these panels ordinarily provide me with things that: (1) I already know only too well or can readily guess; and (2) I do not really need to know to get on with my work. The situations editors of journals find themselves in vary widely, and therefore at roundtables we usually talk about things that are not immediately relevant for many of those present. I have decided that I can generally spend my time more profitably cruising about, searching for likely articles or book manuscripts. This is, of course, a matter of judgment and my colleague editors may feel otherwise. But I tend to side with

Alexander Pope: "Tis with our judgments as our watches, none go just alike, yet each believes his own."

PNQ is a regional journal that occasionally publishes articles of wider scope. It long doubled as the state historical journal, until the Washington State Historical Society began publishing its own, *Columbia*. What makes *PNQ* perhaps unique among regional historical journals is its funding — it is owned and operated by a state university. Its salaries come from the budget of the Graduate School of the University of Washington. Its publication costs are usually covered by the sale of subscriptions, around half from members of the WSHS (who get a reduced rate). Occasionally, a small subsidy from the Graduate School is necessary to balance accounts at the end of the year. The History Department chairman gives the managing editor an occasional reduction in teaching load and freedom from some routine chores — but no extra pay.

Now what I might tell you about most of the nuts-and-bolts aspects of editing "my" regional history journal would probably not even interest my good friends and colleague editors. They are polite people and they might feign an interest; but I know they either already know most of the things we do or they realize that their conditions are so different that they could not do it our way even if they wanted to do so. Even more likely, they have enough of their own problems without looking for new ones they will not have to deal with. Again my old favorite Alexander Pope realized how to put it: "I never knew any man in my life who could not bear another's misfortunes perfectly like a Christian."

Therefore, I feel that I should talk about what we have in common with all scholarly history journal editors everywhere. This is the ardent desire to locate the best scholarship in our respective areas of coverage and to see it into print in the best possible form. This is basically what we seek to do, no matter how far short of the ideal some of us may, on occasion, fall. Success is most likely to come to an editor if he (using "he" in a generic sense, unrelated to gender) combines what appear to be extremes — *watchful waiting* and *purposeful searching*, a technique that combines passivity, or apparent passivity, with aggression, which is always real even if it is not always readily apparent.

We must also admit that we need to have luck, that quality that Napoleon said he prized most in his generals. I remember some rather lugubrious popular songs of self-pity from my youth ("I'm waiting for ships that never come in" and "I'm always chasing rainbows" — or "I'm forever blowing bubbles"). While I do not recommend popular songs as a source of wisdom, I submit that these do make the point that mere waiting, watchful or otherwise, will not always bring success, even if it seems to be purposeful. I also remember one of my much-loved Berkeley professors, a most resolute and purposeful searcher, an utterly tireless scholar, who sought in vain to demonstrate to a Phi Alpha Theta banquet how one could manage data on West Indian trade. He rammed needles into punch cards with ever increasing vigor and shook them again and again, until he finally had to admit that apparently no lemons went from Martinque to New Orleans that year.

But still, the editor needs to employ both watchful waiting and purposeful searching if he is to make the best of his opportunities, or maybe even survive in his position, assuming that he wants to do so. At times I have done much more of the one than the other, and which one may well depend upon the editor's backlog of accepted articles as much as anything else. If an editor has a good many interesting — or at least publishable — manuscripts in the box, he will not have to employ purposeful searching as much as he would if he does not know where his next issue is coming from. There is nothing quite so comforting to an editor, if not to his usually impatient authors, as a nice backlog when one is looking at newly submitted manuscripts. On those occasions, if not too harried by outside obligations, the editor can have what Mark Twain called "the calm confidence of a Christian with four aces." Thus, ironically, the very time that is ripest for purposeful searching is the time when watchful waiting is the easier way. History journal editing is not really a quiet and contemplative career, and I doubt that it ever was or ever will be.

Emily Johnson, our late and much-lamented chief, the founder-director of the University of Washington's Office of Scholarly Journals, loved to put us managing editors in our place by contrasting what we did with what she called "real editing." By "real editing" she meant checking quotations and footnotes, copyediting, layout, and proofreading. She felt that the two types of editor were very different, although their tasks were interrelated. In her view, the scholars who were managing editors had the job of finding the manuscripts, of evaluating them (with the aid of whatever outside experts he needed or could find), of securing the necessary revisions, and of writing the letters of rejections and acceptance. After that, she firmly believed, the managing editor should go on about his duties and let the real editor get on with the rest of the job.

Emily was always glad to have the managing editor be a follow-up proofreader (she herself was the first or second). He might well catch something that should have been caught earlier, but she made it clear that she considered it to be a minor chore. She told me more than once that she thought that university professors who edited journals and also trained graduate students got their fill of real editing when they worked over theses and dissertations. As she also told me more than once, she believed that a good real editor needed to have very special skills and that few faculty members had these skills or could be trained to have them. She was always polite about it, of course, coating the meaning with remarks about "better things to do with your time," but her message was clear and quite unforgettable.

It should be said that each history journal seems to have a kind of tendency or momentum of its own. The editor must not act upon the assumption that he can do anything he wants about turning policy around. A journal has its obligations to those who started it, to those who support it, and to those who merely read it. The last group often give it moral support by word of mouth and add to its prestige by citing it in their own writings. The editor also has his own obligations: to the institution that pays his salary (whether it be university or historical agency); to his advisory board (which must share his responsibilities); and to whomever else he depends upon to get out his journal.

This situation accounts for the fact that the managing editor, even on a new journal and perhaps especially on an old one, has a certain framework within which he must operate. Some manuscripts are going to come to him naturally because his journal is there. They will not all be fresh manuscripts—some of them will (no matter how carefully they have been retyped) already have had a long shelf-life or drawer-life or desk-life before he sees them. Even if these long-lived manuscripts might seem worthy of consideration, with luck somebody will advise the editor of their longevity. This is not to say that some previously rejected papers are not worth considering—several fine articles published by us are things that seem to have fallen through the cracks somewhere, because of publishing policies at other journals. My point is that some articles come to you without any effort on your part. Here, more than elsewhere, is the need for *watchful waiting*. Nowhere else is an editor more dependent upon his advisors, some of them people who have read papers for other journals for many years and most of whom know intimately at least one or more of the fields covered by the *Pacific Northwest Quarterly*.

Although the managing editor inherits a framework, he soon finds out that it can be altered. Indeed, I have found that the framework I inherited over twenty years ago, when I first became acting managing editor when Charles Gates went abroad on a Fulbright stint, began to alter a bit almost at once. First, of course, came manuscripts that Gates had rejected or would have rejected (or so the authors must have thought). I was the new boy in town and worth a try. Since my own situation at the University of Washington was not yet firm, to put it mildly, and since Pacific Northwest history had not been my speciality in graduate school, and since this was my first experience in scholarly editing, I needed lots of help. It came, in the first instance, from Emily Johnson, that remarkable woman who had been Gates's long-time assistant. Her incredible memory, shrewd judgment, and supreme confidence made the task tolerable, even if she could do nothing to convert it into much fun for me at that stage of my career. I assumed that this would be only a temporary role and often wonder if I would have had the same attitude had I realized my future longevity with *PNQ*.

Old friends I had known in Berkeley, particularly Herman Deutsch of Washington State University, Earl Pomeroy of the University of Oregon, and Merle Wells of the Idaho Historical Society, pitched in to help me in my time of troubles, telling me things that I desperately needed to know and introducing me to their colleagues and students. Thanks to my previous travels to the other colleges and universities in the region, to regular participation in meetings, and to forays with Richard Berner to collect manuscripts and archives for the University of Washington Library, I had already become acquainted with most of the college teachers concerned with Pacific Northwest history. Editing, at least the way I learned to practice it, involves a very considerable amount of what is today called *networking*. At the outset it was the only way I could manage to do my job while learning it.

PNQ was a journal with a half-century of life already behind it when I came on the scene. It had had three managing editors: Edmond S. Meany (1906-35); Merrill Jensen (1935-41); and Charles M. Gates (1941-63). Meany was, of course, the Great Spirit of Pacific Northwest history — the founding father and an indefatigable popularizer and enthusiast as well as professor at the University of Washington. He advanced the journal as he was promoting the Alaska-Yukon-Pacific Exposition of 1909. He also saw it as a manifestation of the Seattle Spirit, in defiance of what his associate Clarence Bagley called "the Tacoma Bunch" (the Washington State Historical Society). Meany titled the new journal *The Washington Historical Quarterly* and called its sponsor (in reality a group of his wealthy friends) the University of Washington State Historical Society. After a couple of years the money gave out but the journal was revived, in part at least because of the interest of University Librarian Charles "Bookie" Smith, who saw that the *Quarterly* was a magnet for books and serials that the library desperately needed.

Under Meany the *Quarterly* published scholarly articles, chiefly on Washington but also on the whole region, including British Columbia and Alaska. Its greatest contribution was probably the systematic publication of an amazing variety of sources of Pacific Northwest history. Its emphasis was on the early period at a time when many of the pioneers or their children were still around to testify. We have published a stimulating piece about Meany's regime at the *Quarterly* by George Frykman, whose full-length biography of our own founding father is eagerly awaited. I have come to have the highest regard for Meany's work on the *Quarterly* and think that it may well be his most lasting contribution to scholarship.[1]

Merrill Jensen, a young University of Washington historian specializing in the era of the American Revolution, took over the *Quarterly* after Meany's sudden death and transformed it into a regional journal with its present title. He made a rapprochement with "the Tacoma Bunch," securing a much larger circulation by blanketing in Washington State Historical Society members, who henceforth got *PNQ* with their membership. The arrangement gave to the society an affiliation with a journal and gave to its members something tangible to show for their dues. This strange, perhaps unique, arrangement has persisted to this time. A casual browse through the Jensen period *PNQ*, as well as memories of many conversations with him over the years after he moved on to teach at the University of Wisconsin, convinces me that he fully intended to make *Pacific Northwest Quarterly* into something like the *New England Quarterly*.

Charles M. Gates, who took over from Jensen, was Meany's successor as professor of Pacific Northwest history at the University of Washington. He moved the journal back a bit from Jensen's tendencies toward a national and multidisciplinary scope. Gates published documentary sources when he could find them, but they were no longer as abundant as they had been in Meany's time and he discovered that many unpublished documents deserved to remain unpublished. Gates's own interest was in economic development. He not only opened his pages to articles on major themes in regional economic and institutional history, both in the pioneer period and in more recent times, but he engaged in actively promoting such pieces. He found articles in many places, but some of the most important papers came out of the newly established Ph.D. program in history at the University of Washington.

Gates worked very closely with doctoral candidates, helping them find suitable topics that would fill in gaps, sometimes becoming coauthor himself. While working on his two major books, *Empire on the Columbia* and *The First Century at the University of Washington,*[2] Gates and several graduate assistants turned out a number of lively and informative spin-off pieces for the journal. Outside articles continued to flow in during the Gates era, frequently in response to some of the recent-period economic and institutional articles that came out of the University of Washington graduate program in history.

After Gates's tragic death, we lured Vernon Carstensen out from the University of Wisconsin to join the department as the specialist in Pacific Northwest history and managing editor of *PNQ*. He brought with him a galaxy of graduate students, soon attracted many more, and almost at once began to take a leading role in university affairs. Seeing that he was going to be seriously overloaded, he took advantage of the fact that I was coming to the end of my term as departmental chairman to persuade me to return to the managing editorship. He himself accepted the position of "adjunct editor," a term he had previously invented for me. As adjunct editor he has been exceedingly helpful and influential — scouting articles, getting many manuscripts each year, and advising us on book reviewing. In this manner the Carstensen era has persisted down to the present. Pieces written by Carstensen's own Ph.D.s have been among our most original articles on nineteenth-century topics.

This brings me to some thoughts about the general matter of topics. One of the things that nearly always used to catch me by surprise is what might be called a Historical Boom. Suddenly we would find ourselves inundated by related articles. This often occurred after we had published something rather different from our usual fare. If we ever have doubts about whether we are really being read or at least noticed in the scholarly world, we can take reassurance from this sort of phenomenon. After twenty years or so I can now usually foresee what might well set off a boom—or at least a boomlet. Indeed, our decision on acceptance or rejection is often made in full awareness of possible consequences.

For some time *PNQ* has been in the throes of a full boom in historic photographs. Since 1953, when Charles Gates and Emily Johnson converted *PNQ* from its book format to a two-column layout as an economy measure during one of the university's Great Financial Crises, we have been able to illustrate our articles. Indeed, we were one of the pioneers in two-column format for scholarly journals.

In recent years the national boom in historic photography has developed enormously. Robert D. Monroe, an expert in this field (now, alas, retired from his direction of the University of Washington Library's special collections), was our stalwart helper in all things concerning historic photography. When it came time for us to hire a new editorial associate, we were able to secure a member of Bob's staff, Carol Zabilski. Her expertise and zeal in this area, combined with her artistic sensibilities, enabled *PNQ* to move quickly into greatly expanded use of illustrations. The success of her own photo spreads attracted the attention of both scholars and custodians of photographs. As a result, we have been able to do several photo spreads a year, with no let-up in sight. Our larger, three-column format actually gives us more space than we had before and therefore we have not had to sacrifice space devoted to scholarly writing in order to accommodate the photos. Fortunately the historic photography boom dovetails into our traditional first area of coverage—the history of this state. Year after year, about half of our twelve or thirteen articles deal directly with Washington.

Another boom also fits almost as well into our pattern of coverage, since most of the articles on labor and radical movements give major emphasis to this state. I have said something about this before in my paper "Searching for the Soviet of Washington" at the Walla Walla meeting of the Pacific Northwest History Conference in April 1980. This boom is the result of a coincidence of: (1) recent accessioning and processing of manuscript collections, both at our university library and elsewhere; (2) intense interest of our graduate students and faculty in the subject; and (3) an international upsurge in labor history, often given a special dignity as part of the "new social history." One of my special problems at *PNQ* is to restrain my own interest in labor and radical history lest we become in reality what I understand we have sometimes been called in jest, *The Pacific Northwest Labor History Quarterly*. We tend to publish the first articles of our young labor historians, but we generally tell the more prolific of them to seek other outlets for at least some of their later efforts.

I should say, parenthetically, that I have on occasion tried to start my own booms only to have them bust. Business history, with the single but exceedingly important exception of forest history (for which we surely have to thank the Forest History Society), has never developed into boom proportions. I have had to conclude that the possibility of such a boom is still remote, unless the interest of faculty and students can somehow be aroused.

Then there are booms that are healthy and natural but that have to be contained by us, lest they absorb a vastly disproportionate amount of space. Here the best example is the Great Alaska History boom, which started not long before statehood and shows no sign of abating. Edmond S. Meany published many important Alaska articles in the early days of the *Washington Historical Quarterly*, but scholarly interest in Alaska fell off in the 1920s and 1930s. It is understandable why general interest in Alaska declined then, but it is harder to determine why scholars seem to have turned their backs on Alaska.

There is no doubt how the Alaska history boom began in the 1950s. A group of young, aggressive, enthusiastic scholars emerged as Alaska specialists. Some of them had themselves been attracted to the Great Land or spent time there in the military service. By the 1950s, research support had become available as a result of renewed general interest in Alaska's resources and its people and as the possibility of statehood loomed. Many of these historians seem either to have been trained in western history or to have drawn their initial teaching assignments in the Far West (or even in Alaska). They and their mentors, as well as journal editors and other publishers, saw the great opportunities in the field, since so little of any phase of Alaskan history had been researched adequately (to say nothing of "definitively").

We editors had relatively little to do with the Alaska boom except to offer outlets for the best articles and to rely upon our specialist advisors to help us find them. At *PNQ* we have often published several articles a year on Alaska, although last year we ran only one. But there are several promising Alaska pieces in our pipeline, including two different articles centering on Nome at the turn of the century.

This brings me back to the matter of the editor's advisors. I cannot speak with authority about how my predecessors operated or even about how my present colleagues manage such matters. But from the very first I have relied upon a group of specialist advisory editors to help find good articles and to help improve them once they are located. The only way I have been able to reward them is by putting their names on the masthead as members of the editorial advisory board. Although I have experimented with terms of service and other ways of alternation, I have tended to use these people, or the people they recommend, fairly steadily over the years. We have added to their number, to the limit of our masthead size, or subtracted a few (often at their own urging). But in reality, we tend to call upon people no longer on our board whenever something particularly appropriate (or troublesome) comes along. There seems no way to escape our board, once you have been on it.

I never accept an article without the positive recommendation of at least one or two of these advisors, no matter how much the article appeals to me. It is something like wanting a cosigner or two on a note, but I like to think that I am deferring to those with expertise on a subject on which I know too little or too much.

Some of my most unpleasant experiences as managing editor (and there have been many unhappy times on *PNQ* over these last twenty years) have come when I have heard a paper at a meeting and asked the author to let us consider it, only to find that nobody except me and, presumably, the author found it suitable for *PNQ*. In my early years as acting managing editor I hovered around sessions at meetings ready to snatch papers from the authors' hot little hands. If it appears that I do not do this much any more, it is because we probably have already had the paper in our shop, sent it out to readers, had Carol Zabilski check it out, accepted it for *PNQ*, and then suggested it for the program. It may sound unsporting, perhaps even incestuous, but it has been a way to build some worthy sessions at meetings in the last decade or so.

Each issue is an adventure in itself, especially for our full-time associate editor. The life of a real editor, like Carol Zabilski, is full of surprises, many of them unpleasant. We envy those who can put together "thematic" issues that have involved lots of planning and lead time. More often we find ourselves having to soothe justifiably irate authors, maddened by our slowness.

This opportunity to reflect a bit on my experience as managing editor leads me to one firm conclusion. Whatever we have been able to do to find new writers with fresh materials and to help them polish their manuscripts, and whatever we have been able to do to brighten up our appearance, *PNQ* essentially reflects the state of regional historical scholarship. This may not sound very heroic, but I suspect that is what we must continue to do in order to live up to our obligations.

¹For early descriptions of the Northwest coast see Douglas Cole and Maris Tippett, "Pleasing Diversity and Sublime Desolation: The 18th-Century British Perception of the Northwest Coast," *Pacific Northwest Quarterly* 65 (January 1974): 1-5; James Burney, *A Chronological History of the Voyages and Discoveries in the South Sea or Pacific Ocean* (London: Payne and Foss, 1819), 2: 108-17.

²The details of early competition between Spain and the other European nations may be found in Warren L. Cook, *Flood Tide of Empire: Spain and the Pacific Northwest, 1543-1819* (New Haven: Yale University Press, 1973), chaps. 3-5.

³For Meares's own account see John Meares, *Voyages Made in the Years 1788 and 1789, from China to the North West Coast of America* (London: Logographic Press, 1790).

⁴Cook, *Flood Tide of Empire*, 117-29; Henry R. Wagner, "Creation of Rights of Sovereignty Through Symbolic Acts," *Pacific Historical Review* 7 (December 1938): 312-19. See also Cecil Jane, trans., *A Spanish Voyage to Vancouver and the Northwest Coast of America* (London: The Argonaut Press, 1930), xii-xiv.

⁵Cook, *Flood Tide of Empire*, 129-33, 147, 152, 159, 162-65, 184.

⁶Ibid., 151-58, 162, 167, 174-77, 182, 186-87; Wagner, "Sovereignty Through Symbolic Acts," 322-23. In part, the Spanish motivation in removing the British lay in the desire to control the fur trade. See Adele Ogden, "The Californias in Spain's Pacific Otter Trade, 1775-1795," *Pacific Historical Review* 1 (December 1932): 464-67.

⁷Cook, *Flood Tide of Empire*, 205-07, 212-15, 217.

⁸John Rutledge, Jr., to Jefferson, May 6, 1790, Julian P. Boyd, ed., *The Papers of Thomas Jefferson*, 19 vols. (Princeton, N.J.: Princeton University Press, 1950-1974), 16: 413-15.

⁹Cook, *Flood Tide of Empire*, 225-29, 232-35; William Ray Manning, "The Nootka Sound Controversy," *Annual Report of the American Historical Association, 1904* (Washington, 1905), 450-62.

¹⁰Cook, *Flood Tide of Empire*, 327, 331-33. For late Spanish activities in the region of Nootka and the surrounding waterways see Henry R. Wagner, *Spanish Explorations in the Strait of Juan de Fuca* (Santa Ana, Calif.: Fine Arts Press, 1933); Jane, *A Spanish Voyage to Vancouver*, 96-121.

¹¹Wagner, "Sovereignty Through Symbolic Acts," 320-22; Cook, *Flood Tide of Empire*, 333-35.

¹²Bernard DeVoto, *The Course of Empire* (Boston: Houghton Mifflin, 1952), 324-27.

¹³Spanish explorers Manuel Quimper and Francisco Elisa preceded Vancouver into Fuca Strait in 1790 and 1791, but Vancouver noted important features that had eluded the Spaniards, including the inland waterway that he named Puget Sound after Peter Puget, one of his officers. Vancouver encountered two Spanish vessels. The four vessels pushed northward through the inland passage independently. The Spaniards concluded that there was nothing along the interior waterways worth further examination or acquisition. See Cook, *Flood Tide of Empire*, 335, 355. For Vancouver's explorations see Edmond S. Meany, ed., *Vancouver's Discovery of Puget Sound* (New York: Macmillan Company, 1907), *passim;* Robert B. Whitebrook, "From Cape Flattery to Birch Bay: Vancouver's Anchorages on Puget Sound," *Pacific Northwest Quarterly* 44 (July 1953): 115-28.

¹⁴Cook, *Flood Tide of Empire*, 362-82; Meany, *Vancouver's Discovery of Puget Sound*, 306-21.

¹⁵Wagner, "Sovereignty Through Symbolic Acts," 323-24; Herman J. Deutsch, "Economic Imperialism in the Early Pacific Northwest," *Pacific Historical Review* 9 (December 1940): 385-88; Cook, *Flood Tide of Empire*, 397, 402-05, 421-23.

¹⁶Quoted in Meany, *Vancouver's Discovery of Puget Sound*, 121.

¹⁷John Bartlet Brebner, *North Atlantic Triangle: The Interplay of Canada, The United States, and Great Britain* (New Haven: Yale University Press, 1945), 459-64; Boyd, *Papers of Thomas Jefferson*, 9: 261.

¹⁸Instructions to André Michaux for Exploring the Western Boundary, January, 1793, Paul Leicester Ford, ed., *The Writings of Thomas Jefferson,* 10 vols. (New York: G. P. Putnam's Sons, 1892-1899), 6: 158-61.

¹⁹Jefferson to Lewis, June 20, 1803, Ford, *Writings of Jefferson,* 8: 194-99.

²⁰For a brief account of Mackenzie's travels to the Pacific Coast see DeVoto, *Course of Empire,* 348-55. See also Roy Daniells, *Alexander Mackenzie and the North West* (New York: Barnes and Noble, 1969), 104-60. More recent is James K. Smith, *Alexander Mackenzie, Explorer: The Hero Who Failed* (New York: McGraw Hill, Ryerson, 1973).

²¹Herman J. Deutsch, "The Evolution of the International Boundary in the Inland Empire of the Pacific Northwest," *Pacific Northwest Quarterly* 51 (April 1960), 64-68.

²²Charles Francis Adams, ed., *Memoirs of John Quincy Adams* (Philadelphia: J.B. Lippincott, 1874-1877), 6: 163; *American State Papers: Foreign Relations* (Washington, 1858), 5: 443, 445.

²³See Samuel Flagg Bemis, *John Quincy Adams and the Foundations of American Foreign Policy* (New York: Knopf, 1949), 514-15, 523-24.

²⁴Deutsch, "International Boundary of the Inland Empire," 64, 66-70; Norman A. Graebner, *Empire on the Pacific: A Study in American Continental Expansion* (New York: Ronald Press, 1955), 23-24.

²⁵Frederick Merk, *Albert Gallatin and the Oregon Problem: A Study in Anglo-American Diplomacy* (Cambridge: Harvard University Press, 1950), 67-69.

²⁶Canning to the Earl of Liverpool, June 24, July 7, 1826, Edward J. Stapleton, ed., *Some Official Correspondence of George Canning* (London: Longman's, Green, and Company, 1887), 2: 62, 74.

²⁷Graebner, *Empire on the Pacific,* 29-30; Merk, *Albert Gallatin and the Oregon Problem,* ·74-82.

²⁸Frederick Merk, "The Oregon Question and the Webster-Ashburton Negotiations," *Mississippi Valley Historical Review* 43 (December 1956): 379-404.

²⁹Charles Wilkes, *Narrative of the United States Exploring Expedition During the Years 1838, 1839, 1840, 1841, 1842* (Philadelphia: Printed by C. Sherman, 1845), 4: 293, 305.

³⁰Everett to Webster, October 19, November 2, 18, December 3, 1842, Despatches, Great Britain, Reel 45, 46, Vol. 49, 50, National Archives.

³¹Webster to Everett, November 28, 1842, Fletcher Webster, ed., *The Private Correspondence of Daniel Webster* (Boston: Little, Brown and Company, 1857), 2: 153-54. The role of the waterways in determining the minimum goals of American diplomacy in both Oregon and California during the 1840s is the central theme of Graebner, *Empire on the Pacific.*

³²Ibid., 154; Everett to Webster, January 2, February 21, 1843, Webster Papers, Reel 18, University Microfilms, Ann Arbor, Michigan, 1971.

³³*Cong. Globe,* 27 Cong., 3 Sess., XII, 33.

³⁴Ibid., 74; Webster to Everett, January 29, 1843, Webster Papers, Reel 18.

³⁵Aberdeen to Fox, February 3, 1843, Instructions to the British Minister, Foreign Office 115, Vol. 81, Public Record Office, London (Photostat, Division of Manuscripts, Library of Congress); *Cong. Globe,* 27 Cong., 3 Sess., XII, 240.

³⁶Daniel W. Howe, "The Mississippi Valley in the Movement for Fifty-Four Forty or Fight," *Proceedings of the Mississippi Valley Historical Association, 1911-1912* (Cedar Rapids, Iowa, 1912), 100-01.

³⁷Everett to Upshur, August 15, 17, 1843, Despatches, Great Britain, Reel 47, Vol. 51; Aberdeen to Fox, August 18, 1843, Instructions to the British Minister, F.O. 115, Vol. 81, Public Record Office.

[38]Upshur to Everett, October 9, 1843, Instructions, Great Britain, Reel 74, Vol. 15, National Archives; Everett to Upshur, November 14, December 2, 1843, Despatches, Great Britain, Reel 47, Vol. 51; Everett to Webster, December 28, 1843, Webster Papers, Reel 19.

[39]*Cong. Globe*, 28 Cong., 1 Sess., XIII, 6.

[40]Aberdeen to Pakenham, December 28, 1843, Instructions to the British Minister, F.O. 115, Vol. 83, Public Record Office.

[41]Richard K. Cralle, ed., *The Works of John C. Calhoun* (New York: Appleton, 1853-1855), 4: 238.

[42]Pakenham to Calhoun, August 22, 1844, Notes from the British Legation, Reel 22, Vol. 22, National Archives; Memorandum of a conference between Calhoun and Parkenham, August 23, 26, 1844, ibid.

[43]Pakenham to Calhoun, September 12, 1844; Memorandum of a conference between Calhoun and Pakenham, September 20, 1844, ibid.

[44]Memorandum of a conference between Calhoun and Pakenham, September 24, 1844, ibid.; Aberdeen to Peel, September 25, 1844, Robert C. Clark, ed., "Aberdeen and Peel on Oregon, 1844," *Oregon Historical Quarterly* 34 (September 1933): 237-38.

[45]Peel to Aberdeen, September 28, 1844, ibid., 238; Aberdeen to Peel, October 17, 22, 1844, ibid., 239-40.

[46]Calhoun to Pakenham, January 21, 1845, Notes to the British Legation, Reel 36, Vol. 7, National Archives.

[47]*Cong. Globe*, 28 Cong., 2 Sess., XIV, 400.

[48]For the British reaction see Frederick Merk, *The Oregon Question: Essays in Anglo-American Diplomacy and Politics* (Cambridge: Belknap Press of Harvard University Press, 1967), essay 10.

[49]Thomas Hart Benton, *Thirty Years' View* (New York: D. Appleton and Company, 1856), 2: 661; Robert L. Schuyler, "Polk and the Oregon Compromise," *Political Science Quarterly* 26 (September 1911): 446-47; Buchanan to Louis McLane, July 12, 1845, John Bassett Moore, ed., *The Works of James Buchanan* (Philadelphia: J.B. Lippincott, 1909), 6: 193-94.

[50]Milo Milton Quaife, ed., *The Diary of James K. Polk* (Chicago, 1910), 1: 4-5, 63, 75, 106-07.

[51]*Cong. Globe*, 29 Cong., 1 Sess., Appendix, XV, 3.

[52]Buchanan to McLane, July 12, 1845, Moore, *Works of James Buchanan*, 6: 190-91.

[53]*Cong. Globe*, 29 Cong., 1 Sess., Appendix, XV, 4; Quaife, *Diary of Polk*, 1: 135; Hunter Miller, ed., *Treaties and Other International Acts of the United States of America* (Washington: United States Government Printing Office, 1937), 5: 60.

[54]Buchanan to McLane, January 29, February 4, 26, 1846, Moore, *Works of James Buchanan*, 6: 367, 372, 377.

[55]Albert K. Weinberg, *Manifest Destiny: A Study of Nationalist Expansionism in American History* (Baltimore: Quadrangle Books, 1935), 145.

[56]*Cong. Globe*, 29 Cong. 1 Sess., XV, 134, 136, 200, 342; *United States Magazine and Democratic Review* 18 (February 1846): 93-94.

[57]Howe, "The Mississippi Valley in the Movement for Fifty-Four Forty or Fight," 104; *Cong. Globe*, 29 Cong., 1 Sess., XV, 249; Calhoun to Thomas G. Clemson, June 11, 1846, J. Franklin Jameson, ed., *The Correspondence of John C. Calhoun, Annual Report of the American Historical Association, 1899* (Washington: Government Printing Office, 1900), 2: 697.

[58]*Cong. Globe*, 29 Cong., 1 Sess., Appendix, XV, 117, 239.

[59]Ibid., 99.

[60]Sturgis to _____, June 6, 1845, Bancroft Papers, Massachusetts Historical Society; William Sturgis, *The Oregon Question: Substance of a Lecture Before the Mercantile Library Association, Delivered January 22, 1845* (Boston: Jordan, Swift and Wiley, 1845), 27-28.

[61]For those who pressed this argument see Albert Gallatin, *The Oregon Question*, included in Henry Adams, ed., *The Writings of Albert Gallatin* (Philadelphia: J.B. Lippincott, 1879), 3: 493-94; Sturgis, *The Oregon Question*, 25.

[62]*Cong. Globe*, 29 Cong., 1 Sess., Appendix, XV, 277.

[63]Ibid., 309-10.

[64]"The Oregon Question," *North American Review* 62 (January, 1846): 230, 234.

[65]Allan Nevins, ed., *The Diary of Philip Hone, 1828-1851* (New York: Dodd, Mead and Company, 1936), 751.

[66]See, for example, "A Democrat" to William Allen, January 10, 1846, William Allen Papers, Manuscript Division, Library of Congress. Similarly the *Louisville Journal* (14 January 1846) insisted that the Old Northwest did not favor the demands exerted by its leaders in Congress.

[67]Quaife, *Diary of Polk*, 1: 246; New York *Journal of Commerce*, quoted in the (St. Louis) *Missouri Reporter*, 9 January 1846.

[68]Buchanan to McLane, February 26, 1846, Miller, *Treaties*, 5: 60; New York *Herald,* January 4, April 6, 1846; Webster to Sears, January 17, 1846, Webster, *Private Correspondence of Daniel Webster*, 2: 215.

[69]Albert Gallup to Robert Walker, March 14, 1846, Robert Walker Papers, Manuscript Division, Library of Congress.

[70]Crittenden to Letcher, March 9, 1846, Chapman Coleman, *The Life of John J. Crittenden* (1871; reprint, New York: Da Capo Press, 1970), 1: 235.

[71]Frederick Merk, "The Oregon Pioneers and the Boundary," *American Historical Review* 29 (July 1924): 696. For similar conclusions see Melvin Jacobs, *Winning Oregon* (Caldwell, Idaho: Caxton, 1938), 219-20; Richard W. Van Alstyne, "International Rivalries in the Pacific Northwest," *Oregon Historical Quarterly* 46 (September 1945), 209; and Leslie M. Scott, "Influence of American Settlement upon the Oregon Boundary Treaty of 1846," ibid. 29 (March 1928): 1-19.

[72]Buchanan informed McLane in February that the administration would use this escape from its political dilemma. See Buchanan to McLane, February 26, 1846, Miller, *Treaties*, 5: 60.

[73]Webster and Pakenham quoted in ibid., 89, 90. See also Calhoun to Clemson, April 25, 1846, Jameson, *Correspondence of Calhoun*, 2: 689. Calhoun wrote: "This great change has been effected by the Senate against the entire influence of the Executive. . . ."

[74]Miller, *Treaties*, 5: 33, 59, 61, 63-66, 71, 77, 79-80.

[75]Frederick Merk, "British Government Propaganda and the Oregon Treaty," *American Historical Review* 40 (October 1934): 40-41, 51, 55-58, 61; *The Edinburgh Review* 82: 165 (July 1845): 263-64; *London Illustrated News*, 27 December 1845, 407; *Quarterly Review*, 77: 104 (March 1846): 564-65, 603.

[76]*Cong. Globe*, 29 Cong., 1 Sess., Appendix, XV, 867; New York *Herald*, 12 June 1846.

[1] See especially such Indian human rights cases as *Bender v. Wolff, Crane v. Erickson, Little Raven v. Crisp, Peck v. Meachum, Sequoyah v. Tennessee Valley Authority, Bear Ribs v. Taylor, Frease v. Griffith, Left Hand Bull v. Carlson, Ross v. Scurr. Marshno v. McManus,* and *Badoni v. Higginson,* as well as cases involving a Kootenai River (Montana) dam, a Jemez (New Mexico) geothermal power plant, a Point Conception (California) liquified natural gas terminal, and the return of a Zuñi sacred war god statue, all described in Native American Rights Fund, *Annual Reports* (Boulder, Colorado, 1977-1981).

[2] Subcommittee on Indian Affairs of the Senate Committee on Interior and Insular Affairs, Hearings on H.R. 3306, S. 1624, and 1625, 90th Cong., 2d sess., September 19-20, 1968, pp. 203-04, 220. Also see, Dean M. Kelley, "The Impairment of the Religious Liberty of the Taos Pueblo Indians by the United States Government," *A Journal of Church and State* 9 (Spring 1967): 1962.

[3] George Gibbs, *Indian Tribes of Washington Territory* (Fairfield, Wash.: Ye Galleon Press, 1978), 12.

[4] Federal Agencies Task Force, *American Indian Religious Freedom Act Report (P.L. 95-341)* (Washington, D.C., August, 1979), Appendix C.

[5] The cases denying Indian religious freedom claims were *Sequoyah v. TVA* and *Badoni v. Higginson.*

[6] There is an extensive anthropological literature on Indian religions. Three accessible summaries of Pacific Northwest religions are in Ruth Underhill, *Indians of the Pacific Northwest* (Washington, D.C.: Bureau of Indian Affairs, 1944); Philip Drucker, *Indians of the Northwest Coast* (New York: The American Museum of Natural History, 1963); and Hermann Haeberlin and Erna Gunther, *The Indians of Puget Sound* (Seattle: University of Washington Press, 1930). Other information can be found in such general works as James G. Swan, *The Northwest Coast* (New York: Harper & Brothers, 1857), and in more recent detailed studies as James A. Teit, *The Salishan Tribes of the Western Plateaus,* 45th Annual Report (Washington, D.C.: Bureau of American Ethnology, 1930); Leslie Spier, *The Prophet Dance of the Northwest and Its Derivates,* General Series in Anthropology 1 (Menasha, Wisc.: George Banta Pub., 1935); Marion W. Smith, *The Puyallup-Nisqually* (New York: Columbia University Press, 1940); Click Relander, *Drummers and Dreamers* (Caldwell, Idaho: Caxton Press, 1956); Deward E. Walker, *Indians of Idaho* (Moscow, Idaho: University of Idaho Press, 1978), and *Conflict and Schism in Nez Perce Acculturation* (Pullman, Wash.: Washington State University Press, 1968); and Theodore Stern, *The Klamath Tribe* (Seattle: University of Washington Press, 1966).

[7] "Journal of Alfred Seton," Sleepy Holly Restoration, Tarrytown, New York (unpublished manuscript), 175.

[8] Underhill, *Indians of the Pacific Northwest,* 16-17.

[9] Gibbs, *Indian Tribes of Washington Territory,* 9.

[10] Clifford M. Drury, *Chief Lawyer* (Glendale, Calif.: Arthur H. Clark, 1979), 268.

[11] Alvin M. Josephy, Jr., *The Nez Perce Indians and the Opening of the Northwest* (New Haven: Yale University Press, 1965), 325-26. Minutes of the council are in the L. V. McWhorter Manuscript Collection, Manuscripts, Archives and Special Collections, Washington State University Holland Library, Pullman, Washington.

[12] Josephy, *Nez Perce Indians and the Opening of the Northwest,* 326.

[13] James Mooney, "The Ghost Dance Religion" 14th Annual Report (Washington D.C.: Bureau of Ethnology, Smithsonian Institution, 1896), 721.

[14] Oliver O. Howard, *Nez Perce Joseph* (Boston, n.p., 1881), 64.

[15] "Chief Joseph's Own Story," *North American Review* (April 1879).

[16] Gibbs, *Indian Tribes of Washington Territory,* p. 34.

[17] Alvin M. Josephy, *Now That the Buffalo's Gone* (New York: Knopf, 1982), 129.

[1]Norman H. Clark, *The Dry Years: Prohibition and Social Change in Washington* (Seattle: University of Washington Press, 1965), *Mill Town: A Social History of Everett, Washington* . . . (Seattle: University of Washington Press, 1970), and *Washington: A Bicentennial History* (New York: W. W. Norton, 1976).

[2]Dorothy O. Johansen, *Empire of the Columbia: A History of the Pacific Northwest.* 2nd ed. (New York: Harper & Row, 1967); the first edition, published in 1957, was coauthored by Charles M. Gates.

[3]In addition to Clark, *Washington*, each of the following Bicentennial histories was published in New York by W. W. Norton with the subtitle, *A Bicentennial History*: Gordon B. Dodds, *Oregon*, (1977); F. Ross Peterson, *Idaho* (1976). An appraisal of these and other volumes is Earl Pomeroy, "Bicentennial Histories of the Far Western States: An Essay Review," *Pacific Northwest Quarterly* 73 (April 1982): 62-65.

[4]Allen Smith, "The Writing of British Columbia History," *B.C. Studies* 45 (Spring 1980): 73-102.

[5]Claus-M. Naske and Herman E. Slotnik, *Alaska: A History of the 49th State* (Grand Rapids: William B. Eerdmans, 1979); Claus-M. Naske, *An Interpretative History of Alaskan Statehood* (Anchorage: Alaska Northwest, 1973); John McPhee, *Coming into the Country* (New York: Farrar, Straus, and Giroux, 1977); Joe McGinnis, *Going to Extremes* (New York: Alfred A. Knopf, 1980).

[6]Carlos A. Schwantes, *Radical Heritage: Labor, Socialism, and Reform in Washington and British Columbia, 1885-1917* (Seattle: University of Washington Press, 1979); Richard White, *Land Use, Environment, and Social Change: The Shaping of Island County, Washington* (Seattle: University of Washington Press, 1980); Michael P. Malone, *The Battle for Butte: Mining and Politics on the Northern Frontier, 1864-1906* (Seattle: University of Washington Press, 1981).

[7]Michael K. Green, "A History of the Public Rural Electrification Movement in Washington to 1942" (Ph.D. dis., University of Idaho, 1967); Wesley Arden Dick, "Visions of Abundance: The Public Power Crusade in the Pacific Northwest in the Era of J. D. Ross and the New Deal" (Ph.D. dis., University of Washington, 1973); Peter K. Simpson, "A Social History of the Cattle Industry in Southeastern Oregon, 1869-1912" (Ph.D. dis., University of Oregon, 1973).

[8]Ivan Doig, *Winter Brothers: A Season at the Edge of America* (New York: Harcourt Brace Jovanovich, 1980).

[9]Recent general treatments of Pacific Northwest history include Raymond D. Gastil, "The Pacific Northwest as a Cultural Region," *Pacific Northwest Quarterly* 64 (October 1973): 147-56; Thomas Vaughan, ed., *The Western Shore*. . . (Portland: Oregon Historical Society, 1976); Edwin R. Bingham and Glen A. Love, eds., *Northwest Perspectives: Essays on the Culture of the Pacific Northwest* (Seattle: University of Washington Press, 1979); Kent D. Richards, "In Search of the Pacific Northwest: The Historiography of Oregon and Washington," *Pacific Historical Review* 50 (November 1981): 415-43; and Williams G. Robbins, Robert J. Frank, and Richard E. Ross, eds., *Regionalism and the Pacific Northwest* (Corvallis: Oregon State University Press, 1983).

[10]I treat the New Regionalism and the Old Regionalism at much greater length in "The New Regionalism in America, 1970-1981," in Robbins, Frank, and Ross, eds., *Regionalism and the Pacific Northwest*, 37-96.

[11]On Odum and his institute: Guy Benton Johnson and Guion Griffis Johnson, *Research in Service of Society: The First Fifty Years of the Institute for Research in Social Science at the University of North Carolina* (Chapel Hill: University of North Carolina Press, 1980). The conflicting Chapel Hill and Nashville movements of regionalism are well but differently treated in Michael O'Brien, *The Idea of the American South, 1920-1941* (Baltimore: Johns Hopkins University Press, 1979), and Richard H. King, *A Southern Renaissance: The Cultural Awakening of the American South, 1930-1955* (New York: Oxford University Press, 1980).

[12]Among the many books by the two Texans in the 1930s and 1940s were: J. Frank Dobie, *Coronado's Children* (New York: Literary Guild, 1931), and *The Longhorns* (Boston: Little, Brown, 1941); Walter Prescott Webb, *The Great Plains* (Boston: Ginn, 1931), and *Divided We Stand* (New York: Farrar and Rinehart, 1937); James C. Malin's two most significant books were *Winter Wheat in the Golden Belt of Kansas* (Lawrence: University of Kansas Press, 1944) and *The Grassland of North America* (Lawrence: privately published, 1947).

[13]Faulkner and Wolfe are perceptively treated in the context of regionalism in King, *Southern Renaissance*. Emphasizing Steinbeck's regional background is Nelson Valjean, *John Steinbeck . . . An Intimate Biography of His California Years* (San Francisco: Chronicle Books, 1975). On Benton, Curry, and Wood: Matthew Baigell, *The American Scene: American Painting of the 1930s* (New York: Praeger, 1974). On documentary photography: William Stott, *Documentary Expression and Thirties America* (New York: Oxford University Press, 1973).

[14]Jerre Mangione, *The Dream and the Deal: The Federal Writers' Project, 1935-1943* (Boston: Little, Brown, 1972); Monty Noam Penkower, *The Federal Writers' Project* (Urbana: University of Illinois Press, 1977). Richard D. McKinzie, *The New Deal for Artists* (Princeton: Princeton University Press, 1967), treats the Federal Art Project that produced the post office murals.

[15]H. L. Davis, *Honey in the Horn* (New York: Harper, 1935); Stewart H. Holbrook, *Holy Old Mackinaw: A Natural History of the American Lumberjack* (New York: Macmillan, 1938), and *Burning an Empire: The Story of American Forest Fires* (New York: Macmillan, 1943); Richard L. Neuberger, *Our Promised Land* (New York: Macmillan, 1938).

[16]James Agee and Walker Evans, *Let Us Now Praise Famous Men* (Boston: Little, Brown, 1941); Warren I. Susman, "The Thirties," in Stanley Coben and Lorman Ratner, eds., *The Development of an American Culture* (Englewood Cliffs: Prentice-Hall, 1970), 217; `Stott, *Documentary Expression,* x and chaps. 14-15.

[17]Merrill Jensen, ed., *Regionalism in America* (Madison: University of Wisconsin Press, 1951), is, in effect, an intellectual epitaph for the Old Regionalism of the 1930s and 1940s. Although eclipsed in the 1950s and 1960s, regionalism did not die as the remarkable creative efforts of C. Vann Woodward, Earl Pomeroy, Wallace Stegner, and A. B. Guthrie (to name only a few) attest. Of great importance also was Bernard DeVoto, who published the last volume, *The Course of Empire* (Boston: Little, Brown), of his Far West trilogy in 1952. The survival of regionalism in the 1950s and 1960s is worthy of a separate paper. For the Old Regionalism, see, also, Cornelius H. Sullivan, "Regionalism in American Thought: Provincial Ideas From the Gilded Age to the Great Depression" (Ph.D. dis., University of Chicago, 1977).

[18]John Shelton Reed, *The Enduring South: Subcultural Persistence in Mass Society* (Lexington, Mass.: D.C. Heath, 1972); Raymond D. Gastil, *Cultural Regions of the United States* (Seattle: University of Washington Press, 1975).

[19]Nathan Weinberg, *Preservation in American Towns and Cities* (Boulder: Westview, 1979). *Historic Preservation* (1949-) is a significant journal documenting that movement.

[20]See the new journal, *The Public Historian* (1978-).

[21]James Morton Smith, general editor, *The States and the Nation Series* (50 vols.: New York: W. W. Norton, 1976-1981).

[22]On the *American Guide Series* of the 1930s and 1940s: Mangione, *Dream and Deal*; Penkower, *Federal Writers' Project.*

[23]Receiving support from the Oregon Committee for the Humanities were two stunning documentary films by Ron Finne, *Natural Timber Country* (1972) and *Tamanawis Illahee* (1982), dealing with Pacific Northwest history and culture.

²⁴Published in New York by Oxford University Press. Treating the South are two other outstanding examples of regional cultural and intellectual history: O'Brien, *Idea of American South*, and King, *Southern Renaissance*.

²⁵Published in New York by Harcourt Brace Jovanovich.

²⁶Published in Chicago by the University of Chicago Press.

²⁷Jane Kramer, *The Last Cowboy* (New York: Harper & Row, 1977); Rob Schultheis, *The Hidden West: Journeys in the American Outback* (New York: Random House, 1982).

²⁸Wallace Stegner's recent works include four books (three novels and a biography) all published in Garden City, New York, by Doubleday: *Angle of Repose* (1971), *The Spectator Bird* (1976), *Recapitulation* (1979), and *The Uneasy Chair: A Biography of Bernard DeVoto* (1974). Wright Morris's most recent books include a novel, *Plain Song* (New York: Harper & Row, 1980), and a memoir, *Will's Boy* (New York: Harper & Row, 1981); Ken Kesey, *Sometimes a Great Notion* (New York: Viking, 1964). Published in New York by Simon and Schuster was Larry McMurtry's fictional trilogy of the modern urban West, *Moving On* (1970), *All My Friends Are Going to be Strangers* (1972), and *Terms of Endearment* (1975); notable, also, is McMurtry's earlier collection, *In a Narrow Grave: Essays on Texas* (Austin: Encino, 1968). John Nichols's New Mexico fictional trilogy (all published in New York by Holt, Rinehart and Winston), *The Milagro Bean Field War* (1974), *The Magic Journey* (1978), and *The Nirvana Blues* (1981), is complemented by *If Mountains Die: A New Mexico Memoir* (New York: Alfred A. Knopf, 1980), with text by John Nichols and photographs by William Davis. Ivan Doig has produced two novels (both published in New York by Atheneum), *The Sea Runners* (1982) and *English Creek* (1984), and a biography, *Winter Brothers* (New York: Harcourt Brace Jovanovich, 1980). Joan Didion's recent books (both published in New York by Simon and Schuster) include a novel, *A Book of Common Prayer* (1977), and her reportage of the 1960s and 1970s, *The White Album* (1979). Recent publications by the poets include William Stafford, *Stories That Could Be: New and Collected Poems* (New York: Harper & Row, 1977); Richard Hugo, *31 Letters and 13 Dreams: Poems* (1977) and *The Triggering Town: Lectures and Essays on Poetry and Writing* (1979)—both published in New York by W. W. Norton; Gary Snyder, *Turtle Island* (New York: New Directions, 1974).

²⁹Michael Kammen, ed., *The Past Before Us: Contemporary Historical Writing in the United States* (Ithaca: Cornell University Press, 1980). Supplementing *The Past Before Us* are the essays on "The New History: The 1980s and Beyond," in *The Journal of Interdisciplinary History* 12 (Summer and Autumn 1981).

³⁰Editor Kammen assigned an essay on the new economic history, but the unnamed author failed to provide it. Kammen, *Past Before Us*, 9.

³¹Bingham and Love, eds., *Northwest Perspectives*; Roger Sale, *Seattle: Past to Present* (Seattle: University of Washington Press, 1976). See, also, Robbins, Frank, and Ross, eds., *Regionalism and Pacific Northwest*.

³²Originally published in New York by Viking in 1960, 1962, and 1963, respectively, *Trask, Moontrap*, and *To Build a Ship* were all reprinted in 1977 in Sausalito, California, by Comstock.

³³Robin Skelton, ed., *Five Poets of the Pacific Northwest* (Seattle: University of Washington Press, 1968), presents the poetry of Kenneth O. Hanson, Richard Hugo, Carolyn Kizer, William Stafford, and David Wagoner. See also Allan Seager, *The Glass House: The Life of Theodore Roethke* (New York: McGraw-Hill, 1968); Kermit Vanderbilt, "Theodore Roethke as a Northwest Poet," 187-216, in Bingham and Love, eds., *Northwest Perspectives*.

³⁴For example, art critic Mark Stevens in *Newsweek*, August 3, 1981, 73. A convenient collection of reproductions including those of Mark Toby, Morris Graves, Kenneth Callahan, and Guy Anderson is Puget Sound Group of Northwest Painters, Inc., *The Puget Sound Group of Northwest Painters: First Fifty Years: 1928-1978* (Seattle: Puget Sound Group of Painters, Inc., 1979). The Oregon painter, C. S. Price, is treated in Edwin R. Bingham,

"A Contour of Culture in the Pacific Northwest: C.S. Price, Richard Hugo, and Ken Kesey" (unpublished paper, University of Oregon, 1979).

[35]Thomas Vaughan and Virginia Guest Ferriday, eds., *Space, Style, and Structure: Building in Northwest America*, 2 vols. (Portland: Oregon Historical Society, 1974).

[36]Barry Halston Lopez, *Of Wolves and Men* (New York: Charles Scribner's Sons, 1978).

[37]Oscar Osburn Winther, *The Great Northwest: A History,* 2nd ed. (New York: Alfred A. Knopf, 1952); Earl Pomeroy, *The Pacific Slope: A History of California, Oregon, Washington, Utah, and Nevada* (New York: Alfred A. Knopf, 1965); Johansen and Gates, *Empire on the Columbia.*

[38]Frederick C. Luebke, *Immigrants and Politics: The Germans of Nebraska, 1880-1900* (Lincoln: University of Nebraska Press, 1969); Ronald P. Formisano, *The Birth of Mass Political Parties: Michigan 1827-1861* (Princeton: Princeton University Press, 1971); Richard J. Jensen, *The Winning of the Midwest: Social and Political Conflict, 1888-1896* (Chicago: University of Chicago Press, 1971); Paul Kleppner, *The Cross of Culture: A Social Analysis of Midwestern Politics, 1850-1900* (New York: Free Press, 1970); J. Morgan Kousser, *The Shaping of Southern Politics: Suffrage Restriction and the Establishment of the One-Party South, 1880-1910* (New Haven: Yale University Press, 1974).

[39]Some of the leading studies are Robert D. Saltvig, "The Progressive Movement in Washington" (Ph.D. dis., University of Washington, 1966); Thomas C. McClintock, "J. Allen Smith and the Progressive Movement" (Ph.D. dis., University of Washington, 1959); Warren M. Blankenship, "Progressives and the Progressive Party in Oregon, 1906-1916" (Ph.D. dis., University of Oregon, 1966); Robert C. Woodward, "William Simon U'Ren" (M.A. thesis, University of Oregon, 1949).

[40]Michael P. Malone and Dianne C. Dougherty, "The Montana Political Culture: A Century of Evolution"; R.H. Limbaugh, "Territorial Elites and Political Power Struggles in the Far West, 1865-1890."

[41]Douglass C. North, *The Economic Growth of the United States: 1780 to 1860* (Englewood Cliffs: Prentice-Hall, 1961), was a pioneering work of scholarship. James N. Tattersall, "The Economic Development of the Pacific Northwest to 1920" (Ph.D. dis., University of Washington, 1960).

[42]Robert C. Nesbit, *"He Built Seattle": A Biography of Judge Thomas Burke* (Seattle: University of Washington Press, 1961); Albro Martin, *James J. Hill and the Opening of the Northwest* (New York: Oxford University Press, 1976) — for a critique of this book see the review by Edwin R. Bingham in *Canadian Journal of History* 13 (April 1978): 138-40; Ralph W. Hidy et al., *Timber and Men: The Weyerhaeuser Story* (New York: Macmillan, 1963); Edwin T. Coman, Jr., and Helen M. Gibbs, *Time, Tide and Timber: A Century of Pope & Talbot* (Stanford: Stanford University Press, 1949) — with a revised edition published by Pope & Talbot in Portland, Oregon, 1978; Robert E. Ficken, *Lumber and Politics: The Career of Mark E. Reed* (Seattle: University of Washington Press, 1979); Keith C. Petersen, *Company Town: Potlatch Idaho and the Potlatch Lumber Company,* (Pullman, Wash.: Washington State University Press, 1987). See also George David Smith and Laurence E. Steadman, "The Value of Corporate History," *Journal of Forest History* 26 (January 1982): 34-40, followed on pp. 40-41, by a checklist of company histories of selected firms including many in the Pacific Northwest.

[43]Gordon B. Dodds, *The Salmon King of Oregon: R. D. Hume and the Pacific Fisheries* (Chapel Hill: University of North Carolina Press, 1959); John Newhouse, *The Sporty Game* (New York: Alfred A. Knopf, 1982).

[44]Stephan Thernstrom, *Poverty and Progress: Social Mobility in a Nineteenth Century City* (Cambridge: Harvard University Press, 1964).

[45]William G. Robbins, "Opportunity and Persistence in the Pacific Northwest: A Quantitative Study of Early Roseburg, Oregon," *Pacific Historical Review* 39 (August 1970): 279-96, and "Social and Economic Change in Roseburg, Oregon, 1850-1885: A Quantitative

View," *Pacific Northwest Quarterly* 64 (April 1973): 80-87; Janice L. Reiff, "Urbanization and the Social Structure: Seattle, Washington, 1852-1910" (Ph.D. dis., University of Washington, 1981); William H. Mullins, "San Francisco and Seattle during the Hoover Years of the Depression" (Ph.D. dis., University of Washington, 1975); see also Alexander Norbert MacDonald, "Seattle's Economic Development" (Ph.D. dis., University of Washington, 1959). A significant comparative study is Rodman W. Paul, "After the Gold Rush: San Francisco and Portland," *Pacific Historical Review* 51 (February 1982): 1-21.

[46]Sale, *Seattle*; Clark, *Mill Town*. There is no space here for a full canvas of the growing urban history of the Pacific Northwest, but among newer works are the following books by Carl Abbott and E. Kimbark MacColl on Portland, Murray Morgan on Tacoma, and Paul Loeb on the atomic Tri-Cities of Richland, Kennewick, and Pasco: Carl Abbott, *The Great Extravaganza: Portland and the Lewis and Clark Exposition* (Portland: Oregon Historical Society, 1982); E. Kimbark MacColl, *The Shaping of a City: Business and Politics in Portland, Oregon, 1885-1915* (1976), and *The Growth of a City: Power and Politics in Portland, Oregon, 1915-1950* (1979), both published in Portland by Georgian Press; Murray Morgan, *Puget's Sound: A Narrative of Tacoma and the Southern Sound* (Seattle: University of Washington Press, 1979); Paul Loeb, *Nuclear Culture: Living and Working in the World's Largest Atomic Complex* (New York: Coward, McCann & Geoghegan, 1982).

[47]James T. Lemon, *The Best Poor Man's Country: A Geographical Study of Early Southeastern Pennsylvania* (Baltimore: Johns Hopkins University Press, 1972).

[48]William A. Bowen, *The Willamette Valley: Migration and Settlement on the Oregon Frontier* (Seattle: University of Washington Press, 1978); Samuel N. and Emily F. Dicken, *The Making of Oregon: A Study in Historical Geography* (Portland: Oregon Historical Society, 1979); Donald W. Meinig, *The Great Columbia Plain: A Historical Geography, 1805-1910* (Seattle: University of Washington Press, 1968). A remarkable piece of scholarship is William G. Loy et al., *Atlas of Oregon* (Eugene: University of Oregon Books, 1976).

[49]Paul George Hummasti, *Finnish Radicals in Astoria, Oregon, 1904-1940: A Study in Immigrant Socialism* (New York: Arno, 1979); Kenneth O. Bjork, *West of the Great Divide: Norwegian Migration to the Pacific Coast, 1847-1893* (Northfield: Norwegian-American Historical Association, 1958); Erasmo Gamboa, "Mexican Migration into Washington State. . .1940-1950," *Pacific Northwest Quarterly* 72 (July 1981): 121-31.

[50]Ruth B. Moynihan, *Rebel for Rights: Abigail Scott Duniway* (New Haven: Yale University Press, 1983); Margaret N. Haines, "Women in Jackson County, Oregon, 1875-1885: A Group Portrait" (M.A. thesis, University of Oregon, 1980); *Montana*, 32 (Summer 1982).

[51]Vernon H. Jensen, *Lumber and Labor* (New York: Farrar and Rinehart, 1945); Harold M. Hyman, *Soldiers and Spruce: Origins of the Loyal Legion of Loggers and Lumbermen* (Los Angeles: Institute of Industrial Relations, 1963); Robert L. Friedheim, *The Seattle General Strike* (Seattle: University of Washington Press, 1964); Robert L. Tyler, *Rebels of the Woods: The I.W.W. in the Pacific Northwest* (Eugene: University of Oregon Books, 1967); Clark, *Mill Town*; Schwantes, *Radical Heritage*.

[52]The contributions of Thompson, Gutman, Montgomery, and Brody are treated in David Brody, "Labor History in the 1970s: Toward a History of the American Worker," 252-69, in Kammen, ed., *Past Before Us*.

[53]Carlos A. Schwantes, "The Pacific Northwest Working Class and Its Institutions."

[54]Vaughan and Ferriday, eds., *Space, Style, and Structure*; Bingham and Love, eds., *Northwest Perspectives*.

[55]White, *Land Use*; Malin, *Winter Wheat* and *Grassland*.

[56]Stephen Dow Beckham, *Requiem for a People: The Rogue Indians and the Frontiersmen* (Norman: University of Oklahoma Press, 1971); Theodore Stern, *The Klamath Tribe* (Seattle: University of Washington Press, 1965); Philip Drucker, *Indians of the Northwest* (New York: McGraw-Hill, 1955), and *Cultures of the North Pacific Coast* (San Francisco: Chandler, 1965); Keith A. Murray, *The Modocs and Their War* (Norman: University of Oklahoma Press, 1959).

57Bernard Bailyn, "The Challenge of Modern Historiography," *American Historical Review* 87 (February 1982): 1-24.

58Webb, *Great Plains*; Gregory M. Tobin, *The Making of a History: Walter Prescott Webb and "The Great Plains"* (Austin: University of Texas Press, 1976).

59*Pacific Northwest Quarterly* 64 (October 1973): 157.

60*West Shore*, February 1880, 57, 13 September 1890, 80. Portland *Morning Oregonian*, 17 April 1889, 8. Obviously, the old saying applied only to Oregon west of the Cascades.

61My concepts of the precipitation salient and the 60-inch rainfall line are based on material in the following works: Richard M. Highsmith and A. Jon Kimerling, eds., *Atlas of the Pacific Northwest*, 6th ed. (Corvallis: Oregon State University Press, 1979); David W. Baker, "The Climate of the Willamette Valley, 1900-1953" (M.A. thesis, Oregon State University, 1955); Loy et al., *Atlas of Oregon*; Albert L. Farley, ed., *Atlas of British Columbia: People, Environment, and Resource Use* (Vancouver: University of British Columbia Press, 1979); Arch Clive Gerlach, "Precipitation of Western Washington," 2 vols. (Ph.D. dis., University of Washington, 1943); John Clinton Sherman, "The Precipitation of Eastern Washington," 2 vols. (Ph.D. dis., University of Washington, 1947); Robert DeC. Ward et al., *The Climates of North America*, in W. Koppen and R. Geiger, eds., *Handbuch der Klimatologie*, Band II, Teil J. (Berlin: Verlag von Gebruder Borntraeger, 1936).

62Wilson Duff, *The Indians of British Columbia* (Victoria: Provincial Museum of Northwest History and Anthropology, 1965); Tom McFeat, ed., *Indians of the North Pacific Coast* (Seattle: University of Washington Press, 1967).

63Holbrook, *Holy Old Mackinaw*; White, *Land Use*; Finne, *Natural Timber Country*. General studies of the Pacific Northwest lumber industry, in addition to works already cited in these notes, include: Edmond S. Meany, Jr., "The History of the Lumber Industry in the Pacific Northwest to 1917" (Ph.D. dis., Harvard University, 1935); Thomas R. Cox, *Mills and Markets: A History of the Pacific Coast Lumber Industry to 1900* (Seattle: University of Washington Press, 1974); William G. Robbins, *Lumberjacks and Legislators: Political Economy of the U.S. Lumber Industry, 1890-1941* (College Station: Texas A & M Press, 1982). Two outstanding brief essays are Thomas R. Cox, "Lumber Industry" and "Lumberjack," 685-92, in Howard R. Lamar, ed., *The Reader's Encyclopedia of the American West* (New York: Thomas Y. Crowell, 1977).

64Dick, "Visions of Abundance." Green, "Rural Electrification"; Kai N. Lee et al., *Electric Power and the Future of the Pacific Northwest* (Seattle: University of Washington Press, 1980). There is as yet no thorough study of the Washington Public Power Supply System's ill-fated venture into nuclear-power generated electricity, which is jeopardizing the region's low electric rates based on hydroelectric power.

65Elmo Richardson, *David T. Mason: Forestry Advocate* (Santa Cruz: Forest Historical Society, 1983).

66See the sources cited in note 64, above.

67James Stevens, *Big Jim Turner: A Novel* (New York: Charles Scribner's Sons, 1944); Archie Binns, *The Timber Beast* (Garden City: Doubleday, 1948); Robert Cantwell, *The Land of Plenty* (New York: Farrar & Rinehart, 1934); Kesey, *Sometimes a Great Notion*.

68See the work of Mark Toby, Morris Graves, Kenneth Callahan, and Guy Anderson reproduced in Northwest Painters, *Puget Sound Group*, and the characterizations of the paintings by the members of this school by Mark Stevens in *Newsweek*, 3 August 1981, 73, and by the art critic and novelist, Tom Robbins, in his *Another Roadside Attraction* (New York: Ballantine, 1972), 57.

69Among nature-oriented writers of fiction are H. L. Davis, Don Berry, Ken Kesey, and Tom Robbins; nature-oriented poets include H. L. Davis, William Stafford, Theodore Roethke, and Gary Snyder. Brown, "New Regionalism," 49-53; George Venn, "Continuity in Northwest Literature," 103-17, in Bingham and Love, eds., *Northwest Perspectives*.

[70]Vaughan and Ferriday, eds., *Space, Style, and Structure*, 1: 83-85, 219-22; 2: 476, 631-32, 644-46; Richard V. Francaviglia, "Western American Barns: Architectural Form and Climatic Considerations," Association of Pacific Coast Geographers, *Yearbook* 34 (1972): 156-57, 159.

[71]Dodds, *Oregon*, 185, 226-28, whose generalizations about Oregon seem to me to apply to the region as a whole.

[72]Richard Maxwell Brown, "Rainfall and History: Perspectives on the Pacific Northwest," in G. Thomas Edwards and Carlos A. Schwantes, eds., *Experiences in a Promised Land: Essays in Pacific Northwest History* (Seattle: University of Washington Press, 1986).

[73]Dodds, *Oregon*, 42; Clark, *Washington*, 61; Winther, *Great Northwest*, dedication.

[74]John Rawls, *A Theory of Justice* (Cambridge: Harvard University Press, 1971), 178-79, 426, 441-42, 587, and *passim*. For calling my attention to Rawls's concept of the self-respecting person and suggesting its applicability to our community of Eugene, Oregon, and ultimately to our region as a whole, I am indebted to Mr. Dennis Snook.

[1]For a discussion of America's Oceanic Empire see Jack E. Eblen, *The First and Second United States Empires: Governors and Territorial Government, 1784-1912* (Pittsburgh: University of Pittsburgh Press, 1968), 8-9. See also, Richard W. Van Alstyne, *The Rising American Empire* (New York: Oxford University Press, 1960), and Alpheus H. Snow, *The Administration of Dependencies: A Study of the Evolution of the Federal Empire, With Special Reference to American Colonial Problems* (New York: G. P. Putnam's Sons, 1902).

[2]Alaska Statehood Commission, *More Perfect Union: A Preliminary Report* (Fairbanks, Ala., January 19, 1981), 2-6.

[3]*United States Statutes at Large,* Vol. 94 (1980), 2371.

[4]Richard A. Cooley, *Politics and Conservations: The Decline of The Alaskan Salmon* (New York: Harper & Row, 1963).

[5]For a general discussion of this topic see Ted C. Hinckley, *The Americanization of Alaska, 1867-1897* (Palo Alto, Calif.: Pacific Books, 1972), and Stuart Ramsey Tompkins, *Alaska: Promyshlennik and Sourdough* (Norman, Okla.: University of Oklahoma Press, 1945).

[6]Claus-M. Naske and Herman E. Slotnick, *Alaska: A History of the 49th State* (Grand Rapids: William B. Eerdmans Publishing Co., 1979), 5-6.

[7]Stanley R. Remsberg, "United States Administration of Alaska: The Army Phase, 1867-77: A Study in Federal Governance of an Overseas Possession" (Ph.D. dis., University of Wisconsin, Madison, 1975), 416-29.

[8]Hinckley, *Americanization of Alaska,* 22-49.

[9]Ibid., 49-52.

[10]Ernest Gruening, *The State of Alaska* (New York: Random House, 1968), 52.

[11]*United States Statutes at Large,* Vol. 23 (1884), 24.

[12]Ibid.

[13]Ernest Gruening, "Let Us End American Colonialism," November 9, 1955, 1-7, pamphlet in my files.

[14]Jeannette Paddock Nichols, *Alaska: A History of Its Administration, Exploitation, and Industrial Development During Its First Half-Century Under the Rule of the United States* (New York: Russell & Russell, 1963), 12; Earl S. Pomeroy, *The Territories and the United States, 1861-1890: Studies in Colonial Administration* (Seattle: University of Washington Press, 1969), 2; Eblen, *First and Second United States Empires,* 151.

[15]Gruening, "Let Us End American Colonialism," 7-9.

[16]William H. Dall, "Is Alaska a Paying Investment?" *Harper's Monthly,* January 1872, 257; Roy Robbins, "Preemption — A Frontier Triumph," *Mississippi Valley Historical Review* 18 (December 1931): 349.

[17]*Annual Report of the Governor of Alaska* (1898), 198-99; (1901), 10-11, (1899), 38.

[18]University of Wisconsin School of Natural Resources, *Federal Land Laws and Policies in Alaska: A Summary of Issues and Alternatives,* for the Public Land Law Review Commission, April 1969, 57-67.

[19]George W. Rogers, *The Future of Alaska: Economic Consequences of Statehood* (Baltimore: Johns Hopkins University Press, 1962), 17; Notes of Oscar L. Chapman of Conference on May 1, 1944, Office Files of Secretary of the Interior Oscar L. Chapman, Box 1, folder Alaska, Record Group 48, National Archives.

[20]Nichols, *Alaska,* 343-44; Robert M. La Follette, *La Follette's Autobiography: A Personal Narrative of Political Experiences* (Madison: Robert M. La Follette Co., 1913), 380; Theodore Roosevelt to Ethan A. Hitchcock, December 13, 1906, in *The Letters of Theodore Roosevelt,* ed. Elting E. Morison et al. (Cambridge: Harvard University Press, 1952), 6: 525.

[21]Franklin Ward Burch, "Alaska's Railroad Frontier: Railroads and Federal Development Policy, 1898-1915" (Ph.D. dis., Catholic University of America, 1965), 308-09.

[22]William H. Wilson, *Railroad in the Clouds: The Alaska Railroad in the Age of Steam, 1914-1945* (Boulder, Colo.: Pruett Publishing Co., 1977), 16-31; Hugh A. Johnson and Harold T. Jorgenson, *The Land Resources of Alaska* (New York: University Publishers, 1963), 262.

[23]Claus-M. Naske, *The Board of Road Commissioners for Alaska, 1905-1917* (Anchorage: Arctic Environmental Information and Data Center, 1980), 12-46.

[24]Wilson, *Railroad in the Clouds*, 4; Naske and Slotnick, *Alaska*, 82-83.

[25]Ibid., 99-100, 125.

[26]The information for this section on salmon fisheries is taken from Cooley, *Politics and Conservation*, 24-26, 76-80, 90-97.

[27]Ibid., 52, 96-98; Claus-M. Naske, *An Interpretative History of Alaskan Statehood* (Anchorage: Alaska Northwest Publishing Company, 1973), 163; Rogers, *Future of Alaska*, 179.

[28]Constitution of the State of Alaska, Ordinance No. 3.

[29]Rogers, *Future of Alaska*, 179.

[30]Ibid.

[31]Naske and Slotnick, *Alaska*, 204-05.

[32]Ibid., 211-12.

[33]Ibid., 221-22, 237.

[34]*Alaska Out of Doors*, October, 1979.

[35]Naske and Slotnick, *Alaska*, 193.

[36]Ibid., 193-94.

[37]Naske, *Alaskan Statehood*, 48-51.

[38]*United States Statutes at Large*, Vol. 94 (1980), 2371.

[39]Ibid.

[40]Alaska Statehood Commission, *More Perfect Union: A Preliminary Report*, 1.

[1]Carl L. Becker, *The History of Political Parties in the Province of New York, 1760-1776* (Madison: University of Wisconsin, 1909), 22.

[2]*Owyhee Daily Avalanche* (Silver City, Idaho), 22 December 1875; *Idaho Tri-Weekly Statesman* (Boise), 23 February 1878.

[3]Frederick Jackson Turner, "The Significance of the Frontier in American History," quoted in Ray Allen Billington, ed., *The Frontier Thesis* (New York: Holt, Rinehart and Winston, 1966), 16.

[4]Harold D. Lasswell and Abraham Kaplan, *Power and Society: A Framework for Political Inquiry* (New Haven: Yale University Press, 1950), 75.

[5]David M. Ricci, "Democracy Attenuated: Schumpeter, the Process Theory, and American Democratic Thought," *Journal of Politics* 32 (May 1970): 242-246; Samuel H. Beer, "Federalism, Nationalism and Democracy in America," *American Political Science Review* 72 (March 1979): 10-14; Howard R. Lamar, *The Far Southwest, 1846-1912: A Territorial History* (New Haven: Yale University Press, 1966), 10-16.

[6]Madison recognized and attempted to reconcile the apparent contradiction between factional practices and majoritarian principles in the 10th Federalist. For an analysis see Douglass Adair, " 'That Politics May be Reduced to a Science': David Hume, James Madison and the Tenth Federalist," *Huntington Library Quarterly* 20 (1957): 343-360. See also Jack P. Greene, ed., *The Reinterpretation of the American Revolution, 1763-1789* (New York: Harper & Row, 1968), 27-31; Kenneth Prewitt and Alan Stone, *The Ruling Elites: Elite Theory, Power and American Democracy* (New York: Harper & Row, 1973), 31-52.

[7]Peter Bachrach, *The Theory of Democratic Elitism: A Critique* (Boston: Little, Brown, 1967), 10-17.

[8]Joseph A. Schumpeter, *Capitalism, Socialism and Democracy*. 3rd ed. (New York: Harper & Row, 1976, 1950), 284-285.

[9]Bachrach, *Theory of Democratic Elitism*, 7.

[10]Ibid., 26-36.

[11]Ibid., 75-88.

[12]C. Wright Mills, *The Power Elite* (New York: Oxford University Press, 1956).

[13]David Riesman et al., *The Lonely Crowd* (New Haven: Yale University Press, 1950). For a comparison of the Mills and Riesman theses, see William Kornhauser, "Power Elites or Veto Groups," in Seymour Martin Lipset and Leo Lowenthal, eds., *Culture and Social Character: The Work of David Riesman Reviewed* (New York: Free Press of Glencoe, Inc., 1961), 252-267.

[14]William A. Kelso, *American Democratic Theory: Pluralism and its Critics* (Westport: Greenwood Press, 1978), 147-148.

[15]Lamar, *The Far Southwest*, 146-170, 126-289, 443-459. See also his "Political Patterns in New Mexico and Utah Territories, 1850-1900," *Utah Historical Quarterly* 28 (October 1960): 363-387.

[16]Kent D. Richards, "The American Colonial System In Nevada," *Nevada Historical Society Quarterly* 13 (Spring 1970): 29-38.

[17]James Bryce, *The American Commonwealth*, 2nd ed., revised (New York: Commonwealth Publication, Co., 1908), 2: 628-629.

[18]Lewis L. Gould, *Wyoming: A Political History, 1868-1896* (New Haven: Yale University Press, 1968), 106-268.

[19]Kenneth N. Owens, "Frontier Governors: A Study of the Territorial Executives in the History of Idaho, Montana, Wyoming, and Dakota Territories" (unpublished Ph.D. dis., University of Minnesota, 1959), 171-75, 222-24, 347-50.

[20]Clark C. Spence, *Territorial Politics and Government in Montana, 1864-1889* (Urbana:

²¹William E. Foley, "The American Territorial System: Missouri's Experience," *Missouri Historical Review* 65 (July 1971): 415-21.

²²Merrill D. Beal and Merle W. Wells, *History of Idaho* (New York: Lewis Historical Publication, Co., 1959), 1: 582-96. See also R. H. Limbaugh, "The Idaho Spoilsmen: Federal Administrators and Idaho Territorial Politics, 1863-1890" (unpublished Ph.D. dis., University of Idaho, 1966), 180-97.

²³Limbaugh, "The Idaho Spoilsmen," especially chapters eight and nine.

²⁴Robert W. Johannsen, *Stephen A. Douglas* (New York: Oxford University Press, 1973).

²⁵George M. Dennison, "An Empire of Liberty: Congressional Attitudes Toward Popular Sovereignty in the Territories, 1787-1867," *Maryland Historian* 6 (Spring 1975): 19-40.

²⁶Johannsen, *Frontier Politics and the Sectional Conflict: The Pacific Northwest on the Eve of the Civil War* (Seattle: University of Washington Press, 1955), 131-51.

²⁷Lamar, "Political Patterns in New Mexico and Utah Territories," 387.

²⁸William N. Neil, "The American Territorial System Since the Civil War: A Summary Analysis," *Indiana Magazine of History* 60 (September 1964): 235.

²⁹Kenneth N. Owens, "Pattern and Structure in Western Territorial Politics," *Western Historical Quarterly* 1 (October 1970): 373-92.

³⁰Lamar, "Carpetbaggers Full of Dreams: a Functional View of the Arizona Pioneer Politician," *Arizona and the West* 7 (1956): 187-206.

³¹Paul Kleppner, *The Third Electoral System, 1853-1892: Parties, Voters and Political Cultures* (Chapel Hill: University of North Carolina, 1979), 143.

³²Public land offices were said to be the most lucrative in the Territorial service. A Boise Grand Jury in 1885 summed up the prevailing, if unconfirmed, opinion of how land officials obtained their wealth: "Extortion by demanding and receiving illegal fees from settlers on the public domain has been the rule rather than the exception." *Boise City Republican*, 25 April 1885.

³³Jack E. Eblen, *The First and Second United States' Empires: Governors and Territorial Government, 1784-1912* (Pittsburgh: University of Pittsburgh Press, 1968), 302-19. For examples of printing and appointment controversies, see Everett L. Cooley, "Carpetbag Rule: Territorial Government in Utah," *Utah Historical Quarterly* 26 (April 1958): 115-16; Robert H. Simmons, "The Transition of the Washington Executive from Territory to Statehood," *Pacific Northwest Quarterly* 55 (1964): 76-79; Richards, "The American Colonial System in Nevada," 33-34; Owens, "Frontier Governors," 58-60; Thomas G. Alexander, "Mason Brayman and the Boise Ring," *Idaho Yesterdays* 14 (Fall 1970): 23-24.

³⁴R. H. Limbaugh, "The Carpetbag Image: Idaho Governors in Myth and Reality," *Pacific Northwest Quarterly* 60 (April 1969): 77-83; Lamar, "Carpetbaggers Full of Dreams," 188-189; Earl S. Pomeroy, "Carpetbaggers in The Territories, 1861-1890," *The Historian* 2 (Winter 1939): 53-64.

³⁵R. H. Limbaugh, "Ragged Dick in a Black Hat: The Idaho Career of Horace C. Gilson," *Idaho Yesterdays* 11 (Winter 1967-1968): 9-13.

³⁶Foley, "The American Territorial System," 413-14. See also Eblen, *The First and Second United States' Empires*, 302-16.

³⁷Robert H. Blank, "The Federal Government in Idaho Political Culture: Dependency and Resentment," *Rendezvous* 11 (Fall 1976): 45.

³⁸Ibid., 45; Simmons, "The Transition of the Washington Executive," 79-81.

³⁹Robert F. Berkhofer, "Space, Time, Culture and the New Frontier," *Agricultural History* 38 (January 1964): 21-30; Jackson K. Putnam, "The Turner Thesis and the Westward Movement: A Reappraisal," *Western Historical Quarterly* 7 (October 1976): 389-90.

⁴⁰See especially Elazar's *American Federalism, a View from the States* (New York: Crowell, 1966), and *Cities of the Prairie: the Metropolitan Frontier and American Politics* (New

York: Basic Books, 1970). See also Robert Kelley, *The Cultural Pattern in American Politics: The First Century* (New York: Knopf, 1979).

⁴¹Robert H. Blank, *Regional Diversity of Political Values: Idaho Political Culture* (Washington D.C.: University Press of America, 1978); Boyd A. Martin, "Idaho: The Sectional State," in Frank Jones, ed. *Politics in the American West* (Salt Lake: University of Utah, 1969), 180-200.

⁴²Richard D. Brown, *Modernization: The Transformation of American Life, 1600-1865* (New York: Hill & Wang, 1976); Richard Jensen, *Illinois: A Bicentennial History* (New York: Norton, 1978).

⁴³For a full discussion of "covenanted communities" see Page Smith, *As A City Upon A Hill: The Town in American History* (New York: Knopf, 1966). See also Lamar, "Political Patterns in New Mexico and Utah Territories," 382-86.

⁴⁴Elazar, *American Federalism*, 96-103.

⁴⁵Ibid., 97; 108-09. See also his *Cities of the Prairie*, 153-85; and a recent summary in "Political Culture on the Plains," *Western Historical Quarterly* 11 (July 1980): 261-83.

⁴⁶Kleppner, *The Third Electoral System*, xviii, 44-45; U.S. Bureau of the Census, *Historical Statistics of the U.S., Colonial Times to 1970,* Bicentennial Edition (Washington: U.S.G.P.O., 1976): 1071-72.

⁴⁷R. H. Limbaugh, "Some Idaho Carpetbaggers and the Moulton War," *Idaho Yesterdays* 14 (Fall 1970): 13-20. Brayman's career is treated in Limbaugh, "The Idaho Spoilsmen," 119-62. The pietist-ritualist (liturgical) hypothesis, as applied to midwestern politics, is discussed in Richard Jensen, *The Winning of the Midwest; Social and Political Conflict, 1888-1896* (Chicago: University of Chicago, 1971), 58-88.

⁴⁸Elazar, *Cities of the Prairies*, 181-85.

⁴⁹For examples of Civil War politics in the Far West, see Merle Wells, "Idaho and the Civil War," *Rendezvous* 11 (Fall 1976): 9-26; James L. Thane, "An Ohio Abolitionist in the Far West," *Pacific Northwest Quarterly* 67 (October 1967): 151-62.

⁵⁰Richard Maxwell Brown, *Strain of Violence: Historical Studies of American Violence and Vigilantism* (New York: Oxford, 1975), 93, 103-05. For a different view see W. Eugene Hollon, *Frontier Violence: Another Look* (New York: Oxford University Press, 1974).

⁵¹Robert F. Berkhofer, "The Northwest Ordinance and the Principle of Territorial Evolution," in John P. Bloom, ed., *The American Territorial System* (Athens, Ohio: Ohio University Press, 1972), 45-55.

⁵²Robert Blank, "The Federal Government in Idaho Political Culture," 42-44.

⁵³Robert Kelley, "Ideology and Political Culture from Jefferson to Nixon," *American Historical Review* 82 (June 1977): 533.

⁵⁴Ari A. Hoogenboom, "Spoilsmen and Reformers: Civil Service Reform and Public Morality," in H. Wayne Morgan, ed., *The Gilded Age: A Reappraisal* (Syracuse, N. Y.: Syracuse University Press, 1963), 69-80.

⁵⁵Alexander B. Callow, *The Tweed Ring* (New York: Oxford University Press, 1965); William A. Bullough, *The Blind Boss and His City: Christopher Augustine Buckley & Nineteenth-Century San Francisco* (Berkeley: University of California Press, 1979).

[1]Daniel J. Elazar, *American Federalism: A View from the States,* 2nd ed. (New York: Thomas Y. Crowell, 1972), 84-128, quote on 89; and Elazar, "Political Culture on the Plains," *Western Historical Quarterly* 11 (July 1980): 261-83.

[2]Ira Sharkansky, *Regionalism in American Politics* (Indianapolis: Bobbs-Merrill, 1970); Raymond D. Gastil, *Cultural Regions of the United States* (Seattle: University of Washington Press, 1975).

[3]Kenneth N. Owens, "Pattern and Structure in Western Territorial Politics," *Western Historical Quarterly* 1 (October 1970): 373-92; Merrill C. Burlingame, *The Montana Frontier* (Helena: State Publishing Co., 1942), chap. 7; James L. Thane, Jr., "Montana Territory: The Formative Years, 1862-1870" (Ph.D. dis., University of Iowa, 1972).

[4]The authoritative study of Montana Territory is Clark C. Spence, *Territorial Politics and Government in Montana: 1864-89* (Urbana: University of Illinois Press, 1975); K. Ross Toole, *Montana: An Uncommon Land* (Norman: University of Oklahoma Press, 1959), 173; John W. Hakola, "Samuel T. Hauser and the Economic Development of Montana: A Case Study in Nineteenth-Century Frontier Capitalism" (Ph.D. dis., Indiana University, 1961).

[5]Thomas A. Clinch, *Urban Populism and Free Silver in Montana* (Missoula: University of Montana Press, 1970), 51, on Daly's contributions; Clinch, "The Northern Pacific Railroad and Montana's Mineral Lands," *Pacific Historical Review* 34 (August 1965): 323-35.

[6]Michael P. Malone, *The Battle for Butte: Mining and Politics on the Northern Frontier: 1864-1906* (Seattle: University of Washington Press, 1981), chaps. 5-6; K. Ross Toole, "The Genesis of the Clark-Daly Feud," *The Montana Magazine of History* 1 (April 1951): 21-33; Toole, "When Big Money Came to Butte," *Pacific Northwest Quarterly* 44 (January 1953): 23-29; C. P. Connolly, *The Devil Learns to Vote: The Story of Montana* (New York: Covici Friede, 1938); C. B. Glasscock, *The War of the Copper Kings* (New York: Bobbs-Merrill, 1935); K. Ross Toole, "A History of the Anaconda Copper Mining Company: A Study in the Relationships Between a State and Its People and a Corporation, 1880-1950" (Ph.D. dis., University of California at Los Angeles, 1954); Forrest L. Foor, "The Senatorial Aspirations of William A. Clark" (Ph.D. dis., University of California at Berkeley, 1941).

[7]Malone, *Battle for Butte,* chaps. 7-8; Michael P. Malone and Richard B. Roeder, *Montana: A History of Two Centuries* (Seattle: University of Washington Press, 1976), chap. 9; Sarah McNelis, *Copper King at War: The Biography of F. Augustus Heinze* (Missoula: University of Montana Press, 1968).

[8]"Anaconda Copper," *Fortune,* December 1936, 83-94ff.; and "Anaconda II," ibid., January 1937, 71-77ff.; Isaac F. Marcosson, *Anaconda* (New York: Dodd, Mead, 1957), chaps. 5-7; on the formation of Montana power, see *The Montana Power Company: Reclassification of Electric Plant* (Butte: n.p., 1940), copy in possession of the company at its Butte central office.

[9]Arthur Fisher, "Montana: Land of the Copper Collar," *The Nation,* September 1922, 290; Jerre C. Murphy, *The Comical History of Montana* (San Diego: E. L. Scofield, 1912); Richard T. Ruetten, "Anaconda Journalism: The End of an Era," *Journalism Quarterly* 37 (Winter 1960): 3-12, 104.

[10]Elazar, *American Federalism,* 104-09; Gastil, *Cultural Regions,* 225-36; on homesteading, see Joseph K. Howard, *Montana High, Wide, and Handsome* (New Haven: Yale University Press, 1943), 167-209; Malone and Roeder, *Montana,* 178-94; K. Ross Toole, *Twentieth-Century Montana: A State of Extremes* (Norman: University of Oklahoma Press, 1972), 25-98; and Mary Wilma M. Hargreaves, *Dry Farming in the Northern Great Plains, 1900-1925* (Cambridge: Harvard University Press, 1957).

[11]Roeder's most succinct statement (countering K. Ross Toole's argument in *Montana: An Uncommon Land,* 226, that progressivism amounted to little in Montana) is in "Montana Progressivism: Sound and Fury and One Small Tax Reform," *Montana: The Magazine*

of Western History 20 (October 1970): 18-26; see also, Roeder, "Montana in the Early Years of the Progressive Period" (Ph.D. dis., University of Pennsylvania, 1971); and Jules A. Karlin, "Progressive Politics in Montana," in *A History of Montana*, ed. M. G. Burlingame and K. R. Toole, 3 vols. (New York: Lewis Historical Publishing Co., 1957), 1:247-80; and David Sarasohn, "The Election of 1916: Realigning the Rockies," *Western Historical Quarterly* 11 (July 1980): 285-305.

[12]On Dixon, see Jules A. Karlin, *Joseph M. Dixon of Montana*, 2 vols. (Missoula: University of Montana Publications in History, 1974); of the many writings on Rankin, see especially Joan Hoff Wilson, "Jeannette Rankin and American Foreign Policy," *Montana: The Magazine of Western History* 30 (Winter 1980): 28-41, and (Spring 1980): 38-53; and Hannah Josephson, *Jeannette Rankin: First Lady in Congress* (Indianapolis: Bobbs-Merrill, 1974). J. Leonard Bates is the biographer of Thomas J. Walsh; see especially his "Senator Walsh of Montana, 1918-1924: A Liberal Under Pressure" (Ph.D. dis., University of North Carolina, 1952). Similarly, Richard T. Ruetten is preparing a definitive study of Wheeler; see his "Burton K. Wheeler, 1905-1925: An Independent Liberal Under Fire" (Master's thesis, University of Oregon, 1957), and "Burton K. Wheeler of Montana: A Progressive Between the Wars" (Ph.D. dis., University of Oregon, 1961). A colorful memoir is Burton K. Wheeler with Paul F. Healy, *Yankee from the West* (Garden City: Doubleday, 1962).

[13]Karlin, *Dixon,* 1: chaps. 8-12; Toole, *Montana: An Uncommon Land*, 214-15.

[14]The forthcoming study of Montana's socialists by political scientist Jerry Calvert will place that fascinating group in perspective for the first time. There are no complete studies of the I.W.W. and Nonpartisan League in Montana, but see Melvyn Dubofsky, *We Shall Be All: A History of the Industrial Workers of the World* (Chicago: Quadrangle Books, 1969), 301-93, *passim;* Joseph R. Conlin, *Bread and Roses Too* (Westport, Conn: Greenwood, 1969), 129-30, 141; and Robert L. Morlan, *Political Prairie Fire: The Nonpartisan League, 1915-1922* (Minneapolis: University of Minnesota Press, 1955).

[15]Arnon Gutfeld discusses these events in a very narrow and incomplete focus in *Montana's Agony: Years of War and Hysteria, 1917-1921* (Gainesville: University Presses of Florida, 1979), and also in a series of articles that may be found in that volume's bibliography; for a similar viewpoint, see Toole, *Twentieth-Century Montana*, chaps. 6-7; see also Kurt Wetzel, "The Defeat of Bill Dunne: An Episode in the Montana Red Scare," *Pacific Northwest Quarterly* 64 (January 1973): 12-20; and Benjamin G. Rader, "The Montana Lumber Strike of 1917," *Pacific Historical Review* 36 (May 1967): 189-207.

[16]Ellis Waldron and Paul B. Wilson, *Atlas of Montana Elections, 1889-1976* (Missoula: University of Montana Publications in History, 1978), 76-89; Karlin, *Dixon,* 2: chap. 5; Wheeler, *Yankee*, chap. 8.

[17]Karlin, *Dixon,* 2: chaps. 6-11; Toole, *Montana*, 223-27; Toole, *Twentieth-Century Montana*, chaps. 9-10.

[18]Waldron and Wilson, *Atlas*, 97-124; Richard T. Ruetten, "Senator Burton K. Wheeler and Insurgency in the 1920's," in *The American West: A Reorientation*, ed. Gene M. Gressley (Laramie: University of Wyoming Press, 1968), 111-31; Paul A. Carter, "The Other Catholic Candidate: The 1928 Presidential Bid of Thomas J. Walsh," *Pacific Northwest Quarterly* 55 (January 1964): 1-18.

[19]Thomas Payne, "Montana: Politics Under the Copper Dome," in *Politics in the American West*, ed. Frank H. Jonas (Salt Lake City: University of Utah Press, 1969), 202-30; Clark C. Spence, *Montana: A Bicentennial History* (New York: W.W. Norton, 1978), 165-66.

[20]Michael P. Malone, "Montana as a Corporate Bailiwick: An Image in History," in Peter J. Powell and Michael P. Malone, *Montana, Past and Present* (Los Angeles: William Andrews Clark Memorial Library, 1976), 55-76; for an insight into the conservatism of the Montana Stockgrowers Association, see Robert H. Fletcher, *Free Grass to Fences: The Montana Cattle Range Story* (New York: University Publishers, 1960).

[21] See Vernon H. Jensen, *Heritage of Conflict: Labor Relations in the Nonferrous Metals Industry up to 1930* (Ithaca: Cornell University Press, 1950); and Jensen, *Nonferrous Metals Industry Unionism: 1932-1954* (Ithaca: Cornell University Press, 1954).

[22] Michael P. Malone, "The Montana New Dealers," in John Braeman, Robert H. Bremner, and David Brody, eds., *The New Deal*, 2 vols. (Columbus: Ohio State University Press, 1975), 2: 240-42; and Malone, "Montana Politics and the New Deal," *Montana: The Magazine of Western History* 21 (Winter 1971): 2-11.

[23] Michael P. Malone, "Montana Politics at the Crossroads: 1932-1933," *Pacific Northwest Quarterly* 69 (January 1978): 20-29; Waldron and Wilson, *Atlas*, 126-31.

[24] Leonard Arrington, "The New Deal in the West: A Preliminary Statistical Inquiry," *Pacific Historical Review* 38 (August 1969): 314-15; James T. Patterson, "The New Deal in the West," ibid., 317-27; Patterson, *The New Deal and the States: Federalism in Transition* (Princeton: Princeton University Press, 1969); Richard Lowitt, *The New Deal and the West* (Bloomington: Indiana University Press, 1984); Malone, "Montana New Dealers," 246-48; and Malone and Roeder, *Montana*, 229-33.

[25] Richard Ruetten, "Burton K. Wheeler and the Montana Connection," *Montana: The Magazine of Western History* 37 (Summer 1977): 2-19; Ruetten, "Wheeler of Montana," chaps. 7-8; James T. Patterson, *Congressional Conservatism and the New Deal* (Lexington: University of Kentucky Press, 1967), chap. 3.

[26] Richard T. Ruetten, "Showdown in Montana, 1938: Burton Wheeler's Role in the Defeat of Jerry O'Connell," *Pacific Northwest Quarterly* 54 (January 1963): 19-29.

[27] Waldron and Wilson, *Atlas*, 150-64; Malone, "Montana New Dealers," 252-59; John M. Allswang, *The New Deal and American Politics* (New York: John Wiley and Sons, 1978), 105-07.

[28] Waldron and Wilson, *Atlas*, 165-83; Malone and Roeder, *Montana*, 237-40; Joseph Kinsey Howard wrote with flair and partisanship of wartime politics in "The Montana Twins in Trouble," *Harper's*, September 1944, 334-42, "Golden River," ibid., May 1945, 511-23, and in the beautifully written "The Decline and Fall of Burton K. Wheeler," ibid., March 1947, 226-36; and Ruetten, "Wheeler and Montana Connection," 18-19.

[29] U.S. Department of Commerce, Bureau of the Census, *Statistical Abstract of the United States, 1942*, 698; *Statistical Abstract of the United States, 1979*, 689.

[30] There are no definitive biographical treatments of these three individuals, but on Murray see Forrest Davis, "Millionaire Moses," *Saturday Evening Post*, 8 December 1945, 9-10, 103-04, 106; and Joseph K. Howard, "Jim Murray's Chances," *The Nation*, 9 October 1948, 397-99; on Mansfield, Louis Baldwin, *Honorable Politician: Mike Mansfield of Montana* (Missoula: Mountain Press, 1979); and on Metcalf, Robert Sherrill, "The Invisible Senator," *The Nation*, 10 May 1971, 584-89.

[31] Marcosson, *Anaconda*, 136-339; Malone, "Montana as a Corporate Bailiwick," 65-67; "From Riches to Rags," *Forbes Magazine*, 15 January 1972, 24-25; *Billings Gazette*, 20, 21, 22, 23 April 1980; *Butte Montana Standard*, 28, 29, 30 September 1980; Michael P. Malone, "The Close of the Copper Century," *Montana: The Magazine of Western History* 35 (Spring 1985): 69-72.

[32] Kevin P. Phillips, *The Emerging Republican Majority* (New Rochelle: Arlington House, 1969), 402, 407.

[33] The best quick guides to general political trends in Montana after World War II are Waldron and Wilson, *Atlas*, 178-288; and the *Western Political Quarterly*, which from 1949 through 1971 carried western state-by-state election coverages in the spring or summer issues of odd-numbered years; Jules Karlin described the 1948 and 1952 campaigns, Thomas Payne all those through 1968, and Brad Hainesworth the 1970 campaign; Malone and Roeder, *Montana*, chap. 15; J. Hugo Aronsen's autobiography, *The Galloping Swede*, coauthored with L. O. Brockmann (Missoula: Mountain Press, 1970), is politically unrevealing.

[34]*Billings Gazette*, 20 August 1972.

[35]The legislative statistics are drawn from Waldron and Wilson, *Atlas*; the rankings on per capita income and the funding of welfare were graciously supplied to us by John LaFaver, Legislative Fiscal Analyst of Montana. See also, Margaret Scherf, "One Cow, One Vote: A Strenuous Session in the Montana Legislature," *Harper's*, April 1966, 103-09; Payne, "Montana," 222-26; Neal R. Peirce, *The Mountain States of America* (New York: W. W. Norton, 1972), 114-17; and Peirce and Jerry Hagstrom, *The Book of America* (New York: W. W. Norton, 1983), 676-85.

[36]Waldron and Wilson, *Atlas*, 255-69; Richard D. Lamm and Michael McCarthy, *The Angry West* (Boston: Houghton Mifflin, 1982), 106-08.

¹Zane Grey, *The Desert of Wheat* (New York: Grossett and Dunlap, 1919); Carleton Jackson, *Zane Grey* (Twayne's United States Authors Series; New York: Twayne, 1973), 71-73.

²The articles used to make this compilation are listed in the appendix. I emphasize that it is the kind of list to which readers might be expected to make some additions and deletions and to break down the total somewhat differently than I have. Nonetheless, the proportion of writing devoted to violent and/or radical aspects of Pacific Northwest labor history will doubtless remain significant.

³The following is only a sample of the writing on labor-related violence in the Pacific Northwest: Jules A. Karlin, "The Anti-Chinese Outbreaks in Seattle, 1885, 1886," *Pacific Northwest Quarterly* 39 (April 1948): 103-30; Jules A. Karlin, "The Anti-Chinese Outbreak in Tacoma, 1885," *Pacific Northwest Review* 27 (August 1954): 271-83; Robert Edward Wynne, "Reaction to the Chinese in the Pacific Northwest and British Columbia, 1850-1910" (Ph.D. dis., University of Washington, 1964); Melvyn Dubofsky, *We Shall Be All: A History of the Industrial Workers of the World* (New York: Quadrangle/New York Times Book Co., 1973 [1969]); Carlos A. Schwantes, "Making the World Unsafe for Democracy: Vigilantes, Grangers and the Walla Walla 'Outrage' of June 1918," *Montana: The Magazine of Western History* 31 (Winter 1981): 18-29; Norman H. Clark, *Mill Town: A Social History of Everett, Washington, from its Earliest Beginnings on the Shores of Puget Sound to the Tragic and Infamous Event Known as the Everett Massacre* (Seattle: University of Washington Press, 1970); Vernon Jensen, *Heritage of Conflict: Labor Relations in the Nonferrous Metals Industry up to 1930* (Ithaca: Cornell University Press, 1950); Alan A. Hynding, "The Coal Miners of Washington Territory: Labor Troubles in 1888-1889," *Arizona and the West* 12 (Autumn 1970): 221-36; David Grover, *Debaters and Dynamiters: The Story of the Haywood Trail* (Corvallis: Oregon State University Press, 1964); Charles Pierce LeWarne, "The Aberdeen, Washington, Free Speech Fight of 1911-1912," *Pacific Northwest Quarterly* 66 (January 1975): 1-12; Gerald N. Hallberg, "Bellingham, Washington's Anti-Hindu Riot," *Journal of the West* 12 (January 1973): 163-75; Thomas A. Clinch, "Coxey's Army in Montana," *Montana Magazine of Western History* 15 (October 1965): 2-11; Herman C. Voeltz, "Coxey's Army in Oregon, 1894," *Oregon Historical Quarterly* 65 (September 1964): 263-95; W. Thomas White, "Boycott: The Pullman Strike in Montana," *Montana: The Magazine of Western History* 29 (Autumn 1979): 3-13; Carlos A. Schwantes, "Law and Disorder: The Suppression of Coxey's Army in Idaho," *Idaho Yesterdays* 25 (Summer 1981): 10-15, 18-26; Stanley Stewart Phipps, "From Bull Pen to Bargaining Table: The Tumultuous Struggle of the Coeur d'Alene Miners for the Right to Organize, 1887-1942" (Ph.D. dis., University of Idaho, 1983).

⁴Robert L. Tyler, "The I.W.W. and the West," *American Quarterly* 12 (Summer 1960): 175-87; Grey, *The Desert of Wheat*, 246. Stewart Holbrook, a journalist, probably more than any other person was responsible for popularizing Pacific Northwest labor history as folklore.

⁵Carlos A. Schwantes, "Protest in a Promised Land: Unemployment, Disinheritance, and the Origin of Labor Militancy in the Pacific Northwest," *Western Historical Quarterly* 13 (October 1982): 373-90.

⁶Sylvester Pennoyer's 1893 Christmas Letter was reprinted in the *Oregonian*, May 31, 1902, p. 13. See also, Maude Davis Chapman, "Sylvester Pennoyer, Governor of Oregon, 1887-1895" (M.A. thesis, University of Oregon, 1943). Samples of the state labor bureau reports include: *First Biennial Report of the Bureau of Labor of the State of Washington, 1897-1898* (Olympia: Gwin Hicks, 1899), 7-8; [Idaho] *First Annual Report of the State Bureau of Immigration, Labor and Statistics, 1900* (Boise: n.p., 1900); *Third Annual Report of the Bureau of Agriculture, Labor and Industry of Montana, 1895* (Helena: State Publishing Co., 1896); *First Biennial Report: Bureau of Labor Statistics and Inspector of Factories and Workshops in the State of Oregon, June 3, 1903-Sept. 30, 1904* (Salem: J.R. Whitney State Printer, 1904).

[7]Mary Hallock Foote, *Coeur d'Alene* (Boston: Houghton, Mifflin, 1894); May Arkwright Hutton, *The Coeur d'Alenes, or, A Tale of the Modern Inquisition in Idaho* (Denver: M. A. Hutton, 1900); Job Harriman, *The Class War in Idaho: The Horrors of the Bull Pen.*, 3rd ed. (New York: Volks-Zeitung Library, 1900); Walker C. Smith, *The Everett Massacre: A History of the Class Struggle in the Lumber Industry* (Chicago: I.W.W. Publishing Bureau, 1917); Walker C. Smith, *Was it Murder? Authentic Record of the Cases Leading to the Actual Events of, and the Trial that Followed the Armistice Day Tragedy at Centralia, Wash., Nov. 11, 1919*, 2nd ed. (Seattle: Washington Branch General Defense Committee, 1927); Ralph Chaplin, *The Centralia Conspiracy: The Truth About the Armistice Day Tragedy* (Chicago: General Defense Committee, 1924). See also, Ed Delany and M. T. Rice, *The Bloodstained Trail: A History of Militant Labor in the United States* (Seattle: The Industrial Worker, n.d.)

[8]56th Cong., 1st Sess., House Report No. 1999, "Coeur d'Alene Labor Troubles," Senate Document No. 24, "Coeur d'Alene Mining Troubles," and Senate Document No. 42, "Labor Troubles in Idaho." For British Columbia see Canada, Parliament, "Report of the Royal Commission on Industrial Disputes in the Province of British Columbia" (1903); Canada, Parliament, "Evidence Taken Before the Royal Commission to Inquire into Industrial Disputes in the Province of British Columbia" (1904); Canada, Parliament, "Report of the Royal Commission on Losses Sustained by the Japanese Population of Vancouver, B.C., on the Occasion of the Riots in that City in September, 1907" (1908); Canada, Parliament, "Report of the Royal Commission on Losses, Sustained by the Chinese Population of Vancouver, B.C., on the Occasion of the Riots in that City in September, 1907" (1908); British Columbia, Provincial Legislature, "Report of the Royal Commission on Labour" (1914). See also, Cloice R. Howd, "Industrial Relations in the West Coast Lumber Industry," in U.S. Bureau of Labor Statistics, *Bulletin 349* (1924); 64th Cong., 1st Sess., Senate Document 415, "Final Report of the Commission on Industrial Relations," 11 vols.; United States Immigration Commission, Report, 42 vols. (Washington, D.C.: Government Printing Office, 1911); 61st Cong., 2nd Sess., Senate Document 645, "Report on the Conditions of Women and Child Wage-Earners in the United States," 19 vols. An excellent overview of Washington's labor legislation is Joseph F. Tripp, "Progressive Labor Laws in Washington State (1900-1925)" (Ph.D. dis., University of Washington, 1973).

[9]For an encompassing definition of violence see Roger Lane, *Violent Death in the City: Suicide, Accident, and Murder in Nineteenth-Century Philadelphia* (Cambridge: Harvard University Press, 1979). A good overview of violence is Hugh Davis Graham and Ted Robert Gurr, eds., *Violence in America: Historical and Comparative Perspectives,* rev. ed. (Beverly Hills: Sage, 1979). Pioneering studies of industrial accidents are two contributions by Andrew M. Prouty: "Logging With Steam in the Pacific Northwest: The Men, The Camps, and the Accidents" (M.A. thesis, University of Washington, 1973), and "More Deadly than War: Pacific Coast Logging, 1827-1981" (Ph.D. dis., University of Washington, 1982).

[10]Harvey O'Conner, *Revolution in Seattle: A Memoir* (New York: Monthly Review Press, 1964). See also, *History of the Seattle Labor Movement and the Conspiracy of Employers to Destroy It* (Seattle: Union Record, 1919).

[11]Grey, *The Desert of Wheat,* 8.

[12]Ibid., 40-46; *Flour and Grain World* (1918): 121; *Manufacturer and Industrial News Bureau* (June 1919): 2.

[13]Joseph R. Conlin, "The IWW and the Question of Violence," *The Wisconsin Magazine of History* 51 (Summer 1968): 316-26.

[14]Charles P. LeWarne, *Utopias on Puget Sound, 1885-1915* (Seattle: University of Washington Press, 1975); Paul George Hummasti, "Finnish Radicals in Astoria, Oregon, 1904-1940: A Study of Immigrant Socialism" (Ph.D. dis., University of Oregon, 1975), reissued in 1979 in Arno's "Scandinavians in America" series; Jerry Lembcke and William M. Tattam, *One Union in Wood: A Political History of the International Woodworkers of America* (New York: International Publishers, 1984); Cletus Edward Daniel, "Labor Radicalism

in Pacific Coast Agriculture (Ph.D. dis., University of Washington, 1972), the California portion of this dissertation was subsequently reworked and published as *Bitter Harvest: A History of California Farmworkers, 1870-1941* (Ithaca: Cornell University Press, 1981); Paul B. Bushue, "Dr. Hermon F. Titus and Socialism in Washington State, 1900-1909" (M.A. thesis, University of Washington, 1967); Clifton Howard Jones, "The Oregon Socialist Party, 1901-1918" (M.A. thesis, University of Oregon, 1974); Albert Anthony Acena, "The Washington Commonwealth Federation: Reform Politics and the Popular Front" (Ph.D. dis., University of Washington, 1975); Jill Hopkins Herzig, "The Oregon Commonwealth Federation: The Rise and Decline of a Reform Organization" (M.A. thesis, University of Oregon, 1963); Hamilton Cravens, "A History of the Washington Farmer-Labor Party, 1918-1924" (M.A. thesis, University of Washington, 1963); Meridith Allan May, "Everett's Socialist Paper: A Strident Voice in a Hostile Community" (M.A. thesis, University of Washington, 1969); Edwin R. Bingham, "Oregon's Romantic Rebels: John Reed and Charles Erskine Scott Wood," *Pacific Northwest Quarterly* 50 (July 1959): 77-90; Carlos A. Schwantes, "The Churches of the Disinherited: The Culture of Radicalism on the North Pacific Industrial Frontier," *Pacific Historian* 25 (Winter 1981): 54-65. A summary of the writing on Washington and British Columbia radicalism is provided in Carlos A. Schwantes, *Radical Heritage: Labor, Socialism, and Reform in Washington and British Columbia, 1885-1917* (Seattle: University of Washington Press, 1979), 261-73.

[15]Robert H. Bremner, *From the Depths: The Discovery of Poverty in the United States* (New York: New York University Press, 1967), 154-57; Carleton H. Parker, *The Casual Laborer and Other Essays.* Americana Library (Seattle: University of Washington Press, 1973 [1920]); Paul Brissenden, *The I.W.W.: A Study of American Syndicalism* (New York: Columbia University Press, 1919); Ole Hanson, *Americanism versus Bolshevism* (Garden City, N.Y.: Doubleday, Page, 1920).

[16]Robert Wayne Smith, *The Coeur d'Alene Mining War of 1892: A Case Study of an Industrial Dispute* (Corvallis: Oregon State University Press, 1961); Donald L. McMurry, *Coxey's Army: A Study of the Industrial Army Movement of 1894.* Americana Library (Seattle: University of Washington Press, 1968 [1929]); Vernon Jensen, *Lumber and Labor* (New York: Farrar and Rinehart, 1945). Two of the notable popular books that touched on Pacific Northwest labor were Murray Morgan, *Skid Road: An Informal Portrait of Seattle* (Seattle: University of Washington Press, 1982); and Lowell S. Hawley and Ralph Bushnell Potts, *Counsel for the Damned: A Biography of George Francis Vanderver* (Philadelphia: Lippincott, 1953).

[17]The range of subjects treated reflects a highly eclectic approach: Nellie Linda Higgins, "Child Labor in Washington" (M.A. thesis, University of Washington, 1914); Robert B. Pitts, "Organized Labor and the Negro in Seattle" (M.A. thesis, University of Washington, 1941); Arthur Hillman, "The Unemployed Citizens' League of Seattle" (M.A. thesis, University of Washington, 1934); Claude Nichols, Jr., "Brotherhood in the Woods: The Loyal Legion of Loggers and Lumberman, A Twenty Year Attempt at Industrial Cooperation" (Ph.D. dis., University of Oregon, 1959); Norma Smith, "The Rise and Fall of the Butte Miners' Union" (M.A. thesis, Montana State University, 1961); Frederick Eugene Melder, "A Study of the Washington Coal Industry with Special Reference to the Industrial Relations Problem" (M.A. thesis, University of Washington, 1931); William J. Dickson, "Labor in Municipal Politics: A Study of Labor's Political Policies and Activities in Seattle" (M.A. thesis, University of Washington, 1928). This is only a sample of the theses and dissertations.

[18]Robert L. Tyler, *Rebels of the Woods: The I.W.W. in the Pacific Northwest* (Eugene: University of Oregon Books, 1967); Harold M. Hyman, *Soldiers and Spruce: Origins of the Loyal Legion of Loggers and Lumbermen* (Los Angeles: UCLA Institute of Industrial Relations, 1963); Robert L. Friedheim, *The Seattle General Strike* (Seattle: University of Washington, 1964); Roger Buchanan, *Dock Strike: A History of the 1934 Waterfront Strike in Portland, Oregon* (Everett, Wash.: The Working Press, 1975); Ronald Magden and A. D. Martinson, *The Working Waterfront: The Story of Tacoma's Ships and Men* (Tacoma: n.p., 1982).

[19] *Pacific Northwest Quarterly* 61 (April 1970): 71; William Ames and Roger Simpson, *Unionism or Hearst: The Seattle Post-Intelligencer Strike of 1936* (Seattle: Pacific Northwest Labor History Association, 1978).

[20] Jonathan Dembo, *Unions and Politics in Washington State, 1885-1935* (New York: Garland, 1983), and *An Historical Bibliography of Washington State Labor and Laboring Classes* (Seattle: Jonathan Dembo, 1978); W. Thomas White, "A History of Railroad Workers in the Pacific Northwest, 1883-1934" (Ph.D. dis., University of Washington, 1981).

[21] Herbert G. Gutman, "Work, Culture, and Society in Industrializing America," *American Historical Review* 78 (June 1973): 531-587; Herbert G. Gutman, *Work, Culture and Society in Industrializing America: Essays in American Working-Class and Social History* (New York: Knopf, 1976); E. P. Thompson, *The Making of the English Working Class* (New York: Vintage Books, 1966 [1963]); David Montgomery, *Workers' Control in America* (Cambridge: Cambridge University Press, 1979). For an overview and analysis of the new labor history, see David Brody, "Labor History in the 1970s: Toward a History of the American Worker," in Michael Kammen, ed., *The Past Before Us: Contemporary Historical Writing in the United States* (Ithaca: Cornell University Press, 1980), 252-69; and David Brody, *Workers in Industrial America: Essays on the Twentieth Century Struggle* (New York: Oxford University Press, 1980).

[22] Milton Cantor, ed., *American Workingclass Culture: Explorations in American Labor and Social History*, Contributions in American History, No. 7 (Westport, Conn.: Greenwood, 1979). One notable study of Pacific Northwest labor that makes use of Gutman's insights is Mark J. Stern, " 'To Bring Forth the Hidden Wealth': The Knights of Labor in the Coal Fields of King County, Washington, 1885-1891" (B.A. thesis, Reed College, 1973).

[23] Ronald Steel, *Walter Lippmann and the American Century* (Boston: Atlantic Monthly Press, 1980); *The Scab* (Portland, Ore.: n. p.[ca. 1918]), 4.

[24] Carlos A. Schwantes, "Washington State's Labor-Reform Press, 1885-1917: An Essay and Annotated Checklist," *Pacific Northwest Quarterly* 71 (July 1980). A good overview of Oregon's early labor movement is Jack E. Triplett, Jr., "History of the Oregon Labor Movement Prior to the New Deal" (M.A. thesis, University of California, Berkeley, 1961).

OREGON HISTORICAL QUARTERLY

Herman C. Voeltz, "Coxey's Army in Oregon, 1894" 65 (September 1964): 263-95.

Hugh T. Lovin, "Toward a Farmer-Labor Party in Oregon, 1933-38" 76 (June 1974): 135-51.

Daniel T. Strite, "Hurrah for Garibaldi" 77 (September 1976): 213-37.

_____, "Hurrah for Garibaldi, 2" 77 (December 1976): 341-68.

Carlos A. Schwantes, "Free Love and Free Speech on the Pacific Northwest Frontier: Proper Victorians vs. Portland's 'filthy Firebrand' " 82 (Fall 1981): 271-93.

MONTANA: THE MAGAZINE OF WESTERN HISTORY

Thomas C. Clinch, "Coxey's Army in Montana" 15 (October 1965): 2-11.

Grace Roffey Pratt, "The Great-Hearted Huttons of the Coeur d'Alenes" 17 (April 1967): 20-33.

Charles Vindex, "Radical Rule in Montana" 18 (January 1968): 2-18.

Jay George Ransome as told to Jay Ellis Ransome, "Log Drive to Boise" 19 (April 1969): 2-9.

George A. Venn, "The Wobblies and Montana's Garden City" 21 (October 1971): 18-30.

Theodore Wiprud, "Butte: A Troubled Labor Paradise" 21 (October 1971): 31-38.

Bob Saindon and Bunky Sullivan, "Taming the Missouri and Treating the Depression" 27 (July 1977): 34-57.

W. Thomas White, "Boycott: The Pullman Strike in Montana" 29 (Autumn 1979): 3-13.

Carlos A. Schwantes, "Making the World Unsafe for Democracy: Vigilantes, Grangers and the Walla Walla 'Outrage' of June 1918" 31 (January 1981): 18-29.

Clarence Adami Wendel, "Mining in Butte 40 Years Ago" 31 (July 1981): 60-66.

Arthur W. Thurner, "The Western Federation of Miners in Two Copper Camps: The Impact of the Michigan Copper Miners' Strike on Butte Local No. 1" 33 (Spring 1983): 30-45.

Laurie Mercier, "I Worked for the Railroad: Oral Histories of Montana Railroaders, 1900-1950" 33 (Summer, 1983): 34-59.

IDAHO YESTERDAYS

Stephen Scheinberg, "Theodore Roosevelt's 'Undesirable Citizens' " 4 (Fall 1960): 10-15.

Leedice Kissane, "Steve Adams, The Speechless Witness" 4 (Fall 1960): 18-21.

James H. Hawley, "Steve Adams' Confession and the State's Case Against Bill Haywood" 7 (Winter 1963-64): 16-27.

David Glasser, "Migration in Idaho's History" 11 (Fall 1967): 27-31.

Harold H. Kolb, Jr., "Industrial Millstone" 16 (Summer 1972): 28-32.

Betty Derig, "Celestials in the Diggins" 16 (Fall 1972): 2-23.

B.T. Cowart, "James McParland and the Hayward Case" 16 (Fall 1972): 24-29.

Hugh T. Lovin, "The Red Scare in Idaho, 1916-1918" 17 (Fall 1973): 2-13.

_____, "World War Vigilantes in Idaho, 1917-1918" 18 (Fall 1974): 2-11.

_____, "The Farmer Revolt in Idaho, 1914-1922" 20 (Fall 1976): 2-15.

Merwin R. Swanson, "Student Radicals at the 'Southern Branch': Campus Protest in the 1930's" 20 (Fall 1976): 21-26.

Hugh Lovin, "The Banishment of Kate Richards O'Hare" 22 (Spring 1978): 20-25.

Richard J. Bonney, "The Pullman Strike of 1894: Pocatello Perspective" 24 (Fall 1980): 23-28.

Carlos A. Schwantes, "Law and Disorder: The Suppression of Coxey's Army in Idaho" 25 (Summer 1981): 10-15, 18-26.

John Fahey, "Ed Boyce and the Western Federation of Miners" 25 (Fall 1981): 18-30.

Brant Short, "Socialism in Minidoka County, 1912-1916" 26 (Summer 1982): 30-38.

Hugh Lovin, "Disloyalty, Libel, and Litigation: Ray McKaig's Ordeal, 1917-1920" 27 (Summer 1983): 13-15, 18-24.

Carlos A. Schwantes, "Blessed are the Mythmakers? Free Land, Unemployment, and Uncle Sam in the American West" 27 (Fall 1983): 2-12.

PACIFIC NORTHWEST QUARTERLY

Robert L. Friedheim, "The Seattle General Strike of 1919" 52 (July 1961): 81-98.

Robert L. and Robin Friedheim, "The Seattle Labor Movement, 1919-20" 55 (October 1964): 146-56.

Benjamin H. Kizer, "May Arkwright Hutton" 57 (April 1966): 49-56.

Norman H. Clark, "Everett, 1916 and After" 57 (April 1966): 57-64.

John M. McClelland, Jr., "Terror on Tower Avenue" 57 (April 1966): 65-72.

Benjamin H. Kizer, "Elizabeth Gurley Flynn" 57 (July 1966): 110-12.

Hamilton Cravens, "The Emergence of the Farmer-Labor Party in Washington Politics, 1919-20" 57 (October 1966): 148-57.

Robert E. Wynne, "American Labor Leaders and the Vancouver Anti-Oriental Riot" 57 (October 1966): 172-79.

William J. Gaboury, "From Statehouse to Bull Pen: Idaho Populism and the Coeur d'Alene Troubles of the 1890s" 58 (January 1967): 14-22.

Melvyn Dubofsky, "James H. Hawley and the Origins of the Haywood Case" 58 (January 1967): 23-32.

Larry D. Quinn, " 'Chink Chink Chinaman': The Beginning of Nativism in Montana" 58 (April 1967): 82-89.

Joseph R. Conlin, "The Haywood Case: An Enduring Riddle" 59 (January 1968): 23-32.

Albert F. Gunns, "Ray Becker, the Last Centralia Prisoner" 59 (April 1968): 88-99.

Charles P. LeWarne, "Equality Colony: The Plan to Socialize Washington" 59 (July 1968): 137-46.

Richard C. Berner, "Labor History: Sources and Perspectives" 60 (January 1969): 31-33.

Peter Guy Silverman, "Military Aid to Civil Power in British Columbia: The Labor Strikes at Wellington and Steveston, 1890, 1900" 61 (July 1970): 156-61.

Hugh T. Lovin, "The Fall of Farmer-Labor Parties, 1936-1938" 62 (January 1971): 16-26.

Donald A. McPhee, "The Centralia Incident and the Pamphleteers" 62 (July 1971): 110-16.

Kurt Wetzel, "The Defeat of Bill Dunne: An Episode in the Montana Red Scare" 64 (January 1973): 12-20.

Howard Sugimoto, "The Vancouver Riot and Its International Significance" 64 (October 1973): 163-74.

Cletus E. Daniel, "Wobblies on the Farm: The IWW in the Yakima Valley" 65 (October 1974): 166-75.

Charles P. LeWarne, "The Aberdeen, Washington, Free Speech Fight of 1911-1912" 66 (January 1975): 1-12.

Hugh T. Lovin, "Moses Alexander and the Idaho Lumber Strike of 1917: The Wartime Ordeal of a Progressive" 66 (July 1975): 115-22.

David C. Duke, "Anna Louise Strong and the Search for a Good Cause" 66 (July 1975): 123-37.

James C. Foster, "The Western Federation Comes to Alaska" 66 (October 1975): 161-73.

Joseph F. Tripp, "Toward an Efficient and Moral Society: Washington State Minimum-Wage Law, 1913-1925" 67 (July 1976): 97-112.

James G. Newbill, "Farmers and Wobblies in the Yakima Valley, 1933," 68 (April 1977): 80-87.

Egbert S. Olivery, "Sawmilling on Gray's Harbor in the Twenties" 69 (January 1978): 1-18.

Hugh T. Lovin, "Idaho and the 'Reds', 1919-1926" 69 (July 1978): 107-15.

Stefan Tanaka, "The Toledo Incident: The Deportation of the Nikkei from an Oregon Mill Town" 69 (July 1978): 116-25.

David Jay Bercuson, "The One Big Union in Washington" 69 (July 1978): 127-34.

Eckard V. Toy, Jr., "The Oxford Group and the Strike of the Seattle Longshoremen in 1934" 69 (October 1978): 174-84.

Carlos A. Schwantes, "Leftward Tilt on the Pacific Slope: Indigenous Unionism and the Struggle Against AFL Hegemony in the State of Washington" 70 (January 1979): 24-34.

William J. Williams, "Bloody Sunday Revisited" 71 (April 1980): 50-62.

Carlos A. Schwantes, "Washington State's Pioneer Labor-Reform Press: A Bibliographical Essay and Annotated Checklist" 71 (July 1980): 112-26.

Jonathan Dembo, "John Danz and the Seattle Amusement Trades Strike, 1921-1935" 71 (October 1980): 172-82.

William H. Mullins, "Self-Help in Seattle, 1931-1932: Herbert Hoover's Concept of Cooperative Individualism and the Unemployed Citizens' League" 72 (January 1981): 11-19.

Carlos A. Schwantes, "Coxey's Montana Navy: A Protest Against Unemployment on the Wage Workers' Frontier" 73 (July 1982): 98-107.

Robert A. Campbell, "Blacks and the Coal Mines of Western Washington, 1888-1896" 73 (October 1982): 146-55.

Barbara Cloud, "Laura Hall Peters: Pursuing the Myth of Equality" 74 (January 1983): 28-36.

William L. Lang, "One Path to Populism: Will Kennedy and the People's Party of Montana" 74 (April 1983): 77-86.

Carlos A. Schwantes, "Labor-Reform Papers in Oregon, 1871-1976: A Checklist" 74 (October 1983): 154-66.

ESSAY EIGHT NOTES   183

¹Karen Blair of the University of Washington has recently completed her manuscript for a comprehensive bibliography of women's sources for the Pacific Northwest. Tentatively titled *Northwest Women: An Annotated Bibliography*, it is presently under consideration by several publishers. The best general bibliography is Joan Jensen and Darlis Miller, "Gentle Tamers Revisited: New Approaches to the History of Women in the American West," *Pacific Historical Review* 49 (May 1980): 173-213.

²Gerda Lerner, "New Approaches to the Study of Women in American History," *Journal of Social History* 3 (Fall 1969): 53-62.

³Gerda Lerner, "Placing Women in History: A 1975 Perspective," *Feminist Studies*, 3 (1975): 5-15.

⁴Clifford Drury, *First White Women Over the Rockies*, 3 vols. (Glendale, Calif.: A. H. Clark Co., 1963-66).

⁵Duniway's uneven autobiography *Pathbreaking* was reprinted by Schocken in 1971. Biographers of Rankin have faced difficulties because of scattered and inaccessible papers. Hannah Josephson's *Jeannette Rankin, First Lady in Congress* (New York: Bobbs-Merrill, 1974) is the standard source. Hutton, a flamboyant figure, received sensationalistic treatment from James Montgomery in *Liberated Woman* (Spokane, Wash.: Gingko House, 1974).

⁶All four women are included in Edward T. James, ed., *Notable American Women*, 3 vols. (Cambridge: Harvard University Press, 1971), as well as good citations to their personal papers and biographical materials.

⁷Ronald W. Taber, "Sacajawea and the Suffragettes," *Pacific Northwest Quarterly* 58 (January 1967):7-13. See also David Remley, "Sacajawea of Myth and History," in Stauffer and Rosowski, eds., *Women and Western American Literature* (Troy, N.Y.: Whitson, 1982): 70-89.

⁸T. A. Larson, "Dolls, Vassals and Drudges: Pioneer Women in the West," *Western Historical Quarterly* 3 (1972): 5-16, and numerous other detailed state studies; Richard Roeder, "Crossing the Gender Line: Ella Knowles, Montana's First Woman Lawyer," *Montana* 32 (1982): 64-75 and G. Thomas Edwards, "Dr. Ada M. Weed: Northwest Reformer," *Oregon Historical Quarterly*, 78 (1977): 5-40. For recent eastern work on suffrage see especially Ellen Dubois, *Feminism and Suffrage* (Ithaca: Cornell University Press, 1978).

⁹John Faragher and Christine Stansell, "Women and Their Families on the Overland Trail to California and Oregon, 1842-1867," *Feminist Studies* 2 (1975): 150-166.

¹⁰Lillian Schlissel, "Women's Diaries on the Western Frontier." *American Studies* 18 (Spring 1977): 87-100.

¹¹Sandra Myres, "The Westering Woman," *Huntington Spectator* (Huntington Library, San Marino, Calif.) Winter 1980. She continues this attack in her more recent *Westering Women and the Frontier Experience 1800-1915* (Albuquerque: University of New Mexico Press, 1982).

¹²John Faragher, *Women and Men on the Oregon Trail* (New Haven: Yale University Press, 1979), and Lillian Schlissel, *Women's Diaries of the Westward Journey* (New York: Schocken Books, 1982).

¹³Faragher, *Women and Men on the Oregon Trail*, 178.

¹⁴David Potter, "American Women and the American Character," in John A. Hague, ed., *American Character and Culture*. Contributions in American Studies, no. 42 (Westport, Conn.: Greenwood Press, 1967).

¹⁵Julie Roy Jeffery, *Frontier Women* (New York: Hill and Wang, 1979).

¹⁶Richard A. Bartlett says the masculinity of the frontier society "is as obvious as the sun in the daytime," *The New Country: A Social History of the American Frontier 1776-1890* (New York: Oxford University Press, 1974), 343. See also William A. Bowen, *The Willamette Valley: Migration and Settlement on the Oregon Frontier* (Seattle: University of Washington Press, 1978).

[17]T. A. Larson, "Women's Role in the American West" *Montana* 24 (Summer 1974): 2-11.

[18]Abe Laufe, ed., *An Army Doctor's Wife on the Frontier* (Pittsburgh: University of Pittsburgh Press, 1962).

[19]Gerda Lerner posed this direct question in her 1981 American History Association pamphlet *Teaching Women's History*, in a section entitled "Teaching Questions Designed to Bring Women Into View." The most dramatic example for our region has been the discovery of the vital role of Native American women in the North America fur trade. There are at least five recent doctoral dissertations in the United States and Canada on this topic; see William Swagerty, "Marriage and Settlement Patterns of Rocky Mountain Trappers and Traders," *Western Historical Quarterly* 11:159; and an excellent paper for our region: Mary C. Wright (Rutgers University), "Women and Family in Indian-White Relations in the Oregon Country, 1810-1840," unpublished paper presented at the Conference on the History of Women, St. Paul, Minn. 1977.

[20]I owe this phrase to anthropologist Bea Medicine, who used it to describe how she pieced together an account of women's activities in the early reservation years from scattered documents that mainly talked about men. See her "Native American Women as Change Agents: Reaction to External Forces", abstracted in *Frontiers: A Journal of Women Studies* 5 (Spring 1980): 25-26.

[21]Georgina Blankenship, *Early History of Thurston County, Washington* (Olympia, Wash.: n.p., 1914): 322-23.

[22]Maureen Beecher, " 'Washed Forenoon, Plowed Afternoon': Women's Work on the Mormon Frontier," unpublished paper presented at the Fourth Berkshire Conference on the History of Women, Mount Holyoke College, August 1978; Sue Armitage, "Household Work and Childrearing on the Frontier: The Oral History Record," *Sociology and Social Research* 63 (April 1979): 467-474; Glenda Riley, " 'Not Gainfully Employed': Women on the Iowa Frontier 1833-1870," *Pacific Historical Review* 49 (May 1980): 237-264.

[23]Mary Beth Norton, *Liberty's Daughters* (Boston: Little Brown, 1980).

[24]Karen Anderson, *Wartime Women* (Westport, Conn.: Greenwood Press, 1981), and Karen Skokl, "The Job He Left Behind: American Women in Shipyards During World War II," in Carol R. Berkin and Clara M. Lovett, eds., *Women, War and Revolution* (New York: Holmes and Meier, 1980).

[25]This was a main theme of the exhibit, "Washington Women's Heritage: Working and Caring," funded by the National Endowment for the Humanities 1980-82 and coordinated by the Women Studies Program at Western Washington University.

[26]The best national work is Mary Ryan's Bancroft Award study *Cradle of the Middle Class* (New York: Cambridge University Press, 1981).

[27]Boulder Women's Oral History Project interviews, Boulder Public Library; Sue Armitage, Theresa Banfield, and Sarah Jacobus, "Black Women and Their Communities in Colorado," *Frontiers* 11 (Fall 1977): 45-51.

[28]June Underwood, "Civilizing Kansas: Women's Organizations, 1880-1920," *Kansas History* 7 (Winter/Spring 1985): 291-306.

[29]In Washington, an important finding guide to existing oral history collections is Margot Knight, *Directory of Oral History in Washington State*, Oral History Office, Washington State University, Pullman, Wash. However, many interviews with women are unsatisfactory because the women talk about their fathers, brothers, husbands, and sons, but not about their own lives. Because they were not asked about their own activities, the invisibility of women was perpetuated.

[30]Drury, *First White Women Over the Rockies*, vols. 2 and 3; Narcissa Whitman's letters, 1891, 1894, printed in *Transactions of the Oregon Pioneer Association* (19th and 21st Reunions), 1891 and 1892.

[31]The first women's college, Mount Holyoke College, in South Hadley, Massachusetts, opened its doors in 1837. For a description of its founder and her mission, see Kathryn Sklar, "The Founding of Mount Holyoke College," in Carol R. Berkin and Mary B. Norton, eds., *Women of America: A History* (Boston: Houghton-Mifflin, 1979), 177-201. For the teachers who came West, see Polly Kaufmann, "A Wider Field of Usefulness: Pioneer Women Teachers in the West, 1848-1854," *Journal of the West* 21 (April 1982): 16-25.

[32]Nancy Cott, *The Bonds of Womanhood* (New Haven: Yale University Press, 1977).

[33]Ruth Moynihan's social biography of Duniway, *Rebel for Rights, Abigail Scott Duniway* (New Haven: Yale University Press, 1983), modeled on Katharine Sklar's acclaimed *Catharine Beecher* (New Haven: Yale University Press, 1973), links the development of Oregon as a state with the intellectual and political development of a complex and interesting woman.

[34]A particularly striking example is explored by Jacqueline Hall in *Revolt Against Chivalry: Jessie Daniel Ames and the Women's Campaign Against Lynching* (New York: Columbia University Press, 1979).

[35]Karen Blair has explored some of these questions for eastern women in *The Clubwoman as Feminist* (New York: Holmes and Meier, 1980).

[36]Recent offending examples include James Thore, ed., *A Governor's Wife on the Mining Frontier: The Letters of Mary Edgerton from Montana*, critically reviewed by Gloria Lothrop in the *Pacific Historical Review* 48 (May 1979): 300-01; and Sandra Myres, *Ho For California! Women's Overland Diaries From the Huntington Library*, reviewed by the author in *Frontiers* 5 (Fall 1980): 71-73. A model of sensitive reading is provided by Elizabeth Hamsten, *Read This Only to Yourself* (Bloomington: University Press, 1982).

[37]At the very least, such an approach would add gender to the list of basic categories of historical analysis. However, as the Organization of American Historians-sponsored national project "Integrating Women's Materials into History Surveys" discovered in 1980-81, the inclusion of information about women moves the surveys strongly in the direction of social history. This means a loss of the narrative power and clarity which has distinguished the traditional survey. The problem of how to teach social history is a challenge for us all, feminist and nonfeminist historians alike.

¹George A. Frykman, "Development of the Washington Historical Quarterly, 1906-1935: The Work of Edmond S. Meany and Charles W. Smith," *Pacific Northwest Quarterly* 70 (July 1979): 121-30.

²Dorothy O. Johansen and Charles M. Gates, *Empire of the Columbia: A History of the Pacific Northwest* (New York: Harper, 1957; 2nd ed., 1967); Charles M. Gates, *The First Century at the University of Washington, 1861-1961* (Seattle: University of Washington Press, 1961).